Comments on Kevin James Shay and His Work

Creative abilities show up in window Yule tree and ornaments painted by **Kevin Shay**, **Patty Powers**, **Matt Raines** and **Andy Kingery**.
— The Tampa Times, 1964

Kevin Shay, 14, son of **Mr.** and **Mrs. James J. Shay** of Mapleridge Drive, was awarded the rank of Eagle Scout in court of honor ceremonies held recently in Northminster United Presbyterian Church.
— The Dallas Morning News, 1973

The LH B-Team has seen steady improvement in the second half of district play due to the surging efforts of **John Melanaphy, Jeff Courtwright, Duane Weeks** and junior Kevin Shay.
— **Barry Smith**, The Lake Highlands High Fang, 1976

The newest edition of Wildcat basketball opened **Jerry Wells'** second season at the Lake Highlands helm [first one had 9-22 record] on a winning note at Wildcat Gym with a rather convincing 81-67 romp over the W.T. White Longhorns. And with two starters sidelined, the Wildcat victory tasted that much sweeter. Kevin Shay topped the Wildcat attack as the senior came off the bench to score 20 points and grab 14 rebounds. After trailing 18-15 at the end of the first quarter, [Shay entered the game and] Lake Highlands rallied to gain a 35-28 advantage at intermission.
— **Chad Ferguson**, Richardson Daily News, 1976

I really don't know what motivated your attempt at the creep business [naming former University of North Texas head football coach **Jerry Moore** the first "Sports Creep of the Day" for hastily moving to Texas Tech and taking six assistant coaches].... It was a grossly unfair knock of Jerry. Unfortunately for you, the laugh may be on the Daily sports staff.
— **Fred Graham**, University of North Texas sports information director, memo to North Texas Daily, 1981 [resulted in Shay changing the name of the new feature to "Sports Jerks of the Week"; Moore later went to Appalachian State and made the College Football Hall of Fame]

In examining Shay's shuttle bus scheme, it is similar to most of the Daily's proposals – a nice idea with no research or method of accomplishment…. Non-productive, ill-informed critics are a burden those of us lifting must bear.
— **Steve Player**, president, UNT Student Association, NT Daily, 1981

While Shay may have a point to make, his tone can be characterized by a word he used appropriately in his column: arrogant.
— **William Holmes**, reader, NT Daily, 1981

Shay is certainly obsessed with victimization…..What has all this brutalization and inhumane mental torture that our crusader of the stinging wit must endure in a hostile environment got to do with anything?... Any day, our star reporter might go from plain old Kevin "Doc" Shay to Kevin "Doc, Sometimes I Just Feel Like Breaking Rules" Shay.
— **David Landrum**, reader, NT Daily, 1981

Shay almost hit the spot when he pointed out the immature way some public figures respond to publicity…. The graduate with stars in his eyes and illusions of integrity at his work place has to take a few bruises before he decides if that's really how he wants to make a living.
— **Gene Douglas**, reader, NT Daily, 1981

Shay has a distinctive style of writing and a perspective in his stories that sets him apart from most college students.
— **Sharon Ware**, Editor, NT Daily. 1981

[Shay makes] some great points. In fact, [he] may have inspired me to do another column.
— **Skip Bayless**, sports columnist and talk show host, 1983

Yours is a fine mission, and I send you every encouragement as you walk across our great nation for the cause of peace and understanding among all peoples.
— **Jimmy Carter,** former U.S. president, 1984

In examining Shay's shuttle bus scheme, it is similar to most of the Daily's proposals – a nice idea with no research or method of accomplishment.... Nonproductive, ill-informed critics are a burden those of us lifting must bear.

— **Steve Player**, president, UNT Student Association, NT Daily, 1981

While Shay may have a point to make, his tone can be characterized by a word he used appropriately in his column: arrogant.

— **William Holmes**, reader, NT Daily, 1981

Shay is certainly obsessed with victimization…..What has all this brutalization and inhumane mental torture that our crusader of the stinging wit must endure in a hostile environment got to do with anything?... Any day, our star reporter might go from plain old Kevin "Doc" Shay to Kevin "Doc, Sometimes I Just Feel Like Breaking Rules" Shay.

— **David Landrum**, reader, NT Daily, 1981

Shay almost hit the spot when he pointed out the immature way some public figures respond to publicity…. The graduate with stars in his eyes and illusions of integrity at his work place has to take a few bruises before he decides if that's really how he wants to make a living.

— **Gene Douglas**, reader, NT Daily, 1981

Shay has a distinctive style of writing and a perspective in his stories that sets him apart from most college students.

— **Sharon Ware**, Editor, NT Daily. 1981

[Shay makes] some great points. In fact, [he] may have inspired me to do another column.

— **Skip Bayless**, sports columnist and talk show host, 1983

Yours is a fine mission, and I send you every encouragement as you walk across our great nation for the cause of peace and understanding among all peoples.

— **Jimmy Carter**, former U.S. president, 1984

Comments on Kevin James Shay and His Work

Creative abilities show up in window Yule tree and ornaments painted by **Kevin Shay**, **Patty Powers**, **Matt Raines** and **Andy Kingery**.
— The Tampa Times, 1964

Kevin Shay, 14, son of **Mr.** and **Mrs. James J. Shay** of Mapleridge Drive, was awarded the rank of Eagle Scout in court of honor ceremonies held recently in Northminster United Presbyterian Church.
— The Dallas Morning News, 1973

The LH B-Team has seen steady improvement in the second half of district play due to the surging efforts of **John Melanaphy, Jeff Courtwright, Duane Weeks** and junior Kevin Shay.
— **Barry Smith**, The Lake Highlands High Fang, 1976

The newest edition of Wildcat basketball opened **Jerry Wells**' second season at the Lake Highlands helm [first one had 9-22 record] on a winning note at Wildcat Gym with a rather convincing 81-67 romp over the W.T. White Longhorns. And with two starters sidelined, the Wildcat victory tasted that much sweeter. Kevin Shay topped the Wildcat attack as the senior came off the bench to score 20 points and grab 14 rebounds. After trailing 18-15 at the end of the first quarter, [Shay entered the game and] Lake Highlands rallied to gain a 35-28 advantage at intermission.
— **Chad Ferguson**, Richardson Daily News, 1976

I really don't know what motivated your attempt at the creep business [naming former University of North Texas head football coach **Jerry Moore** the first "Sports Creep of the Day" for hastily moving to Texas Tech and taking six assistant coaches].... It was a grossly unfair knock of Jerry. Unfortunately for you, the laugh may be on the Daily sports staff.
— **Fred Graham**, University of North Texas sports information director, memo to North Texas Daily, 1981 [resulted in Shay changing the name of the new feature to "Sports Jerks of the Week"; Moore later went to Appalachian State and made the College Football Hall of Fame]

[Shay is walking with] the finest group of young people I've ever seen. Easy to talk to, pleasant in their disagreement with others along the way who try to provoke an argument and very tactful. But sure of their beliefs and firm in their convictions. I'm proud to have met him.

— **Jean Ewing**, Havre de Grace, Md., 1984

I thank you for your march, for your beautiful and sometimes painful march, giving concrete ground to the hope rising now in East and West beyond old ideologies.

— **Raymond Yans,** deputy mayor, Liege, Belgium, 1985

Shay is tanned, relaxed, and in good shape after spending most of last year [walking] on the road to Moscow. And for someone who was forced to stop playing basketball because of a bad knee, Shay shows no ill effects from his long trek.

— **Dennis Phillips**, correspondent, The Dallas Morning News, 1985

There is no hotel space [for you in Moscow].

— telex from **Soviet Union** officials, 1985

To Shay, a former Richland College student, his 18-month walk for peace in the world was like a master's program in life. "I learned more in that 18 months than I ever could in school."

— **Jo Bristow**, staff writer, Richland Chronicle, 1987

[The walk project book is] an important contribution to the cause of peace.

— **Robert Ellsberg**, Orbis Books, Maryknoll, N.Y., 1988

Shay does not write articles about me the way my mother would write them.

— **Max Wells**, Dallas Mayor Pro Tem, Addison/North Dallas Register, 1989

The recent decision to put "cute" titles over crime reports [i.e. "Quick Dough" re: Domino's Pizza assault and robbery] is surely in poor taste. We should be waging a war on crime, not glamorizing/humorizing it.

— **Patrick Beal**, reader, Register,1990

I am angry, disgusted, and will never again read your newspaper. It will go straight into the trash after the trashy "Quick Pull-Out" bit in your Police Blotter. … Are you hard up for material or what? Unctuous material like "Quick…" is low class and a total insult to your readers. My husband is equally shocked.
— **Jackie Winberg**, reader, Register, 1991

In [the book on Dallas civil rights history], **Roy H. Williams** and Kevin J. Shay pick up where other historians left off….Their account of Mr. Williams' voting rights suit is fascinating and sobering…. A good start at providing a history of Dallas for everyone.
— **Craig Flournoy**, journalism professor, University of Cincinnati, SMU, Pulitzer Prize-winning reporter, The Dallas Morning News, 1992

[Williams and Shay provide] a powerful local supplement to several new nationally oriented evaluations, including **Andrew Hacker's** *Two Nations* and **Studs Terkel's** *Race*. Helps provide desperately missing context to what are often interpreted by whites as chaos and caterwauling.
— **Rod Davis**, author, *East of Texas, West of Hell,* D Magazine, 1992

Your book [on humorous police blotter items] is excellent….. That's a great photo of you in shades with the two cops. I'd have had them looking tough, though, instead of smiling. I think I'll try that style for a publicity photo.
— **Chuck Shepherd**, founder, *News of the Weird* syndicated column, 1992

I do not believe that anyone has separated the wheat from the chaff, or the truth from probabilities, possibilities, and lies, more than Kevin Shay reporting for the Metrocrest News. Shay has not allowed the "good old boyism" of local politics to color his reporting. Straight-forward and straight-shooting, Shay really tells it like it is.
— **R. G. Harrell**, reader, Metrocrest News, 1993

On one thing everyone agrees: there is no shortage of political intrigue in Coppell. As Kevin Shay, a journalist who covered Coppell for two years as a reporter for the Metrocrest News and is now an editor with the Arlington News, puts it: "It's a weird little town. There is always some issue for people to get riled up about in Coppell."
— **Ann Zimmerman**, Dallas Observer, 1994

A statewide editorial award is something for which you should be very proud.
— **Daniel Crowe**, president, Dallas-Fort Worth Suburban Newspapers, 1994

Pretty serious stuff on loss of American dream for corporate employees. Not much fun to read, even if we ought to.
— judges, **Texas Press Association** Awards, 1995

I just read [Shay's column] about Arlington ISD students wearing uniforms and comparing them to sweatshops. That's as immature and certainly the least profound kind of thinking I can imagine. Where did he get his journalism degree?
— anonymous reader, "**Sound Off**," Arlington News, 1995

There is an extremely negative and depressing kid who writes a column and may even be some kind of an editor for the Arlington News. His writing is not up to your standards, and I hope you will not include him on your new staff.... Did you see the recent article that I attached? Can you imagine anyone on The Dallas Morning News staff calling presidential candidates "SWINE?"
— **Benjamin Harrison**, letter to DMN executive **Gary Jacobson**, 1996

It's always a relief when you've done a really complicated piece to not hear any complaints, and even better when you get good compliments.
— **Dave Hiott**, Texas and Southwest editor,
The Dallas Morning News, 1999

[Williams and Shay] rip the covers off the beauty queen we call Dallas and expose her ugly scars of racism, bigotry, cronyism, and greed. Those who profess to embrace truth cannot remain sedate and silent after reading the often petrifying story of power. This is must reading for all students and their parents.
— **Martin W. Burrell**, former executive,
American Airlines Center, DART, 1999

Kevin Shay of Arlington received a $500 prize for his unpublished book in the fourth annual International Peace Writing Awards. Sponsored by the **Omni Center for Peace, Justice and Ecology** in Fayetteville, Ark., and the Peace and Justice Studies Association of Evergreen State College in Olympia, Wash., the program was founded in 1998 to honor writings about peacemaking.
— **The Dallas Morning News**, 2002

For the last time, pagans are not devil worshippers! The article [by Shay] was biased toward the Christian view. I'm sick of intolerant and uneducated conservatives painting pagans as sick, evil, blood-sacrificing freaks. Pagans didn't create the devil, the Judeo-Christian belief system did. We've been around a lot longer than 2,000 years.

— **John Lamberth**, Fort Worth Weekly, 2002

Writing under a nom de plume, a Texas journalist has created a roster of journalists who, transgressing conventional media wisdom, opposed the Bush Administration's war in Iraq and were fired.

— **Joel Bleifuss**, In These Times, 2003

If [**George W. Bush**] and their organizations are ever brought to justice, it will happen because a small and careful cadre of journalists, including [**Shay**], kept score.

— **Sara S. DeHart**, Associate Professor Emeritus, University of Minnesota, 2003

Not only are [Shay's] essays and columns usually more well researched than syndicated columnists making big bucks in the national media, they are more passionate and just plain well written. In future centuries, it won't be the essays by the David Broder's and Charles Krauthammer's that will be studied and emulated, it will be the [Kevin Shay]'s.

— **Brad Beachy**, English professor, Butler College, El Dorado, Ks, 2003

[Shay] raises many issues that are still not being openly debated in the mainstream media, let alone acknowledged.

— **R.B. Ham**, webmaster, Truth & Consequences, 2003

[Shay] writes with a sword. His work reads like a bomb.

— **Celia Ramirez**, concert promoter, 2003

Shay was hired as a business reporter for The Gazette, a chain of more than 30 newspapers in Maryland. He was one of several contributors to the book, *Big Bush Lies*, released in June.

— **The North Texan**, 2004

Excellent analysis of the pros and cons of area "buy local" campaigns.... All information presented comes together to provide a complete overview of regional economy.
— judges, "Best of Show," **Maryland-Delaware-D.C. Press Association**
Editorial Contest, 2009

As underwhelming as the White House had seemed up to that point, walking into the foyer was like finally stepping into Willy Wonka's wondrous chocolate room: the air was heady with tradition and formality; colors took on a heretofore unrecognized vibrancy; an atmosphere of excellence and attention to detail took hold.

"You almost made it here [as a player]," said former Dallas Morning News reporter Kevin Shay to former Maverick guard **Rolando Blackman**, who was sitting near the reporter/invited-guest divide. Blackman, who held the Mavericks' record for most points scored until **Nowitzki** broke it…simply smiled, content to enjoy the current Mavericks moment.
— **Peter Voskamp**, Texas Monthly, 2012

[Shay's road trip book is] amusingly chronicled.
— **Roadside America**, 2014

[Shay is] one gutsy guy – two weeks – 7,000 miles with two children. All three of you deserve medals!
— **John Watson**, founder, DriveCrossCountry.net, 2014

[Shay's] latest endeavor is a hoot! Next time you're on a road trip with your family, don't be surprised to see 6-foot-7 inch Kevin Shay and his kids there, too.
— **Lindsay Baronoskie**, Lake Highlands Today, 2014

[Shay's John F. Kennedy book is] well documented cover to cover. Professional old-school journalism at its best.
— **Stephen Michael Berberich**, author, *Night at the Belvedere*, 2017

Shay does a commendable job of remaining objective… [His book on January 6] will be a great addition to any library.
— **JD Jung**, Underrated Reads, 2022

Every generation has an Edmund Pettus Bridge moment. You are a part of an Edmund Pettus Bridge moment. You knew before you got here that there might be some danger associated with what you were doing, but you marched on. You knew that because of current events [associated with the killing of Charles Kirk] that there are threats that are being made, threats that some people are allowing to cause them to change their course. But you didn't change your course. You didn't change your direction. ... You marched on 160 miles, and for this, you are now bringing the Edmund Pettus Bridge moment to Washington, D.C. You're bringing it to fruition.

— **U.S. Rep. Al Green**, We Are America March rally, 2025

The protests today to support democracy and oppose Trump authoritarianism are more important than anything I have stood up for in my life. For the future of democracy, for the future of our children, for liberty and justice for all, we have no choice but to march on.

— **Shay**, "The Valor of Vigils and Marches," 2025

STILL SEARCHING FOR UTOPIA

*Essays and Columns
Written Along a
Road Less Traveled*

Volume I

KEVIN JAMES SHAY

RANDOM PUBLISHERS

* WASHINGTON, D.C. *

ALSO by KEVIN JAMES SHAY

Death of the Rising Sun: A Search for Truth in the JFK Assassination
It's a Mad, Mad, Mad, Mad Trip: On the Road of the Longest Two-Week Family Road Trip in History
Mad Trip Tips, Trivia, and Tourist Attractions
Operation Chaos
Walking through the Wall
A Parent's Guide to Dallas/Fort Worth
And Justice for All: The Untold History of Dallas [with Roy H. Williams]
Sex, Lies & Newsprint: Tales from a North Dallas Police Blotter

Front cover photo by Kevin Shay of Dennis Thomas walking in rural Germany, 1985

Published by Random Publishers

Copyright © 2025 by Kevin James Shay

All rights reserved. Parts of this book may be quoted in reviews and articles, and cited in academic works. This book is for informational purposes only. Every effort has been made to ensure that the information is accurate. The author and publisher disclaim liability to any party for any loss or damage caused by errors or omissions, or any other cause.

ISBN 978-1-881365-88-4
EBOOK ISBN 978-1-881365-89-1
LIBRARY OF CONGRESS CONTROL NUMBER 2025926518

Library of Congress Cataloging in Publications Data
Shay, Kevin James, 1959-
Still Searching for Utopia by Kevin James Shay.
Pages cm.
ISBN 9781881365884 [paper]
1. Memoir, Kevin James Shay. 2. Essays. 3. Activism. 4. History. I. Title.
814.54 SHAY
LCN 2025926518
10 9 8 7 6 5 4 3 2 1
Printed in the United States [USA]
First edition, 2025

Contents

Introduction	17

The Big Issues

Taking on the Big Issues	29
Housing and Society: Searching for Utopia	41
Public vs. Private Land: Who Owns America?	57
Climate Change: Where is the Will for Real Action?	67
Natural Disasters: A Growing Threat	75
Civil Rights and the Danger of Standing Up: The 1960s Assassination Conspiracies	83
Social Justice: Dreams Deferred	108
Authoritarianism: Putin and the Rise of Dictators	127
Democracy: The Valor of Vigils and Marches	144
The Afterlife: Exploring What Happens After Death	159

More Societal Ills

Race and Class: Why was Ruben Triplett Murdered?	171
Education: The Religious Right's Long Campaign to Destroy Public Education	189
Press Freedom: The Last Great Texas Newspaper War	204
Government Power: A Strange but True Tale	237

Getting More Personal

Healthcare and Death: The Aspirin Strain	245
Death and Loss: Bye, for Now	261
Death and Loss: Dancing in the Moment	269

Epilogue: Still Searching for Utopia	286

Appendix
Acknowledgments 289
Notes 290
About the Author 305

Utopia is a paradoxical concept.

As a motivating idea – improvement is desirable – we can't do without it.

But every time we try to implement it on a grand scale,

we accomplish its disastrous opposite.

Perhaps that is why the word itself means "no place."

— **MARGARET ATWOOD**, The New York Times Magazine, 1999

Introduction

During the oppressive year of 1985, Romania ranked among the most tyrannical countries in the world, down there with the former Soviet Union, Iraq, and Vietnam. Police in that southeastern Europe Soviet satellite arrested people for innocent, seemingly harmless acts like smuggling coffee and books into their country.

So as I stood in a compartment of the crowded Romanian train, with gypsies leering at my belongings, with police approaching to search my pack that contained coffee grounds and philosophy books, I pondered my options. At age 26, I questioned my decisions, if not my sanity.

It seemed I had spent my life going against the grain. My career choice as a journalist in a dwindling job market, when aptitude tests and employment trends showed a computer scientist was a wiser path, bewildered more than just my mom. I attempted to be an idealistic journalist who wasn't afraid to leave my typewriter to take action, not merely write about others doing so. I shunned binge drinking bouts in smoky watering holes and late-night parties. I joined a health club and used it religiously three times a week. I volunteered at soup kitchens and food banks. I delivered meals to the needy. Besides writing for some Dallas-area newspapers to pay the bills, I worked for free for an underground paper that published stories about labor strife and peace demonstrations.

I didn't always go to church; I would rather spend an hour delivering meals or loading food than sitting in a building listening to someone's theories on the afterlife. I wanted to make *this* life better; I'd worry about an afterlife when I got there.

I wasn't a communist. I wasn't a socialist. I wasn't a Democrat or a Republican. Though I later voted for mostly Democrats, I cast a 1980 ballot for Libertarian Ed Clark in the only presidential election I had participated in up to that point. I wasn't a liberal or a conservative, though some accused me of being liberal. Independent idealist seemed to best describe my views.

In short, I was woke long before the cons twisted that concept – which dates to African-American leaders and musicians issuing warnings to "stay woke" during Jim Crow days of the early 20th century – into something negative.

In the mid-1980s, narcissistic music videos dominated young people's television screens. Madonna sang about being a "Material Girl." Michael

Douglas' character in the 1987 movie, *Wall Street,* aptly summed up life's motto for many: "Greed, for lack of a better word, is good."

It was the time of $10,000 Rolex watches, $500 running shoes, $7,000 Pentagon coffee makers, and multimillion-dollar yachts. School counselors advised kids to "just say no" to drugs and sex, as if that would work. Cocaine and steroids became popularized to help ladder climbers get ahead in corporate and sports circles. Werner Erhard and other pop psychologists told us how great we were the way we were.

Among the maze of contrasting messages, well before the Internet would really confuse society, I searched for my vision of a utopian community, if not society. As I studied Earth's history and various movements, I found that many had tried to bring forth improvements, only to have gains used for selfish means. Sure, there were positive moments, from Charles Goodyear's rubber tires to U.S. amendments that expanded civil rights and liberties to more people. But eventually, the negatives seemed to outweigh the positives. We could drive for miles to visit relatives, but the costs of vehicles rose out of sight and more people died in auto accidents. More folks could vote, but more wealthy people could rig the system.

I tried to focus on the Big Picture. In the mid-1980s, the biggest picture on the planet was the Cold War between the U.S. and former Soviet Union, seen most notably through the nuclear arms race. While President Ronald Reagan and Soviet heads of state had not as much as met in the four years prior to my Romanian visit, both sides built and tested nuclear arms at a furious pace, practiced detailed military maneuvers, and seemed hell-bent on staging the ultimate war.

Cold War tensions escalated soon after late 1979 when the Soviets invaded Afghanistan. President Jimmy Carter announced a boycott of the 1980 Summer Olympics in Moscow, and NATO deployed nuclear missiles in Western Europe. The Soviets countered with their own SS-20 nuclear weapons on the east side of the Iron Curtain. The concept of a "protracted nuclear war" was a key part of a classified report signed by U.S. Defense Secretary Caspar Weinberger in 1982. That same year, Reagan approved a national security order to develop a "capability to sustain protracted nuclear conflict." In early 1983, he announced the launch of the Strategic Defense Initiative to develop systems to shoot down missiles from space.

U.S.-Russia relations nosedived in September 1983, when the Soviets shot down Korean Air Lines Flight 007 after the pilots mistakenly flew into Soviet airspace, killing 269 passengers and crew members. The victims included U.S. Rep. Larry McDonald, a conservative Democrat from Georgia. He happened to be chairman of the far-right John Birch Society and opposed the creation of Martin Luther King Day because he considered King to be a communist.

As the Soviets accused KAL 007 of conducting a U.S.-sponsored spy mission and deliberately provoking a conflict, Reagan ordered the Federal Aviation Administration to revoke the license of Russia's Aeroflot, and New York's Port Authority denied Soviet landing rights. In late September, the Soviet nuclear warning system mistakenly reported that the U.S. had launched missiles towards Russia. A Soviet officer alertly suspected the false alarm and held off on reporting it to his superior, thus avoiding a potential real launch by Moscow.

Reagan officials soon urged NATO to deploy updated Pershing II and ground-launched cruise missiles in West Germany. The new missiles fueled more massive protests, including as many as 500,000 people forming a human chain around missile bases.

The Reagan administration and Moscow leaders stepped up the nuclear war games, drifting the countries closer to nuclear war than anyone admitted, according to declassified documents published by nonprofit research group National Security Archive in 2013. As some 40,000 U.S. and NATO troops conducted maneuvers across Western Europe in late 1983, officers authorized nuclear strikes in an exercise called Able Archer 83, which could have been interpreted by Soviet spies as the real thing.

"While historians have previously noted the high risk of an accidental nuclear war during this period, the new documents make even clearer how the world's rival superpowers found themselves blindly edging toward the brink of nuclear war through suspicion, belligerent posturing, and blind miscalculation," maintained Douglas Birch, a journalist with the Center for Public Integrity. [1]

The increased danger of nuclear war, along with conventional conflicts in Central America, the Middle East, and other places, caused the Bulletin of the Atomic Scientists to move its "Doomsday Clock" – which had marked worldwide threats to humanity since 1947 – to three minutes until midnight in January 1984. These were not religious zealots holding signs saying, "The end is near." These were scientists, some of whom won prestigious awards like the Nobel Prize, who had set their clock to the closest to midnight since 1953, when it was at two minutes with the testing of thermonuclear hydrogen bombs.

Around that same time, I read a short article in the underground newspaper that I wrote for about a proposed 7,000-mile group march from California to Moscow called A Walk of the People – A Pilgrimage for Life. Something clicked. Perhaps a walking community could be my utopian movement. When the project reached Texas that May with four survivors, I answered the call. The longer we walked, the more it seemed like a real-life *Survivor* television show – but without the promise of riches. As we grew to 15 members, the physical part of walking 20 miles a day wasn't as draining as the mental part of organizing housing, food, meetings, visas, and more. But we were making a difference in people we met and spreading a message of hope through the media.

As we walked through some of the most conservative parts of the country in rural Alabama, Reagan proclaimed that he signed legislation to "outlaw Russia forever" during a radio program microphone check. "We begin bombing in five minutes," he said to a crowd that included National Public Radio engineers. The pre-broadcast remarks hit the media, and Reagan backtracked, saying he was merely "joking." Reagan had previously made public statements that "all mankind would lose" in a nuclear war, though he had also claimed that one could be limited to Europe. Such mixed messages didn't exactly stem the massive anti-nuclear protests in Europe that we would later join.

After the project was turned back by the Russians in Hungary following 18 months on the road in late 1985, I sought another way to reach some people across the Iron Curtain. When Hungarian freedom fighters urged me to visit Transylvania, the disputed section of Romania where many Hungarians had settled before World War II only to be stuck in poverty without the right to freely travel, I could not say no. And when Gyorgy, a history student, handed me a pound of coffee and some Greek philosophy books to hide in my pack to take to his friends, I accepted the contraband.

I took coffee and books on philosophy for granted. To Gyorgy's friends, they were nuggets of gold. But to the Romanian government, they were threats to its reign.

"Don't worry, the guards never check you Americans," Gyorgy had assured me. *Famous last words*, I thought as the slow-moving train ground to a halt and I observed guards rifling through people's bags. The thought of being whisked away to a holding cell without being able to communicate to anyone entered my mind. This was before everyone and his infant had a cell phone, when you had to deposit coins into a pay phone to make a call. I considered slipping the coffee and books out the window.

But something made me stand tall, which at 6-foot-7 is pretty tall. It was ludicrous to me that people could be arrested for carrying coffee and books. Smuggling those items was a small step for liberty in this country, yet an important one. It showed that even in the darkest times, some would take a stand against a dictator, as insignificant as that action might seem. If we couldn't make a stand for the smaller things, what chance did we have standing up for larger ideals?

Rosa Parks made a difference over a seat on a bus. I was among numerous supporters of the Romanian revolution who would make a difference with coffee and books.

A guard searching through the suitcase of the Romanian theology professor next to me pulled out some eyeglasses, tried them on, and pocketed them. The guard skipped over the pack of Adele, the only other fellow walk participant crazy enough to accept the freedom fighters' challenge, and asked me to open mine.

I decided to play the obnoxious American card, one of my better decisions at that time. "What?" I snapped angrily. "Why are you bothering me? I'm from the USA."

I then ripped open my pack and shoved it in the guard's face. The move worked, lending more evidence that the more obnoxious you act, the more you get your way. The guard sheepishly felt around the top of my pack, his hands not going deep enough to discover the contraband. As he moved on, I observed Gyorgy smiling. We'd later have a good laugh, as he called me the "angry American."

Among my first sights in this country, the home of the 15th-century Prince of Wallachia, Vlad Tepes, whose legendary, blood-thirsty killings of Turks and other foes gave Bram Stoker great material for his *Dracula* novel, was a humble railway station. The station looked like it was out of a Podunk, last-edge-of-the-world scene, with its single, one-room waiting area and one hardwood bench.

I crumbled into a corner and waited there for about three hours until some of the two million Hungarians living in this area met us right before dawn. I tried to sleep, but the memory of my close call and chatter of my hosts – which grew louder with each pass of a bottle of vodka – kept me awake.

Finally, I gave up and took a swig of vodka. My tongue burned, but the potion was just what I needed at the time.

Welcome to the End of the World, I thought, as I drifted off to a restless nap.

'All we can do is learn'

At dawn, we walked through a village of decaying frame houses, few people, and fewer cars. Living conditions for the Hungarian minorities worsened after communist dictator Nicolae Ceausescu rose to power in 1965, my hosts said. Hungarians stuck in Transylvania could only visit Hungary once every two years. They lived in houses that were little better than shacks, with clean water, butter, meat, cheese, fruit, and vegetables in short supply.

Since this was market day, where locals had a chance to buy fresh fruit and vegetables, we tried to catch another train towards the village of Bratca. The first few trains were so packed we let them pass. Some people caught rides with families on horse-drawn carts. Finally, we decided to jump on the next train no matter how crowded.

When the train stopped, its cars became engulfed with a surging sea of human bodies. Seeing that Adele was having a tough time climbing up the steep steps with her pack on, I helped propel her into the mass of people in that car. A whistle sounded as I observed I was the only one of my party still on the ground. I leaped onto the next car's steps and grabbed hold of a vertical bar.

As the train began to slowly rumble down the track, I ignored a conductor's yell to get off and started up the steps. At that precise moment, my pack started to slip off my back, hanging precariously on one elbow. I made a frantic effort to yank the pack in, open the train door, and pull myself through, all in one motion. I landed in the middle of a crowd of elderly women and stood up.

"Excuse me," I smiled, pointing at my chest. "American."

The train soon stopped, and I observed everyone leaping out onto sharp rocks by the track. Women who made the six-foot drop moaned in pain as they landed. So I jumped myself, then caught one woman after the next, like I was Salinger's Holden Caulfield in *The Catcher in the Rye*, saving people before they fell off a cliff. This wasn't a dream like Holden's, though it seemed like one.

I joined the mass walking towards the market and realized my companions were nowhere in sight. I suddenly became rather religious and prayed I ran into familiar faces. About a half-mile down that road, I heard Gyorgy's deep baritone. "Kevin, where you been? We been looking all over for you. We thought you might have missed that train."

"Not quite," I replied. "I had to....take care of some business." We reached our home for two nights – a barn we shared with donkeys and horses. I shook off Gyorgy's offer of vodka and sausage to join the animals.

What seemed like days later, I awoke to the smell of donkey dung, taste of straw in my mouth, and sound of a surreal scene just outside the barn. I observed gypsies dancing and singing; merchants hawking fruit, vegetables, pottery, rugs, woolen clothing, paintings, and baskets; children riding carnival rides; and colorfully-dressed magicians and sword-swallowers performing for crowds.

This has to be a dream, I thought.

That evening when everyone assembled for dinner, I whipped out a bag full of buttons and postcards I had collected during the previous 18 months to give to people in Eastern Europe. Thinking that this was as far East as I would get – several in the project would later make it to Moscow via train, as I would with my brother the following year – I gave the bag to a young woman to distribute. She excitedly took it and called everyone she knew together in a circle. She then threw the bag into the air like a basketball referee does a jump ball. The scramble for the buttons and other treasures was more intense than any hoops contest I had played.

A man wearing glasses and a stocking cap approached me while I observed the scene to say, "These people, they're not for peace. They want a violent revolution. They want to take back this part of Romania for Hungary."

Jozsef, a former Romanian schoolteacher, said he quit that job because he got tired of "lying to students." He spent his work days translating technical manuals from English into Romanian. He was not happy with the work but shrugged, "It is a job, and what else can I do?"

He eagerly read illegal books brought to him by Budapest friends. He told me about a journal some Hungarians had tried to publish three years before in Romania. The publication that criticized Ceausescu's regime had lasted only seven months before two of the Hungarian founders were imprisoned and the other exiled for life, Jozsef said.

Of the political revolts that would ensue throughout Eastern Europe from 1989 to 1991, the only one that would contain a wide stench of violence and result in the execution of its leader was in Romania, which was also one of the few Eastern Bloc countries not to boycott the 1984 Olympics. After a bloody week-long battle that claimed the lives of more than 1,000 people, mobs would drive Ceausescu from the presidential palace in Bucharest. After his execution, people like Jozsef would eventually be free to leave Transylvania and return at their pleasure.

Four years before that rebellion, Jozsef agreed progress needed to be made somehow. "We are such a poor country," he said. "We cannot do anything. Most government officials take bribes. If we try to say something against these officials, we are beaten or put in jail. If someone finds out I have these books or was talking to you this way, they would beat me."

He looked away, sighing, "All we can do is learn."

I looked at Jozsef, listening in silence. I wanted to tell him that he could do more, that in reading the books and talking to me "this way" he was doing more. I wanted to tell him about the fine things some people I had met in the West were doing, despite most citizens wallowing in the excesses. But as I stood there in the mist, realizing how much my way of life contrasted with Jozsef's, all I could do was nod my head and listen. *Who the hell was I to give this guy a pep talk?* I was not Werner Erhard.

On the walk back to the train station to get on with my journey, some Hungarian women thanked me for the coffee, books, and buttons. They offered me a golden bell and vest, not accepting my polite refusal. I handed them the rest of my Romanian currency, which they refused. "You need this more than me," one said, pecking my cheek.

"No, really, I don't," I protested. Nothing I said changed their minds. That kind of will was what would drive out Ceausescu.

From my perch on the evening train as I left my new-found friends that dark, misty evening in 1985, I caught Jozsef and his girlfriend smiling and waving from the platform. I waved back and watched their faces grow dimmer.

To this day, I don't know the fate of Jozsef, Gyorgy, and others I befriended in Romania. Their situation shook my belief that a nonviolent revolution, as Gandhi had led in India, was always possible. "Sometimes the only response to brutality can be violence," Gyorgy had said. "We all can't be revolutionaries. But we can all do something."

In a 1986 letter, Gyorgy invited me back to Transylvania. "I hope [to] see you again, and wish you many good things and more," he wrote. That was the last I would hear from him.

Potential revolutionaries from Romania and Hungary wait for an approaching train in 1985 in rural Romania.   Photo by Kevin Shay

Trying to maintain idealism

In the years since, I tried to maintain a semblance of that daring brand of idealism while juggling a career and family amid changing times. I continued to volunteer through my kids' schools, scouting groups, and youth sports teams. After Republicans took the 2000 presidential election under questionable circumstances, I authored articles and columns that strongly criticized the George W. Bush administration under a pen name. When Barack Obama was elected as the first African-American U.S. president in 2008, I really thought the country and society were changing.

But the threats to the planet were still increasing, according to the atomic scientists. They had set their clock all the way back to 17 minutes in 1991 as the Cold War ended and the U.S. and Russia honored new treaties and reduced their nuclear arsenals. But since then, the clock has climbed steadily, getting closer to midnight in 2025 than it has ever been.

The rise of far-right leaders in the U.S., Russia, Holland, Italy, Hungary, and other nations, Russia's aggressive war in Ukraine, a potential three-way nuclear arms race involving the U.S. Russia, and China, record heat, massive floods, wildfires, and technologies such as artificial intelligence that spread disinformation make these times more perilous than ever, the scientists said in 2025. "Trends that have deeply concerned the Science and Security Board continued, and despite unmistakable signs of danger, national leaders and their societies have failed to do what is needed to change course," they said. "Consequently, we now move the Doomsday Clock from 90 seconds to 89 seconds to midnight – the closest it has ever been to catastrophe." [2]

So what can our response be now, as we continue to pursue utopian visions? In 1984, there were several other groups of marchers walking across the U.S. at the same time as the one in which I participated. In the Internet Age, such actions seem archaic. Massive protests and citizens lobbying their leaders could help, if leaders really act.

"Blindly continuing on the current path is a form of madness," the scientists said. "The United States, China, and Russia have the collective power to destroy civilization. These three countries have the prime responsibility to pull the world back from the brink, and they can do so if their leaders seriously commence good-faith discussions about the global threats outlined here. Despite their profound disagreements, they should take that first step without delay. The world depends on immediate action."

Freedom House, an organization co-founded by Eleanor Roosevelt in 1941 to monitor political rights and civil liberties worldwide, reported that global freedom declined for the 19th consecutive year in 2025. Citing Ukraine, the continued rise of authoritative regimes in nations that included Turkey, Hungary, Myanmar [formerly Burma], and Tunisia, and political repression that destabilized a wide range of countries, the organization found that 60 nations saw their level of freedom decrease while only 34 experienced an uptick. El Salvador, Haiti, Kuwait, and Tunisia showed the largest declines, while Bangladesh, Bhutan, Sri Lanka, and Syria recorded the most significant gains.

A sobering trend remained: The number of nations classified by Freedom House as "not free" rose to 67 in 2025 from 51 in 2014, while those deemed "free" declined to 86 from 89. Those in the "not free" category included Russia, Belarus, Syria, North Korea, Nicaragua, Haiti, and Sudan – all countries that the Trump administration sided with in opposing a 2025 UN resolution that condemned Russia for invading Ukraine.

The U.S. slide towards a form of competitive authoritarianism – in which voter suppression increased and elections were stacked against opposition candidates – was barely noted in Freedom House's report. The group slightly upgraded the U.S. score to 84 from 83 in 2024 [still well below Canada and most Western European nations] and claimed that the 2024 election, which was marred by GOP vote suppression laws, bomb threats at polling sites, and thrown-out ballots, was "free, fair, and credible." Freedom House reported that Trump "warned that he would prosecute his political opponents and reduce the independence of institutions – including federal law enforcement agencies, the civil service, and the media – that have traditionally protected the rule of law, ensured transparency, and served as beneficial checks on presidential discretion." Throughout 2025, the Trump administration furiously engaged in a scheme to dismantle democratic institutions and further authoritarianism, as Trump and allies like Elon Musk did exactly what they promised and more. [3]

As a journalist, my main response is to expose harmful actions and outline possible real solutions. As an idealist, I have no choice but to continue the search for a utopian something. The following pages contain some of the hundreds of essays and columns I have written in my 40-plus years in journalism. Many started with articles or columns, and blossomed into larger essays. Where relevant, I have updated them. This first volume contains more serious, timely topics, while the next volume will include lighter subjects, including sports and travel, as well as attempted humor.

Ultimately, I don't know what our response to the apparent approaching midnight should be. I became involved up to my teeth back when the atomic scientists said we were so close to midnight in the 1980s, to see such efforts apparently pay off and then be negated once again. It seems to be one of those vicious cycles in which humanity is forever destined to be stuck.

We have lived on this precipice ever since I can remember, and not much seems to change, no matter what we do. Somehow, we're still here. And many still believe that we can improve our society in both large and small ways.

Sometimes, my mind wanders to my climactic conversation with Jozsef in 1985 a few years before his country erupted in a bloody revolution. I cannot help but think that, amid the noise and confusion, Jozsef's conclusion contained an amazing dose of clarity.

In 1985, Freedom House issued Romania its lowest scores for political rights and civil liberties, something only the former Soviet Union, Iraq, Vietnam, Somalia, Afghanistan, Bulgaria, and 12 others recorded. Even Hungary and Nicaragua were rated slightly better. [4]

By 2025, Romania's total score improved to 82, better than all of the worst 1985 nations except for Mongolia, which shot up to 84. Romania was only two points behind the U.S. while surpassing China [9], Russia [12], Nicaragua [14], Vietnam [20], Iraq [31], Hungary [65], Israel [73], and many more. People had to rise up, take action, risk their lives and security, and die, for that to occur.

Perhaps, Jozsef did have a point. At least in nations where freedoms are severely curtailed, there may be little citizens can really do but bide their time and take notes. Meanwhile, in the countries where we still have liberties, we must keep standing up and using them. Or else we all risk falling into the abyss, where we can be arrested for carrying coffee and books.

The Big Issues

Taking on the Big Issues

First published in Medium, January 2, 2019

Never depend upon institutions or government to solve any problem. All social movements are founded by, guided by, motivated, and seen through by the passion of individuals.

— **MARGARET MEAD**, 1901-78

While watching a public television documentary in 2018, I focused on a clip that showed 1961 Freedom Riders on a bus stopped along a country road in the Deep South. The terror on the faces of the reformers sitting in their seats grew more intense as they observed white middle-aged men and youth carrying pipes, bats, and other weapons walking towards their vehicle.

As the attackers smashed the bus windows and started to enter through the door, one rider confronted his fear by running to the door and standing against it, temporarily blocking their assailants' passageway. The segment ended with him sacrificing his body to the mob, as hands reached in to execute their cruel injustice.

The emotional vividness of the short clip shown from the work of director Sidney Lumet shook me enough to research further into that time. I discovered that my knowledge of the riders' campaign was fairly superficial. I knew it was an important segment of the civil rights movement, one that challenged the notion of segregated public buses, which the U.S. Supreme Court had ruled unconstitutional as early as 1946. Southern states had ignored those decisions, and federal officials did nothing to enforce them. So sadly, it was up to individuals to test and ultimately make the government obey its laws by putting their own lives on the line.

What I didn't fully understand until I unearthed a valuable signed copy of the late David Halberstam's 1998 book, *The Children,* was what it was really like for those civil rights workers, how courageous and creative they had to be to take on the decades-entrenched Jim Crow system. How could a relatively few individuals, armed with nothing but their own consciences and sense of justice, lead the way to such a profound change, which had not occurred through legal means by those whose jobs it was to make such changes?

In doing so, they had to confront the courts, politicians, police, KKK, business community, certain media, and other segments that supported the unequal policies that signified second-class status for many. The unfair Jim Crow codes included separate restrooms, schools, and water fountains, not being able to eat in most restaurants and shop in many stores, sitting in the backs of buses, and obstacles to voting.

In addition, civil rights champions had to take on the apathy in their own communities. Many had to confront unsupportive parents, who feared their actions would get them expelled from college, jailed, and even killed. And they had to deal with resistance from numerous African Americans who preferred being a bigger fish in their own pond to the unknown future that integration would bring.

They joined this war knowing they would not be furnished with weapons beyond training on how to ignore insults and focus on the action, how to curl up in a ball and cover your head during attacks. They knew they could be jailed. They knew they could be beaten. They knew they might even die.

In short, they were some of the most courageous Americans who have ever lived.

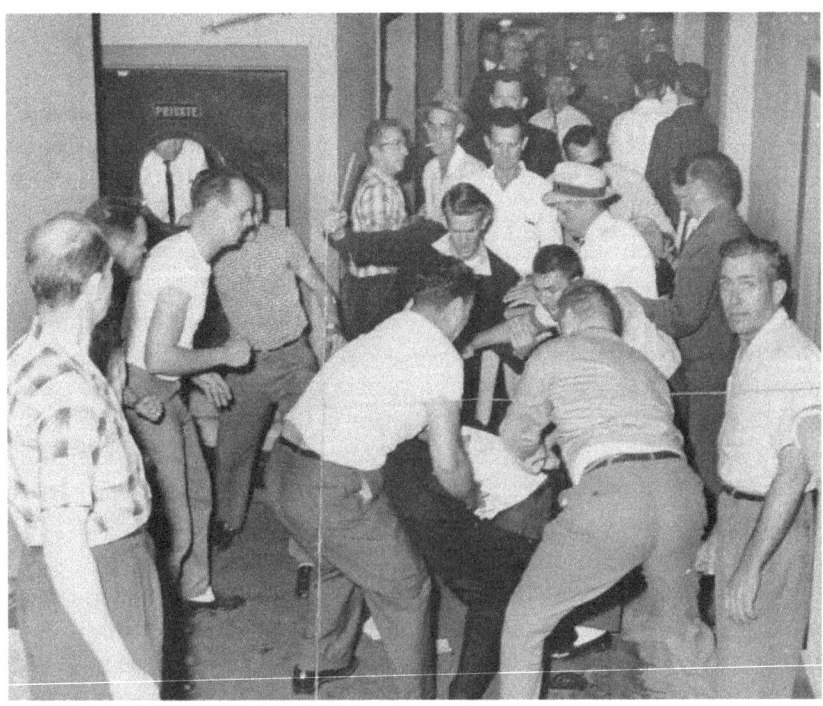

A mob of white men beats a Freedom Rider at a bus station in Birmingham, Ala., in 1961.   Photo from U.S. National Endowment for the Humanities, Public Domain

'Non-ending struggle'

On May 4, 1961, thirteen Freedom Riders – seven African American, six white – departed from Washington, D.C., on a Greyhound bus. Their goal was to reach New Orleans by May 17, the seven-year anniversary of the *Brown v. Board of Education* school desegregation ruling. Organized by the Congress of Racial Equality, which had conducted a similar action in 1947, the group openly tested a Supreme Court decision that segregated buses and terminals were unconstitutional.

As integrated groups sat towards the front of the bus, they did not encounter violence in Virginia and North Carolina. The first ugly incident occurred in Rock Hill, S.C., where Fisk University student and future U.S. Rep. John Lewis and two others were attacked after they tried to enter a whites-only waiting room.

In Atlanta, about half of the group split to join a Trailways bus. The Greyhound bus reached Anniston, Ala., first, where a mob of klansmen attacked the vehicle, slashing tires and breaking windows. The driver continued past the crowd, many of whom followed in cars and pounced on the bus when it soon stalled due to flat tires. After breaking more windows, one attacker threw a firebomb into the vehicle, which exploded into flames. Some assailants pressed against the doors and yelled, "Burn them alive!" [1]

At one point, an exploding fuel tank made the mob back off. Riders escaped through windows and doors, but some mob members assaulted them and talked of lynching them. Original rider Hank Thomas, a 19-year-old Howard University student, was hit in the head with a baseball bat. Alabama highway patrolmen reportedly fired warning shots in the air, helping to disperse the mob.

The Trailways bus arrived in Anniston about an hour after the Greyhound one. Some police officers entered the bus and told riders to switch seats. After they refused, klan members who secretly joined the bus in Atlanta stood up and beat several riders. As some viciously struck 61-year-old Michigan teacher Walter Bergman with hammers and clubs, his wife begged them to stop. They ignored her and threw Bergman's bleeding, unconscious body over other passengers in the back to block them from sitting up front. The assailants did the same with 46-year-old New York union organizer James Peck, 21-year-old South Carolina student Herman Harris, and others. [2]

The bus continued to Birmingham, where another mob entered the vehicle. Eugene "Bull" Connor, Birmingham's notoriously racist police commissioner, allowed klan members to beat riders for about 15 minutes before calling in officers to intervene. Peck required 53 stitches. Bergman suffered a stroke from the blows to his head and was forced to use a wheelchair for the rest of his life, which lasted to the age of 100. The mob went after news photographers, destroying their cameras, although numerous photographs survived. Some journalists, including Howard K. Smith of CBS News, observed attacks, and their reports eventually helped expose the Deep South savagery and attract international sympathy for the cause.

As Peck was treated at a clinic, he told reporters he would continue the rides. "It is my philosophy that the struggle has to be a non-ending one, because I am not one of those idealists who envision a utopia," he later said. Peck was the only participant of both the 1961 and 1947 campaigns. The latter journeyed through Upper South states like North Carolina and resulted in arrests, but only isolated violence. Between the 1930s and 1980s, Peck was arrested more than 60 times for labor, social, civil rights, and environmental causes. [3]

Some participants tried to locate other buses to take them onward, but drivers refused to escort Freedom Riders. A few decided to fly to New Orleans from Birmingham, but flights were canceled due to bomb threats. It took calls to U.S. Attorney General Robert Kennedy's office to get a plane to take some riders to New Orleans, where Xavier University of Louisiana housed them in secret.

Enter Diane Nash, Rev. James Bevel, Rev. C.T. Vivian, Bernard LaFayette Jr., and others. While attending college in Nashville, they had organized sit-ins that integrated drugstore and restaurant lunch counters. Hearing about the Freedom Riders' problems, Nash, LaFayette, Vivian, and Bevel were among those who traveled to Alabama to keep the effort going. Robert Kennedy sent special assistant John Seigenthaler to lobby for an end to the Freedom Rides. When that didn't work, the federal official helped negotiate with local officials to protect riders.

Seigenthaler told Nash that continuing the rides could result in death to participants. She responded, "We know someone will be killed, but we cannot let violence overcome nonviolence." Lewis responded in kind to an older mentor: "We understand that [death] may be the price. But it has to be done." Ironically, Seigenthaler himself was knocked unconscious in Montgomery while trying to protect riders. [4]

On May 20, Lewis, Thomas, and others left Birmingham on a Greyhound bus to Montgomery. As the vehicle entered the terminal, police protection again disappeared. The scene appeared quiet, then a mob carrying clubs, baseball bats, pipes, and more suddenly appeared. Riders debated about whether to exit through the back and attempt to outrun the angry assailants. Ultimately, white rider Jim Zwerg first ventured off the bus in front.

Before the mob reached him, he bowed his head and asked God for strength. "I had the most wonderful religious experience," Zwerg, who had transferred to Fisk from Wisconsin through an exchange program, later told a PBS reporter. "I felt a presence as close to me as breath itself, if you will, that gave me peace knowing that whatever came, it was okay." [5]

Zwerg probably saved numerous riders, said Fred Leonard, who was then a student at Tennessee State and later became a successful businessman. "He walked off the bus in front of us, and it was like those people in the mob were possessed. They couldn't believe that there was a white man who would help us," Leonard said. "When we came off the bus, the attention was on him. It's like they didn't even see the rest of us for about thirty seconds." [6]

Zwerg, who later became a minister before working for IBM and a charity, was not only badly beaten but thrown over a rail several times. Men held him while women and children clawed his face. He suffered a cracked spine, among numerous injuries. Lewis also took a barrage from the mob, being hit with a wooden crate at one point. He later said he thought he was going to die. The group took refuge at the First Baptist Church in Montgomery, where Martin Luther King Jr. arrived to speak. A white mob surrounded the church, and Kennedy sent marshals who used tear gas to disperse the mob.

On May 24, a group made it to Jackson, Miss., but many were arrested. Gov. Ross Barnett instructed guards at Parchman, the state's worst prison, to "break their spirits." That action was typical for Barnett, who said during his 1959 campaign that God "made [black people] different to punish" them. In 1962, he defied a federal order to admit James Meredith to the University of Mississippi, leading to riots. The following year, Barnett opposed allowing the Mississippi State basketball team to compete in the NCAA playoffs to the point he supported a court injunction, but the team avoided being served by sending decoy players to the airport.

Lewis, Thomas, and others appealed the Parchman sentences, and it took several years for them to be reversed by the Supreme Court. More riders descended on Montgomery and Jackson in ensuing months, and at one time, more than 300 riders were held at Parchman.

Lewis, like many, spoke of the persistent fear during those times. But they got beyond the fear mainly through their faith, outrage over injustices, and commitment to fellow participants. Often, what kept them going was they did not want to let down each other, particularly people they had recruited into the movement. It was not unlike the bonds forged by combatants during wars, where ordinary people perform extraordinary deeds for the cause and each other. Their actions transformed them into nonviolent, spiritual warriors who would persevere despite great risks and long odds.

Two years after the Freedom Rides, Fred Shuttlesworth, a Birmingham minister who co-founded the Southern Christian Leadership Conference with King and others, convinced King to help with an integration campaign in what was probably the most segregated U.S. city. King wrote the famed "Letter from Birmingham Jail" after being jailed for exercising First Amendment rights.

Shuttlesworth fought a conviction for parading without a permit to the U.S. Supreme Court, which reversed the conviction years later.

Bull Connor provided graphic media images by ordering officers to use fire hoses and dogs on children during those demonstrations. At the same time, far-right leaders and activists met in New Orleans to plot the killing of President John F. Kennedy and civil rights leaders.

King wanted to call off the Birmingham campaign after merchants told him they couldn't negotiate with demonstrations occurring, said Shuttlesworth, who didn't agree. "If we had just called it off without an agreement, the merchants would've said, 'Well, we never agreed to anything.' And we would not have gotten a victory," Shuttlesworth stated. "And King wouldn't have been immortal today." [7]

A month later, Mississippi NAACP leader Medgar Evers was assassinated by a klan member at his Jackson home as part of a tri-state conspiracy. On the same night, LaFayette, then a Student Nonviolent Coordinating Committee organizer, was brutally attacked at his home in Selma, Ala., and barely escaped death. Rev. Ben Cox, a Congress of Racial Equality organizer who had also participated in the Freedom Rides, eluded other assailants in New Orleans by being out of town.

A few months later, President Kennedy was felled in Dallas by another assassin in what many believe was a conspiracy involving former CIA officials who Kennedy forced to resign and other political enemies. More violent acts ensued, including the June 1964 murders of civil rights advocates James Chaney, Andrew Goodman, and Michael Schwerner in Mississippi. The following year, Malcolm X was gunned down, while Lewis and others were beaten by authorities on the Edmund Pettus Bridge in Selma, Ala., during a famed voting rights march.

The violent wave forced many politicians to support the Civil Rights Act of 1964, the Voting Rights Act of 1965, and other laws that took the shackles off Jim Crow. But such victories remained hollow since many states and municipalities ignored the laws until individuals challenged them, at continued risk.

An often-forgotten axiom: Just because a law is passed doesn't mean it will be enforced. As Peck said, the struggle for "liberty and justice for all" seems to be an unending one.

Students C.T. Vivian, Diane Nash, and Bernard LaFayette lead a 1960 march in Nashville. LaFayette was targeted for assassination on the same 1963 night that NAACP leader Medgar Evers was killed.   Photo from U.S. National Endowment for the Humanities, Public Domain

Segregation 'not going to change by itself'

Even though I grew up in a middle-class, all-white neighborhood in one of the most segregated cities in the South during the 1960s, I was not immune to the social changes. When some black kids were bused to my school, I refused to shun them, unlike many of my peers. I befriended them on the playgrounds in a way that innately made sense to me at a young age. Why should something as insignificant as skin color play a role in defining who you are and what rights you have as a human being? Don't many white people try to get darker skin in the summer by sitting in the sun?

As I played and followed sports, black athletes – Bob Hayes, Bob Gibson, Bill Russell – were among my favorites. I felt outrage as I watched movies and television shows that depicted slavery and other injustices. In 1968, when sprinters Tommie Smith and John Carlos raised black-gloved fists during an Olympic Games medal ceremony, I didn't understand why the adults around me were mad about that. I had seen a lot of athletes raise their fists during games. Why was it so bad to do during a ceremony when the national anthem – written by a slave owner who even supported sending freed slaves back to Africa – played?

I wanted to learn more about why Smith and Carlos did that, and why people were so mad about it, to the point that the athletes were initially ostracized by many and received death threats. Being only nine years old, I was shielded from the harshness of Jim Crow racism, the assassinations of King and another Kennedy, the continued civil rights struggle.

In my teen-age years, I was more interested in sports than social movements. But I read biographies of African-American athletes like Wilt and Russell and sought to understand what they had overcome. I befriended black basketball teammates and even brought some home to play pool or ping pong. The family dog, who ironically was both black and white, wasn't used to seeing nonwhites and barked more than usual at my black friends. Was Boots racist, or was he reflecting the racism in our lily-white neighborhood? Or was it a physical, vision issue, with the barking done more out of confusion?

During college, my biggest stands were exposing shoddy practices by a psychology professor who encouraged students to rappel down the football stadium wall with little training that resulted in one dying, advocating for the Libertarian Party, ranting against female reporters in men's locker rooms, and calling Jimmy Carter "nuts" for believing that his 1980 Olympic Games boycott would sway the former Soviet Union. Four years later, I joined the nuts, believing that a walk from California to Russia could impact the former Soviet leaders.

How did I get there? I started my journalism career as a sportswriter and soon discovered that was too limiting a career path. One thing led to another, and I found myself helping to produce an underground newspaper called the Dallas Advocate for Jobs, Peace and Freedom. As I previously wrote, I sought to be the kind of journalist who wasn't afraid to cross the line into advocacy at times and work on some solutions, rather than merely sit back and watch. That might not be the best approach since you get labeled an activist and worse, but there was one thing I knew: You gotta do what you gotta do.

I wasn't political, but believed in the power of individuals to effect change, as articulated by the late anthropologist Margaret Mead and others. There have been moments when governments, institutions, and individuals worked together to try to solve major problems, resulting in laws like the civil rights bill and programs such as Social Security and Medicare. But those have been relatively fleeting and usually led by individuals.

Halberstam's book showed how young people pushed on with civil rights actions when politicians and some leaders in the SCLC and other organizations wanted to cool off. Moreover, John Kennedy wasn't much of a civil rights advocate during the start of his presidency and saw most actions as irritations, something he didn't want to deal with since his party needed the support of racist, status-quo Democratic leaders in the South.

Some called our long walk to Russia in 1984 and 1985 a brave thing to do, particularly wearing shirts and carrying signs about walking for peace to Moscow and ending the Cold War through some of the country's most conservative Deep

South states. But it wasn't nearly as courageous as what those civil rights workers did.

In 1982, a KKK member drove his truck through a small group walking through the Deep South to New York for a United Nations disarmament conference, injuring one participant. We didn't face such a direct threat, though some large log-carrying trucks came pretty close to us in rural Alabama, due more to the narrow, two-lane roads than intent. Some motorists and others who saw us – even those in northern states like New York – gave us the finger and yelled that we were commies. A grocery store owner in Alabama called us "outside agitators," and someone threw a wad of wax at us, hitting a young walker. A Virginia state trooper threatened to "bust [us] in the chops." Police in a Maryland town demanded we roll up our signs because we didn't have a permit for a "political" march there. But most who stopped were supportive.

Almost 20 years after marchers were assaulted in Selma, Ala., our small group crossed the Edmund Pettus Bridge without incident. There, I met Amelia Boynton Robinson, a local civil rights leader who had been beaten unconscious during the 1965 Bloody Sunday. A photograph of her lying on the bridge was circulated worldwide, sparking much sympathy.

Almost two decades later, she still carried scars from that day. But there was no question she would do it again. "Segregation was not going to change by itself," said Mrs. Robinson, who died in 2015 at the age of 104.

Amelia Boynton Robinson, in wheelchair holding President Obama's hand, was on the front line of a 2015 march across the Edmund Pettus Bridge to commemorate the 50th anniversary of Bloody Sunday. Rep. John Lewis, another 1965 participant, was at Obama's right.   Photo from U.S. White House, Public Domain

By the time I finished various walks, the Cold War had about ended. We had met with high-level government officials from the U.S. and Russia who could not dismiss us because we had backed up our commitment to the cause with powerful action and attracted a large amount of media attention.

While some say the fall of the Berlin Wall and collapse of the Soviet Union in 1989 were caused more by Reagan's hard-line military buildup, others believe that efforts to bridge East-West differences like these walks played a significant role. For one they inspired people in Hungary, East Germany, Romania, and other former Soviet satellites to protest for political reforms.

I have come to see those years as an alternative to military service, community service to my country and the world in which I attempted to do what I could in my own, small way to address the Big Issues of the day.

Some members of Walk of the People meet with Rev. Jesse Jackson in 1985 in Geneva, Switzerland, during the first summit between Gorbachev and Reagan. Photo by Shay friend

Today's Big Issues

Today's young people face a number of challenges, including rocketing costs for housing and education, a decline in good-paying jobs, rising college debt and hate crimes, and climate change. Then there is that democracy issue, as Trump tried to go full authoritarian starting in 2025.

The most important issue cited by Americans between 18 and 34 years old was cost of living and inflation, according to a survey in late 2023 by the Center for Information and Research on Civic Learning and Engagement at Tufts

University in Massachussetts. In 2025, an AP poll still showed the economy as the chief concern among young people. [8]

While some say the times were more perilous for young people during the Great Depression, World War II, Cold War, and turbulent 1960s, there is no doubt that the present age offers unique challenges. One is that many federal officials are no longer that open to causes that the young cite as important, as seen in the many Republican Party leaders' unwillingness to support democracy, international climate treaties, and needed social-uplift programs.

Following the 1963 March on Washington, the Kennedy's invited civil rights leaders to the White House for a discussion. Meanwhile, Trump ignores large marches and other actions for democracy, women's and minorities' rights, the environment, and other causes. He belittles their efforts with demeaning social media messages, such as when he circulated a cartoonish video of him dropping poop on No Kings demonstrators from a plane after more than seven million people hit the streets in 2025.

Still, young people have tools that other generations didn't, such as social media and cell phones with video. As noted before, it's wiser to depend more on individuals than government and institutions, while not ignoring any segment that can provide aid. Approaching issues on a personal, nonpartisan level can be more effective. The No Kings movement of 2025 attempts to point out a concept that most Americans hate without mentioning the elephant in the White House – the idea that one person should control the government. Thus, people from all political persuasions are among the millions of people protesting in the streets against Trump excesses.

The bottom line is that every generation faces fresh challenges, and the Big Issues can be tackled with characteristics that play to young people's advantage, such as passion and perseverance.

Know that even as you may confront an issue that seems insurmountable, there is a playbook to win through studying the tactics of the civil rights movement.

In short: Embrace these challenges. Follow your consciences. Stay nonviolent in your dissent. Let the cons continue to be the violent ones, as they have throughout our history. Have each others' backs. And even if the mainstream media ignores your protest, record everything on social media.

No Kings protests signs at 2025 rallies often focused on concepts such as the Bill of Rights, rather than individual politicians. Kevin Shay photo

Housing and Society: Searching for Utopia

First published in the Eternal Flame, Dallas, Texas, February 1982; and Medium, May 6, 2018

Human beings will be happier – not when they cure cancer or get to Mars or eliminate racial prejudice or flush Lake Erie – but when they find ways to inhabit primitive communities again. That's my utopia.
— **KURT VONNEGUT JR.**, Playboy, 1973

Like many people, Bob and Ruth Foote spent much of their lives searching for a better way to live.

They took their children out of public schools and educated them through experiences such as a California-to-Bolivia sailing excursion. They lived in the backwoods of Oregon without access to numerous modern conveniences. They built a 55-foot schooner and schemed about taking the family to a deserted island for a Swiss Family Robinson-style adventure.

The island idea was eventually beached due to excessive costs and porting regulations, so the Foote's decided to establish a self-sufficient community of earth-sheltered homes that would use the smallest environmental footprint possible and also shield homeowners from escalating mortgage rates and energy costs. Ruth Foote worked in the real estate, insurance, and title industries, while Bob was an engineer and designed experimental aircraft. While he considered rising coastal sea levels, potential nuclear strikes, and a collapsed economy real possibilities, he was drawn to building an off-the-grid community more for the challenge than being a diehard survivalist.

"The story as I was told as a child was that Bob Foote had built a ferro-cement boat that was so nice that his wife, Ruth, suggested they live in it," Ben Huttash, who lived in the Foote's community for part of his childhood, told Preserve Denton. [1]

Finding 80 acres of fairly cheap land near Denton, Tx., the Foote's named the community Whitehawk Valley after an albino hawk they observed during their initial glimpse of the area in 1977. Soon, 30 other families put down $2,500 each for a plot of land to build their own version of their visions. Many knew the Foote's through a spiritual group.

Holding onto the attitudes hatched during the cataclysmic societal changes of the 1960s, most Whitehawk pioneers were fed up with the waste and bureaucracy of modern society, Bob Foote told me in 1982, as I surveyed numerous ferro-cement, underground homes. They wanted not only to advocate for conservation and simplicity, but to live those ideals.

"We were a group taking an apocalyptic viewpoint," Foote said. "We didn't think the world would end literally, but would end as to how we are currently living. Natural resources are finite. When they are used up, there is nothing left. We took a viewpoint that someone had to do something about finding a more conservative, simpler lifestyle." [2]

Between that visit and 2025, the median cost of a single-family home in the United States more than quintupled to about $421,000, according to the National Association of Realtors. Even when adjusted for inflation, home prices almost doubled. Soaring home mortgage, insurance, and inflation costs made the median monthly mortgage payment on a 30-year loan rise by almost 50 percent from 2021 to 2025, to $2,259, Bankrate reported.

Underground homes made of ferro-cement, such as this one, still exist in Whitehawk Valley, Tx. Photo by Steve Spurlock

Meanwhile, the average renter spent about $23,400 in 2025, about 40 percent more than in 2015, according to Zillow. Often priced out of their homes, the homeless population continued to increase to almost 1 million by 2025, federal figures show. More people not only lived in shelters and camps, but in their vehicles and on friends and relatives' couches, the latter of whom were mostly not counted in government surveys.

As of 2025, society has avoided the dire predictions by author Jeffrey Goodman and others of coastal cities falling into oceans, cataclysmic earthquakes, and massive planetary shifts. Still, climate change has sparked hotter weather and more intense storms and wildfires.

Short history of utopian communities

All utopias face a problem: what do you do with those who don't agree with you?

— MARGARET ATWOOD, 1999

The Whitehawkers weren't the first – and wouldn't be the last – people to seek a utopian community. Plato's *Republic*, written around 380 B.C., outlined a proposal for a better societal system. British lawyer and author Sir Thomas More created probably the first definitive work about an Atlantic Ocean island society in his 1516 book, *Utopia*.

Native peoples in the Americas formed communities for centuries that shared resources and were ruled not by a king but by a council of elders. American Indians like the Iroquois likely inspired founding fathers Thomas Jefferson and Ben Franklin by incorporating separation of powers and similar principles in their governing system, according to *Forgotten Founders* author and college professor Bruce E. Johansen. [3]

Many families left Europe for America seeking religious freedom, their own land, and more favorable taxes. The colony of Plymouth, Mass., formed in 1620, was among those that spoke to such desires, though reality often did not match expectations. One of the longest-running early American communes was established by a Christian separatist group, the Harmony Society, near Pittsburgh in the early 1800s. Led by George Rapp, the Rappites practiced celibacy and shared all goods and property, while preparing for the second coming of Christ. The group moved to Indiana for a decade before returning to Pennsylvania, where they existed for about a century.

While the Rappites didn't attract many converts, the Shakers, another religious group that formed communes in the U.S. around the same time, added about 6,000 members across 20 sites by the 1830s. Founded by Mother Ann Lee, the Shakers devised an equal labor system, engaged in musical sessions, and embraced the celibacy philosophy. Canadian writer and inventor Margaret Atwood thought this group produced the most effective utopian model. "They didn't kill anyone; they didn't try to impose their ideas by force," Atwood wrote in The New York Times Magazine. "They made a lasting contribution to furniture design and music, which is more than some can say, and best of all, they were self-limiting." [4]

The Oneida Community, a New York socialist commune formed by John Humphrey Noyes, was another that made a concrete contribution. While its communes that practiced complex marriage based on the concept of free love only lasted about three decades, its silverware-making operation blossomed into a big company.

Transcendentalists, who believed that humans had the capacity to transcend the chaos in the world to bring forth a higher nature, started their own utopian communes, Brook Farm and Fruitlands, in the 1840s in Massachusetts. Fruitlands, guided mostly by reformist educator Bronson Alcott, dissolved in less than a year. Brook Farm, primarily steered by Unitarian minister George Ripley, who became an advocate of the utopian socialist ideas espoused by French philosopher Charles Fourier, lasted about six years.

Journalist Charles Dana, one of its leaders, wrote that Brook Farm showed a way to abolish domestic servitude and provide better education for all students. "Although it passed away with little more than a whimper, Brook Farm cannot be considered a failure," noted Aaron McEmrys, a Unitarian minister in Arlington, Va. "Brook Farm left an indelible mark on American history, and remains a model for intentional communities throughout the world." Intentional communities are a voluntary, residential, structured group that shares values and duties, such as ashrams that existed in Asia before Christ, income-sharing communes, survivalist retreats, and cohousing projects. [5]

La Réunion, also inspired by Fourier, formed in 1855 near present-day downtown Dallas with about 350 settlers primarily from France, Belgium, and Switzerland. Unlike most other early communes, both men and women could own property and vote. Members were mostly artisans and shopkeepers, while some were musicians and artists. They honed skills that enabled them to form Dallas' first butcher shop and brewery, but their farming competence amidst the chalky terrain was lacking.

The colony disbanded in less than two years, with many returning to Europe or moving to San Antonio or New Orleans. Those who stayed included acclaimed botanist Julien Reverchon, who had a park and street named after him, and Benjamin Long, who became a Dallas mayor. "Although it functioned for only 18 months or so, La Reunion brought more to Dallas and Oak Cliff than most folks realize," Gayla Brooks wrote in the Oak Cliff Advocate. "It brought culture." [6]

Most such communities created in the 20th century were short-lived like Brook Farm. Many failed to live up to utopian ideals and died out due to internal conflict and economic problems.

An extreme example was Jonestown, a Guyana religious commune that practiced a form of socialism founded by Peoples Temple leader Jim Jones. The cult ended with the tragic 1978 mass suicide of more than 900 members. The Branch Davidians religious group led by David Koresh in Texas was another notorious cult, culminating in a 1993 fire and law enforcement standoff that left more than 80 dead.

The Centrepoint community in New Zealand saw some of its leaders convicted of drug charges and sexual assault of minors in the 1990s. The fundamentalist Seven Tribes commune in Germany faced allegations of child abuse after a television reporter filmed instances of adults striking young children with willow canes in 2013. [7]

The Foundation for Intentional Community listed about 1,050 communities in its online directory in 2025, with almost 800 in the U.S. Many groups don't choose to list themselves, said Laird Schaub, former executive secretary of the FIC. He estimated that there were more like 4,000 intentional communities with a combined population of some 100,000 in the U.S. alone. [8]

Those numbers, which are hard to obtain since many groups are not interested in answering inquiries from the general public, "have been rising over the quarter century that we've been collecting the data," Schaub said. "Some groups are afraid that open publicity will lead to more negative attention than positive attention and thus choose to be discreet about what they say in public."

Some called Arden, a Delaware single-tax village of about 500 people founded in 1900 based on the philosophy of political economist and writer Henry George, an intentional community. If it is, Arden has to be one of the most structured such entities. Residents own homes and pay taxes, or land rent, while about half of Arden's land is publicly-owned forests and greenways. Many residents are artists and musicians. Among its former residents were President Joe Biden and writer Upton Sinclair.

If Arden is not really an intentional community, then the 350-acre Twin Oaks, founded in 1967 on a former tobacco farm in a hilly section of rural Virginia, is likely the oldest existing one, as of 2025. Adhering to the beliefs of psychologist B.F. Skinner, author of the 1948 utopian novel *Walden Two*, the group grew to about 90 people by 1984 and remains about that size in 2025.

Residents work full-time at jobs such as making hammocks and growing tofu. They receive housing, food, health care, and spending money rather than a direct salary. In the 1970s, the group won a big contract with national retailer Pier 1 Imports to produce handcrafted hammocks. Twin Oaks had so many orders that leaders, or planners, had to subcontract with neighboring communes such as

Acorn Community, which formed in 1993. But in 2004, Pier 1 faced financial problems and ended the contract.

In response, Twin Oaks had to cut $50,000 from the overall budget that year, with the tofu business replacing hammock manufacturing as the most lucrative enterprise. Members grow much of their own food and raise cows and other animals, while some earn income through book indexing and seed farming. While the planners, managers, and decentralized committees make decisions, a majority vote by members can overturn the leaders' choices.

A member of Twin Oaks in Virginia works on a hammock. Photo by Rashaun, Wikimedia Commons

In 2025, there were seven large group houses, a children's building, community center with a kitchen, work buildings, a hospice, and cemetery. Most buildings utilized some form of solar energy. Some members ran errands in Richmond and other neighboring cities, taking care of other residents' needs like returning library books.

"Our resource-sharing lifestyle enables us to live lightly on the earth, minimize waste and inefficiency, and invest wisely in collective goods," Twin Oaks member Raj Ghoshal wrote in 2002. Those public amenities included an artificial pond, volleyball court, miniature home theater, computers, and music equipment. [9]

I met one Twin Oaks member in 1984 while walking through Virginia on the Walk of the People project. Taylor Frome, a cousin of walk participant Barbara Hirshkowitz, had given most of her possessions to Twin Oaks and traveled with just a small pack. Some of us had several suitcases and much larger packs in tow.

On a rest day, Frome led a group therapy session, where we discussed the true potential of being able to change another person and related concepts. We tried a listening exercise practiced at Twin Oaks, where we broke into pairs and explained our ideas further on a one-to-one level. When we reconvened, we had to summarize what our partner said. Most discovered we were better talkers than listeners.

"You learn a lot about how to work with others through living in a community," said Frome, who later moved to the Philadelphia area but maintained communication with former and current members. "You gain tools that really help you."

Keenan Dakota, who joined Twin Oaks in 1983, told a Richmond, Va., television news reporter in 2015 that the simpler lifestyle was a key factor in her living there so long. "The things that kept me here are different," she said. "I wanted to raise my kids. I like the work with my hands. I like to build things. I think that's true for a lot of people who live here." [10]

Rachelle Ellis, who lived at Twin Oaks from 2005 to 2007, commented on a 2014 Al Jazeera America article that income-sharing communities "provide an incredible security that you'd never find in the mainstream culture…. You have to work, but you also don't have to pay bills, worry about upkeep for your car, try to find the cheapest organic brown rice at the co-op, or find a doctor that's covered under your health care plan. All of those activities are worked into the labor structure of the community and become someone's job, which is perfect motivation for taking care of those things and making them the problems of a small group of people who get 'paid' to do so." [11]

Another older, thriving income-sharing commune was The Farm, which dated to 1971 when about 300 mostly Californians purchased cheap land in central Tennessee. They built structures from recycled materials and became agriculturally self-sufficient within four years without government aid. By 1980, the population had swelled to more than 1,200 people, but financial problems like medical bills forced the farm to start charging residents rent.

The Farm became known for natural childbirth, midwifery, vegetarianism, creative arts, alternative technologies, and working with native tribes. By the 1990s, the commune had established a solar power educational program, its own electrical and water systems, a construction company, and tofu plant. Some group members helped rebuild homes in Guatemala after a 1976 earthquake.

"Unlike other high-profile communes that often morphed into dangerous [or murderous] cults, The Farm kept its leaders mostly in check, focusing instead on becoming self-sufficient through the communal infrastructure, organic farming, a plant-based diet, and natural childbirth," Jill Ettinger stated in a 2023 Ethos article. "While today it's a much smaller collective and its organizational structure has changed from the early days, The Farm in Summertown is still thriving." [12]

Visiting European intentional communities

In the mid-1980s, I ran into others who lived in intentional communities and stayed in a few. In Baudenbach, a German village nestled among picturesque scenery between Wurzburg and Nuremberg, Swami Gerhard Unger allowed us the run of two rooms and an entire attic within a 20-member commune. He had studied yoga in Bombay for four years and traveled extensively throughout Europe, Africa, and the U.S.

During a rest day, I took a hike through nearby woods with fellow walker Dennis Thomas, a California engineer who joined the project in France. Working at IBM "figuring out how much computers cost," Thomas had made enough money to afford two houses, a Datsun sports car, and tax breaks, before he felt like something was missing and decided to radically alter his lifestyle. He heard about the walk around the same time I did and was about to join it from California with intentions of going the distance, but something made him hang on to job security for one more year.

Like myself, Thomas had not been a formal member of a peace organization, though the former collegiate swimmer and water polo player sympathized with the aims. We propped ourselves on a decaying picnic table and munched on cheese sandwiches and apples. Our chatter eventually gravitated to issues revolving around living in a group setting.

Thomas, who had ignored walk member Tammy Leffler's request a few nights earlier to help her with the dishes, explained his non-cooperative behavior. "I just don't like to be told what to do, even on that simple level," he stated. "If I'm not in the mood to do something, I just don't like to do it. In a utopian community, everyone should be able to do what they want automatically, and it would work that easily." [13]

"But you forget. We have yet to find a real utopian community," I reminded him.

I had been looking for such a community even before that walking project when I helped start one in a large lakeside house near Dallas in 1982. The experiment existed about a year before succumbing to squabbles and money problems. For almost two years, the Walk of the People itself was a nomadic intentional community – not unlike an old-fashioned tribe.

At the Baudenbach community, Harold Greubel detailed his experiences from a journey that took him through the Himalayas, Australia, New Zealand, and the western U.S. He stayed at several communities, including the Moonies for about a month. One Moonie rule became difficult to follow while there: No sex. "They don't believe in invoking that sense of guilt, here," he disclosed.

Europe has numerous intentional communities. One in Regnitzlosau, Germany, hosted peace projects in the 1980s.   Photos by Kevin Shay

The Baudenbach commune was not listed in the Foundation for Intentional Community's online directory and was apparently inoperable in 2025. Others we visited, such as L'Arche communities in Alabama, Washington, D.C., France, and Belgium, were still active.

Our walk stalled at the former East German border, and we moved into a seven-bedroom mill house in the 750-year-old village of Regnitzlosau. Called Frieden Zentrum Dreilandereck, which meant "peace house near the triple-border point," the residence had been home to two other international peace contingents in the previous two years, so it was a temporary commune of sorts.

Members of a project called *A Walk to Moscow* had stayed there for some nine months in 1982 and 1983, before securing visas to walk through Czechoslovakia and Poland. The other contingent was comprised of primarily Australian natives who cycled for peace in 1984 and were eventually granted visas to enter Czechoslovakia.

During our two months, we started a garden and made home improvements, including to the upstairs plumbing. We built community relations through projects like helping neighbors paint their homes.

Our stationary, temporary commune broke up when former peace campers at a base in southwest Germany needed to take over the mill house. We then continued into Austria, where the project's walking portion essentially ended in Vienna. We arranged a train trip into Hungary and later walked through part of Switzerland before some members visited Russia and other nations by train.

'Rather keep a bachelor's room in Hell than go to board in Heaven'

The walk project lent a good idea of what intentional communities were like, both in visiting some and attempting to live out a nomadic version. Having people around to share tasks and do jobs most cannot, like unplugging a centuries-old plumbing system, is a definite advantage. Keeping expenses down, conserving resources, and fellowship with like-minded friends are other benefits in such living arrangements.

But there are drawbacks to living in communes, like limited privacy. You have to be willing to wait in line for the bathroom. Hearing others talk loudly when you're trying to sleep or focus can be annoying. But it wasn't much different from living in an apartment complex, particularly one with thin walls, or a large family.

Another drawback is dealing with inevitable conflict, which can be fueled by lack of space or getting on each others' nerves. Even close friends who have known each other for years can face conflict when in a communal living situation; television shows like *Survivor* and *Big Brother* depend on drama like this for ratings.

Studies show that groups that have clear ways of dealing with such conflicts tend to last longer than those that let issues fester. "When conflict is mismanaged, it can cause great harm to a relationship, but when handled in a respectful, positive way, conflict provides an opportunity to strengthen the bond between two people," Jeanne Segal, Lawrence Robinson, and Melinda Smith said in HelpGuide.org. [14]

Successful intentional communities, such as Twin Oaks and The Farm, also don't isolate themselves, Lucy Sargisson, a professor in the School of Politics and International Relations at the University of Nottingham, maintained in a study. They assimilate to some degree into the wider community, she noted.

Finding enough financial resources to survive has long been a challenge for communes, Sargisson said. If they can't sell a product, such as a hammock or tofu, to the wider community or allow members to work outside the communities, they can't raise revenue. And that, in turn, leads to bigger problems. Being part of the wider community is also beneficial to combat feelings of alienation from society, she said. [15]

Of course, one reason many join a commune in the first place is to separate themselves from the greater community. Such communities need a certain amount of separation to accomplish this.

"Just as utopian fiction requires some level of estrangement for critical distance or cognition, so intentional communities require it to pursue their collective projects," Sargisson noted. "These groups need to operate within self-set boundaries that separate them from the wider community... However, this can generate material challenges and, more importantly, can deteriorate into collective alienation."

While boundaries are essential in most intentional communities, a balance between separation and remaining open to the greater community needs to be maintained, she said. For example, the Katajuta community in New Zealand found it had to alter a longtime open-door policy after a new member started walking around naked claiming to be Jesus Christ.

"Nobody minded very much until he began to insist that they kneel and worship him," Sargisson stated. "This hardly fitted with their vision of the good life, and there followed a difficult period from which the group took some time to recover." [16]

Walk of the People had an open-door policy for people joining for the day, but they had to be reviewed via a written letter to a coordinator in Georgia if they wanted to walk longer than that. Some embraced this and others didn't, leading to long, draining debates. We never had a problem with anyone walking around naked and wanting us to kneel before him, but we did have to deal with a new member in England who told a veteran walker to "fuck off" in front of numerous people.

There were also various viewpoints on how much community building was needed within our group. Some wanted to meet for hours to build cohesion during non-walking days; others preferred quick meetings with more free time to do their own thing. We tried to reach a compromise, though there were still some meetings that lasted for hours. Like many progressive groups, we operated on consensus with no set leader. Coordination duties rotated between members from week to week.

Some people are better suited for commune life than others. John Vander Zee Sears, a boarder at 19th-century Brook Farm for several years, appreciated the community's practices of equal pay and dividing duties. "Men and women, boys and girls, drawn together in groups by special likings for the work to be done, made labor not only light but really pleasant," he said. Ardent Brook Farmers wanted "first of all, to be in harmony with the common mind." [17]

Author Nathaniel Hawthorne invested in the Brook Farm community and moved there, thinking he would have much time to write books. But he left after six months and even filed a lawsuit against founder Ripley for $586. He reportedly did not have time to write much more than a letter and grew tired of shoveling manure that was used at the farm as fertilizer. He wrote to his fiancée that he "never suspected that farming was so hard" and wanted to leave "before my soul is utterly buried in a dung heap."

Writers and transcendentalists Ralph Waldo Emerson and Margaret Fuller declined to join Brook Farm, believing in solitude and more of an individualistic vision. Fellow writer Henry David Thoreau was also not a fervent supporter. He amusingly scribbled in his journal after a visit, "As for these communities, I think I had rather keep a bachelor's room in Hell than go to board in Heaven." [18]

I sympathize with such views – it's hard to live with just one person, let alone more than one. Yet, I still prefer some type of community-living arrangement that provides a better way to live than having to lock ourselves into structures, or even gated communities, out of fear of what may occur. Much has changed since the 1840s, and we have to find better methods to share what may be limited resources in the future.

Alternatives like cohousing, tiny homes grow

Perhaps the greatest utopia would be if we could all realize that no utopia is possible; no place to run, no place to hide, just take care of business here and now.

— **Jack Carroll**, legislative representative, Ontario, 1995-99

Since the walk, I have tried various housing arrangements. I bought and sold two single-family houses, rented apartments and single-family dwellings, and leased rooms. I have raised two kids in various dwellings, shared quarters with roommates, and lived almost alone. In 2021, I bought half of a duplex in a community that caters to seniors, where my children can stay.

The arrangements carried their own advantages and disadvantages. Owning a new 2,000-square-foot home on a cul-de-sac for just $105,000 in Arlington, Tx., was a good deal. Most neighbors were friendly and considerate, with the biggest problem being a few parties lasting to the early morning and cigarette butts thrown on our lawn. Owning an almost 60-year-old, 1,900-square-foot home on a cul-de-sac for $275,000 in Rockville, Md., was not such a good deal. The home was in a decent – but not great – neighborhood, dated in many areas, and required substantial plumbing, roof, electrical, and other repairs.

Qualifying for Montgomery County's moderately-priced dwelling program allowed me to rent a two-bedroom apartment in trendy, Main Street-style planned communities for lower than market rate. But still, paying $1,200 a month for such apartments seemed excessive at the time, though not so much later, especially considering we had access to pools, hot tubs, and exercise rooms.

All in all, living in King Farm and Fallsgrove apartments were decent experiences. In King Farm, I could walk or take a free shuttle to a light-rail station, which gave me access to the Washington, D.C., area. I could walk to work, parks, grocery stores, banks, restaurants, and shops. Fallsgrove had a greater variety of retailers, though not a nearby subway station. Bicycling was encouraged, but there were not any covered racks to lock them. There were events like community movie nights, swim parties, and yard sales.

But there was a definite gap between homeowners and "apartment people," with the latter viewed by some as having second-class status. That was an issue in such communities; you didn't feel like you were an equal member when you rented in comparison to homeowners. In the senior community, I feel like I am more on equal footing with my neighbors, but there are other issues, such as restrictive homeowners association rules that even forbids parking a car overnight in front of your own house and putting wind chimes on your back porch.

I can see the benefits of living in an income-sharing commune like Twin Oaks, especially for those in their early 20s. But when you get to a certain age and want a family, a more traditional arrangement typically makes more sense.

Cohousing projects, which combine privately-owned homes with shared amenities such as community and recreation centers, laundry rooms, and lawnmowers, were a great alternative, some said. While that movement began in Denmark in the 1960s, many U.S. projects were along the East and West coasts. Common Place Cooperative in Cambridge, Mass., was the oldest, dating to 1973.

The U.S. Cohousing Association listed more than 300 communities in its online directory in 2025, with about one-third of them starting since 2020. About 30 were for seniors age 55 and older. More were cropping up in Middle America. The first cohousing project in Texas opened in 2025 in Houston, about two miles from the Astros' ballpark. [19]

Besides residing at Twin Oaks, Ellis lived in Blueberry Hill Cohousing in Vienna, Va., from 2008 to 2012. That community, billed as the first cohousing development in Northern Virginia, formed in 2000.

"In cohousing, members own their homes, property, and cars," Ellis noted. "They do their own grocery shopping and are responsible for their own health care needs. It's almost like a conventional neighborhood, but there's true intention as being there really is a choice."

The developments combine private units with community facilities like kitchens for group meals. Homes also have private kitchens. Most have homeowners associations that develop community rules. In short, they generally offer a clearer path to develop a true community that watches out for neighbors, advocates said.

Cohousing has advantages like having people around to help with repairs and disadvantages, such as limited privacy. "People thrive in cohousing when they value the benefits of community life more than they value whatever they have to give up to get it," said Karen Gimnig, a cohousing consultant who lived in River Song Cohousing in Eugene, Oregon. [20]

While she and her husband left the Eugene development in 2023 for their hometown on the Puget Sound in northwestern Washington, Gimnig's opinions about the workability of cohousing remained rosy. "Nothing has changed in our very positive opinion of our neighbors," she said. "The problem is that Eugene, where River Song is located, has a climate and landscape that doesn't work for us. The winter is gray and damp. We miss the rain shadow and frequent bright sun."

While some homes can be pricey, others are more reasonable, often depending on the area and size. In 2025, Wolf Creek Lodge in California had a one-bedroom place listing at $435,000, while a two-bedroom in Fresno's La Querencia was only $300,000. Renting a room at Fat Peach Farm in New Hampshire started at $1,000.

Many cohousing projects have similar values with intentional communities, including cooperation, Sargisson concluded in another study. But most were more focused on individual members than the community as a whole.

"Its members aspire to own their homes, bring up their children in nuclear families and live safe, happy lives in friendly and supportive neighborhoods," she stated. "And, as a movement, there is an observable anti-radical tendency in North American cohousing. They describe themselves as non-ideological, or non-doctrinal. What they mean, I have suggested, is that they are not oppositional. And this may help to explain the success of cohousing." [21]

The anti-radical nature in which cohousing works primarily for the good of members is not meant to be a criticism, Sargisson said. "Cohousing is significant, and it is effective. I have cited studies that suggest that it does indeed create better communities and more active citizenry amongst its members."

Another trend is towards tiny or micro homes – with many residences smaller than 700 square feet – as an alternative to larger, more expensive homes. There is even a Tiny Home Industry Association that began in 2016 in Colorado and had more than 1,000 members in 2025. "Over the past 15 years, the tiny-house movement grew steadily," the group reported on its website. "It is now worldwide, with massive popularity in Australia and burgeoning in several other countries." [22]

Many accessory dwelling units – those built on existing lots behind larger, mostly single-family homes – are smaller, at up to 1,200 square feet. The ADU generally houses relatives, thus some call them "granny flats." In California, ADUs were one of the most popular affordable housing solutions, comprising about one-fifth of new housing permits in 2025. Many are modular, pre-fab units.

Whitehawk Valley in Texas is a sort of gated cohousing and tiny-home community in which residents build and own their homes while sharing common areas, tools, and work. Ferro-cement, which involves applying plaster or mortar over metal such as chicken wire, originated in the 1840s in France and has been used in the building of other sturdy structures like ships and water tanks.

The home construction costs ranged from $25 to $35 per square foot, compared with $100 to $150 with the average brick or siding home. The first 550-square-foot home cost about $3,500 for materials and required 3,000 man hours to construct. All homes had septic tanks, which comprised up to 20 percent of the total cost.

With proper solar-window setups and ground cover, the homes maintained comfortable temperatures without the need for battery-powered heaters or cooling systems, advocates said. During one hot summer when the temperature reached more than 100 degrees Fahrenheit for six consecutive weeks, the temperature inside a Whitehawk residence did not exceed 80 degrees, according a report by builder Loren Impson. [23]

On really cold days, which are fairly infrequent in Texas, the temperature inside the structure dropped to 60 degrees, which required using a heater for most people. Some reported not enjoying the somewhat rustic conditions that could be likened to camping. One homeowner contracting for electricity on the power grid caused controversy among members who thought it went against the founders' ideas. Lots were sold through memberships, not individual deeds.

Many homes had wind generators, composting toilets, solar energy panels, and greenhouses. The Foote's also started another community, Rainbow Valley, in 1978 and formed an agricultural co-op that made decisions through a voting system by members. They provided 75 acres of land to the Texas Land Conservancy to preserve the original Blackland Prairie area. As of 2025, the TLC continued to protect that land with homeowners in the Rainbow Valley Agricultural Co-op.

While Bob Foote passed away in 2013 and Ruth in 2012, their son, Robin, founded Whitehawk Construction Co. to help people build ferro-cement homes. Robin passed away in 2024, but others continued to take up the slack.

"As new people move in, the reason for [Whitehawk and Rainbow Valley's] existence changes," Ben Huttash said. "Sometimes I think about climate change and wonder if the intended purpose of Whitehawk will be realized in a warming climate…. I have a [young daughter] and worry about the world she will inherit from us. The Foote family was on the right track, just 40 years too early."

Keri Ross, who grew up in Rainbow Valley and later lived about an hour away, had fond memories of her childhood. "Me and my friends….used to roam. My mom would ring the dinner bell when it was time to come home. It was great," she said.

The vision changed with disputes over land, membership, and other matters, Ross said. The roads and other areas were badly in need of repair. At one time, co-op members were required to volunteer a certain number of hours working on roads and other sections.

In 1982, Foote told me he foresaw similar communities of low-cost underground homes cropping up around the country, though not necessarily built with ferro-cement. While the number of really successful alternative housing communities remains relatively small, the philosophy that causes many to seek a better life, to strive for an ideal that means "no place" in Greek, continues to thrive.

Public vs. Private Land: Who Owns America?

First published in the North Texas Daily, University of North Texas, Denton, September 16, 1980; and Medium, July 25, 2018

The woods, the streams, everything on it belong to everybody and is for the use of all. How can one man say it belongs only to him?
 — **MASSASOIT SACHEM**, Wampanoag Indian chief, 1581–1661

Who owns the Mississippi River, or any of our great rivers? The water runs out of a mountain down to the sea. It belongs to no individual....Who owns the beaches in Santa Barbara and elsewhere? Who owns the fish, the ducks, and the pelicans?...One has but a lease on ownership during one's lifetime. The success or failure of how something is used depends upon how it is left.
 —**WALTER J. HICKEL**, *Who Owns America?*, 1971

There was a time when New Braunfels was still among the quintessential small American towns, with many more acres of open space than residents.

This central Texas pit stop between Austin and San Antonio had a natural attraction that many similar towns lacked: the Guadalupe and Comal rivers. Locals and visitors had experienced the thrills of fast-moving rapids on those waterways through inner tubes, canoes, and other means since the mid-19th century. There were a few family resorts, such as Camp Warnecke that opened shortly after World War I, and tube rental sites. Many people brought their own tubes and shot the rapids for free.

Now, Camp Warnecke is known more for a water park and condo complex.

In 1979, Bob and Billye Henry opened a resort motel on the Comal River and erected a 60-foot replica of a tower at the Solms Castle in Germany. They built slides and pumped water from the river, establishing the second water park in the country. The Henry's bought Camp Warnecke in 1991 and turned the more natural resort into the Boogie Bahn surfing wave and Dragon Blaster uphill water coaster. Schlitterbahn grew into one of the most popular water parks nationwide, attracting more than a million visitors by 2017. That was more than any such park not in Orlando, according to the Themed Entertainment Association.

During a 1980 visit, I sensed the Wave of Change that was to occur in New Braunfels. The city had taken control of the main spillway, charging an additional $1.50 to shoot it. I had just read Hickel's *Who Owns America?*, in which the former Alaska governor decried excesses such as the privatization of public lands. As U.S. interior secretary under Richard Nixon, Hickel supported stronger public land conservation laws and environmental regulations on offshore oil rigs than most officials. He also wrote a letter critical of Nixon's Vietnam War policy following the 1970 shooting of college students at Kent State University by National Guard troops. Nixon fired him, but Hickel's position appeared even more conscientious when Watergate took down the disgraced president.

So I had to ask the New Braunfels employee collecting the cash how the city could take over this spillway and charge money for people to enjoy it. I was going beyond Hickel to even question the concept of public ownership of natural resources. "Well, it owns the place so it makes the rules," she replied.

That reason made little sense to me. I asked to see the manager, who was right behind her. "What do you want?" he asked.

"I want to know how the city can come in here and charge people money for something it didn't create. I mean, how did they get to own this place?" I asked in all seriousness, as if I really expected an answer.

He looked slightly shaken. "Why do you want to know this?"

"Because I don't think it's right for someone to come in and exploit nature just to make money," I replied, again in all seriousness. I was but 21, naive enough to believe that something besides crass commercialism dominated our society.

"Well, I can't answer that," he finally replied. "You'd have to talk to the city. Now, either pay up or leave."

I left. I found a hole in the fence and entered the park my own way. It was one small act of civil disobedience against the Wave of Change, one small finger in the dike before the hurricane hit and flooded that town and many more towns across the land. In 1980, New Braunfels was still a town of some 20,000 folks. After becoming one of the fastest growing cities in the nation during the 2010s, that town would transform into a suburban San Antonio city with more than 100,000 residents seeking similar tract housing plots.

Even back in 1980, my protest wasn't really worthwhile. I had to wait in a really long line to ride down the spillway. Trash littered the water. The city continued to operate the chute in 2025, charging $7 to ride it and as much as $20 to park. Those fees were cheaper than paying $40 per person to ride the chutes and other features at nearby Schlitterbahn.

A few months after my 1980 visit, I wrote a manifesto for my college newspaper, the North Texas Daily. I noted how American Indians rejected land ownership for the most part, though some tribes recognized general communal land rights. "The first [European] settlers...disregarded the native Indians' ways and rights," I charged. They "set down ownership plots, not caring that [they] didn't make the land....The [European-American's] downfall is in thinking he owns something he doesn't and trying to use this for his own selfish benefit."

I added that I wasn't necessarily against progress and the "American way," but it had to be "done with reason." The European-American of today "can't turn his back on that eternal question: Who owns America?" I concluded.

Numerous J-school professors bristled at my bold musings. I received veiled threats, whose authors had to take the time to compose by written letters in those days. Rather than back up me and the First Amendment, our paper's spineless editor proclaimed to the staff, "From now on, stay away from eternal subjects in future columns."

I considered that edict to be a violation of my First Amendment rights, an ironic example of a media establishment that received substantial public funds engaging in self-censorship. I wanted to launch a Clarence Darrow-like defense about how one purpose of a university should be to make students think of bigger questions than how they will pay for their education and combat the cockroaches in their dorm rooms. But I had to pick my battles; I figured I had done enough damage. And I could always get around that edict by refraining from actually using the word, "eternal," again.

I did learn a larger lesson: If you're going to make waves and stand up for what you believe, be prepared to pay a price.

My 1980 college newspaper column caused a change in editorial policy to not write about "eternal" topics, which I considered to be a violation of my First Amendment rights. Shay photo, Fair Use

This land is my land

When Italian explorer Christopher Columbus landed in the Caribbean in 1492 and established a settlement in present-day Haiti, about 25 million natives lived in the region that would become North America. Throughout the entire New World, including present-day Central and South America, estimates vary from 54 million to 112 million people, which would be more than the population in Europe back then. They had crossed a land bridge that connected Eurasia with the Americas across what is now the Bering Strait into modern-day Alaska. The bridge existed until about 10,000 B.C. when it was covered by flood water.

Columbus was not even the first European to reach land in the Americas; the Viking Leif Erikson explored Newfoundland and other North American regions around 1000. While Europeans were starting to transition from the concept of nobility and churches owning much of the land to lower-income individuals overseeing plots, Columbus' settlement sparked the private land ownership wave in the Americas.

After Columbus' crew landed, the native Arawaks, Tainos, and Lucayans were friendly, even giving them cotton and spears, and helping to repair their ship. So how did Columbus return the favor? By claiming present-day Haiti and the Dominican Republic for Spain – despite natives living there for thousands of years – and killing and enslaving them. Columbus was not only the first slave trader in the Americas, but his son became the first African slave trader, according to former Republican speechwriter Eric Kasum. [1]

With the land grab, Columbus claimed resources such as gold for Spain, as well. The Spaniards reportedly killed and beheaded many natives, raped women, and threw infants headfirst against rocks, Indian Country Today reported. They forced natives to work in gold mines and cut off their hands if they did not produce at least a thimble of gold dust every three months – an almost impossible task since Columbus misjudged the extent of gold on the island. They fed babies to dogs, sometimes in front of horrified parents, and set up butcher shops where the remains of native bodies were sold as dog food. By 1494, about 125,000 natives on the island had died. [2]

As pilgrims landed at Plymouth Rock in 1620, they were also greeted by natives, who lived in a mostly communal style without private property rights. But the tribes did recognize general land rights – the Wampanoag tribe became weakened with disease around this time and agreed to give up rights to more land to the inland rival Narragansett people. The Wampanoag, led by Massasoit Sachem, welcomed the British invaders, helping them to farm and catch fish to survive the early years. In 1621, Sachem even agreed to give up access to some 12,000 acres that the pilgrims used for Plymouth Plantation, though he didn't really understand the differences between communal land use by natives and the European ownership concept.

While pilgrims usually at least worked with natives to gain permission for land, the English Puritans who soon followed just grabbed the land. Puritan leader John Winthrop, who became governor of the Massachusetts colony in 1629, declared that the natives did not have a "civil right" to the land, only a "natural right" that did not have legal standing. John Jay, a Founding Father and first U.S. chief justice in 1789, spoke for many when he remarked, "The people who own the country ought to govern it." Never mind *how* those people came to "own" the country.

Natives fought back, but eventually the English settlers prevailed and made many of them slaves. Many died by smallpox introduced into native communities by the Europeans.

"Behind the English invasion of North America, behind their massacre of Indians, their deception, their brutality, was that special powerful drive born in civilizations based on private property," wrote historian Howard Zinn in *A People's History of the United States*. "It was a morally ambiguous drive; the need for space, for land, was a real human need." [3]

Zinn further noted, "Indian Removal, as it has been politely called, cleared the land for white occupancy between the Appalachians and the Mississippi, cleared it for cotton in the South and grain in the North, for expansion, immigration, canals, railroads, new cities, and the building of a huge continental empire clear across to the Pacific Ocean. The cost in human life cannot be accurately measured, in suffering not even roughly measured. Most of the history books given to children pass quickly over it."

Some founders, such as Ben Franklin and Thomas Jefferson, argued with early American leaders to work with natives, or at least abide by signed treaties to stay off their land. But even Jefferson as president supported the removal of Creek and Cherokee natives from Georgia. In North Carolina, land speculators stole thousands of acres of native land from the Chickasaw people, though they were among the few tribes to fight on the American side against the British.

Andrew Jackson, the country's seventh president, was a notorious proponent of removing natives so whites could claim the land, particularly through the 1830 Indian Removal Act that he pushed through Congress. He reportedly believed he was doing natives a favor by protecting them from white settlers and land speculators who soon outnumbered natives.

Some tribes, such as the Seminoles, refused to move and fought the settlers. Others like the Cherokees used legal means to fight back and even won a U.S. Supreme Court case in 1832 that recognized them as an independent entity entitled to federal protection from the actions of state governments that took their land. But the state of Georgia and Jackson ignored that ruling and forced the

Cherokees on the Trail of Tears to the West. An estimated 4,000 Cherokees died of cold, hunger, and disease on that 800-mile march in 1838 and 1839.

By 1844, the number of natives living east of the Mississippi River declined to about 30,000 from some 120,000 in 1820. Red Cloud, an Oglala Lakota chief, summed up the removal campaign: "They made us many promises, more than I can remember, but they never kept but one: They promised to take our land, and they took it."

Activists demonstrate for Native Americans' rights to clean water and other matters in the shadow of the Washington Monument in Washington, D.C.
Photo by Kevin Shay

Land grabs help new American elite concentrate wealth

Following the American revolution, many leaders focused on not just pushing natives off Western land, but on concentrating wealth for the New World elite.

Robert Morris Jr., a Declaration of Independence signer who was U.S. superintendent of finance from 1781 to 1784, was one of the more egregious. He reportedly steered public contracts to his own company and implemented other measures to profit from the Revolutionary War, as he and others like Alexander Hamilton built the new nation's financial system.

Securing more land became a primary means of amassing New World wealth. In 1812, the feds established the General Land Office to oversee land grabs, particularly in the expansive Western region. That office became the Bureau of Land Management in 1946.

The federal government owned most of the western land that was taken through force and battles against natives, until states such as Kansas and Utah entered the union. Much of the land was given away free to settlers through the Homestead Acts; about 816 million acres of public land was transferred to individuals and railroads between 1781 and 2018, according to the Congressional Research Service. [4]

Landowners, particularly landlord, railroad, lumber, oil, and mining barons, dominated the U.S. Super Richest Club in the 18th and 19th centuries. Initially, Southern states contained most of the wealthiest landowners because of slavery. Some 60 percent of the 7,500 Americans with net worth of more than $111,000 in 1860 lived in the South; most were plantation owners.

After the Civil War, going West proved lucrative. James G. Fair built a $53 billion fortune by 1894 largely through a Nevada silver and gold mine, the largest mining discovery in the country at that time. Lumber magnate Frederick Weyerhauser's adjusted earnings totaled $91 billion by the time he died in 1914. By 1910, the share of wealth owned by the richest ten percent of Americans had grown to 80 percent from 58 percent in 1810. That share declined to about 67 percent by 2025, though it threatens to rise again with the Trump-MAGA emphasis on aiding the wealthiest Americans at the expense of lower-income people. [5]

The feds did retain some land for mineral rights, national parks, and other uses. Yellowstone became the first national park in 1872. The feds still owned about 640 million acres in 2025, mostly through the BLM and Forest Service, valued at about $1.8 trillion. That was 28 percent of the 2.3 billion acres in the country.

About 60 percent of U.S. land was in private hands – either through individuals, corporations, or trusts – and another 12 percent owned by state and local governments. Western states tended to have much more publicly owned land than Eastern ones; some 61 percent of Alaska was publicly owned, while more than 99 percent of Connecticut and Iowa were in private hands.

So of the 60 percent in private hands, who owned the most land in 2025? West Coast lumber magnate Red Emmerson with 2.4 million acres, according to The Land Report. Others controlling more than two million acres were John

Malone, chairman of Liberty Media and former CEO of cable giant TCI, and CNN founder Ted Turner. Both own Western ranches. [6]

To little surprise, some 75 percent of the private land was owned by just 5 percent of landowners.

Super Rich get super richer

While owning land was once the quickest way to wealth, most of the richest people in the U.S. and other countries in the 21st century got that way through leading large multinational companies that saw their stock prices skyrocket.

In 2025, Elon Musk, who fired tens of thousands of federal workers while gaining access to Americans' financial data as a Trump adviser, topped the worldwide wealth list at $489 billion, an astonishing increase since 2020 when he was worth about $25 billion. Google co-founder Larry Page [$260 billion], Oracle leader Larry Ellison [$244 billion], Amazon founder Jeff Bezos [$242 billion], Facebook head Mark Zuckerberg [$223 billion], French fashion and cosmetics magnate Bernard Arnault [$189 billion], and investment services tycoon Warren Buffet [$146 billion] followed. Eight of the ten wealthiest individuals lived in the U.S.

The number of billionaires reached a record 3,028 in 2025, with the most in the U.S. at 902. China's wealthy class has dealt with a real estate bust, but that nation still had the second most billionaires [516], well ahead of third place India [205]. [7]

Displaying more evidence that the Super Rich have gotten super richer, the 400 wealthiest Americans were worth a record $6.6 trillion in 2025, about triple the amount a decade earlier. From 1982, when the richest 400 Americans were "only" worth $127 billion, the Super Richest have improved their holdings by 52 times.

Meanwhile, the median net worth of the average American adult was about $193,000 in 2022, according to the Federal Reserve. While that may sound fine to some, numerous other countries were better places for the middle class. Twelve countries, led by Belgium [$250,000] and Australia [$247,500], had higher figures than the U.S., according to Credit Suisse The richest one percent of Americans owned 34.2 percent of assets, while the poorest half only held 3 percent. Most other wealthier nations spread out money more fairly, with Japan and Australia better than most. [8]

When the wealth inequality is as great as it is in the U.S., that affects not just the earning power of the middle and lower classes but their political and social power, noted University of California at Santa Cruz sociology professor G. William Domhoff, author of the book, *Who Rules America?* Many Super Rich individuals may strive to be publicly apolitical or contribute to both major parties; that doesn't mean they don't employ well-paid lobbyists to grease the wheels to keep the money flowing to them. Some of them, such as the Koch brothers, outright fund pols and movements.

The result is that substantial changes in helping those at the bottom gain more income and own a greater piece of the pie are practically impossible. Barack Obama tried to help lower-income Americans more than most presidents; yet the share of citizens at the bottom of the wealth class only increased by about one percentage point between 2010 and 2017. Meanwhile, the share of wealth owned by the richest Americans increased by about five points.

"The United States is a power pyramid," Domhoff wrote on his website. "It's tough for the bottom 80 percent – maybe even the bottom 90 percent – to get organized and exercise much power." [9]

So who does own and control America?

So, do the members of the U.S. Super Rich Club own the country and deserve to rule it as they please, as some of its first leaders suggested?

While most agree an elitist cabal should not control nations, reality begs to differ. Dictatorships in Russia, China, and Saudi Arabia more directly exhibit this control, while the super wealthy yield a more subtle influence in democracies. In the U.S., the owners of corporations, banks, other financial institutions, and agri-businesses pretty much run the country, with help from pols, private managers, and leading experts they hire, according to Domhoff.

Consumer crusader Ralph Nader singled out corporations as largely controlling the direction of the U.S. "The financial, industrial, and commercial stock corporations care far less about ownership than about control," Nader wrote in his 2014 book, *Unstoppable*. "Ironically, the greatest wealth in this country is still owned by the people but controlled by the corporations under the approving aegis of the federal and state governments. These assets are owned under individual claims, in the case of pensions and stocks, and as a commons in the case of the public lands, the public airwaves, and the varieties of government research, development, and other public assets. All are peoples' assets controlled and taken by corporate power for profit." [10]

Nader longed for bolder social critics, saying that 1930s writers, such as Troy J. Cauley, an economist and author of *Agrarianism: A Program for Farmers*, were more willing to go out on a limb. "If there is to be a stable and permanent foundation for a redistribution of income, the foundation must be a general diffusion of property ownership, that is, a general diffusion of the control of the sources of income," Cauley stated in his book.

Democracies convey the notion that every citizen has a voice in voting; yet when you cast your vote, do you really think your decision ultimately has much impact on the politicians sitting in Congress or the White House? There may be an impact on certain politicians, some more than others. But more seem to be influenced by their mentors and more highly-ranked colleagues who badger them into voting their way, their large campaign contributors who are mostly Super Rich Club members and corporations, and their personal ambitions.

So, who does wield the most control of the U.S.? The president? Speaker of the House? Supreme Court chief justice? Federal Reserve Board chairman? CIA? High-ranking military officials? Musk? The growing number of Japanese, Chinese, and other foreign investors who own a substantial portion of the nation's escalating $38 trillion public debt? The Trilateral Commission? A secret group of alien invaders being investigated by the X-Files team?

All of the above?

Even if all of the above parties mostly fight it out to control the direction of the U.S., there are times when a single person from a more humble background can have far-reaching impact. Look at the short life of Mattie Stepanek, whose writings inspired the likes of Oprah and Jimmy Carter before he died in 2004 from a rare form of muscular dystrophy just before his 14th birthday. There are many other examples of individuals having a greater impact than expected.

As I reread my 1980 "Who Owns America?" column, much of it seems simplistic and unreasonable. I wasn't the first to criticize Europeans' treatment of natives or question the private ownership system. I'm sure not advocating a total government-ownership system; that doesn't work, either. Perhaps a fairer hybrid is the best we can do, for now.

We should try to emulate nations like Australia more. For such a system to work, you need individuals not motivated by private greed running it. Such leaders are difficult to find, much less help get into positions of power.

I still believe in the premise of the final sentence in that college paper column. We can't turn our collective backs on this ownership – and ultimately this control – question. To do so is to give up all hope of ever living in a better society, one with true liberty and justice for all, not just for the United States but for the world.

Climate Change: Where is the Will for Real Action?

First published in The Dallas Morning News, May 23, 2000; Maryland Gazette of Politics and Business, October 26, 2007; Democracy Guardian, April 19, 2024; and NewsBreak, April 20, 2024.

Some call Lonnie Thompson the Indiana Jones of the environmental movement.

Since the 1970s, the Ohio State University climate scientist has risked frozen extremities and falling into dangerous crevasses to preserve proof on how glacial ice masses change under warming temperatures. Thompson, who was born in the small coal-mining town of Gassaway, W.V., has probably spent more time "above 18,000 feet than any other person on Earth" as part of his research, Rolling Stone wrote. Former Vice President Al Gore praised him as the scientist who has taken the greatest risks to document global warming. [1]

Thompson was the first to retrieve samples from a remote tropical ice cap in the Peruvian Andes Mountains to analyze them for global warming clues. As an OSU grad student who earned a doctorate in geology, he created an ice core research program. He helped develop solar-powered drilling equipment that weighed less than predecessors, thus making it easier to haul across high-altitude places like the Himalayas and Africa's Mount Kilimanjaro.

In 1992, more political leaders were open to address climate change than these days. When Thompson testified in a 1992 U.S. Senate hearing, he was optimistic that top public and private officials would spark enough action to help reverse the worldwide melting of glaciers. His hopes heightened after pro-environment Bill Clinton and Gore, who held the first congressional hearing on global warming in 1981 and Bush famously mocked as "Ozone Man," won the 1992 presidential race.

"I thought [in the 1990s] that change was going to come from the top down, and it looked very positive," Thompson said via remote video during the 2024 Environmental Film Festival in the Nation's Capital, billed as the world's premier eco film fest. [2]

But obviously, that did not happen. 2024 was the warmest year on record with an average temperature of 15.1 Celsius, or 59.2 Fahrenheit. "Multiple global records were broken, for greenhouse gas levels, and for both air temperature and sea surface temperature, contributing to extreme events, including floods, heatwaves, and wildfires," reported the European Union's Copernicus Climate Change Service. [3]

While 2025 was expected to finish as high as second warmest, the nine years before 2024 also yielded the warmest average temperatures since at least 1850. "Global heating is a cold, hard fact," United Nations Secretary-General Antono Guterres said in a statement. "We need to fight even harder to get on track. Blazing temperatures in 2024 require trail-blazing climate action in 2025. There's still time to avoid the worst of climate catastrophe. But leaders must act – now." [4]

In 2025, Arctic and Antarctic glaciers were melting faster than usual. Global sea ice fell to 6.9 million square miles in January 2025 from 7.9 million a decade earlier, according to the NOAA-affiliated National Snow and Ice Data Center at the University of Colorado Boulder. Arctic sea ice dropped to a record low in February 2025, while the Antarctic level tied for the second lowest since 1979. [5]

Climate scientists predicted that sea levels along coastlines will rise by as much as six feet by 2100 due to melting glaciers entering waterways and the expansion of warmer ocean water. Some estimated an even greater increase, which would have dramatic impact on coastal infrastructure and homes. Numerous coastal villages in Alaska were relocating or at least being fortified, while the polar bear population declined. More communities built seawalls along coastal properties. [6]

Due to warming and forest clear-cutting trends, carbon dioxide readings at Hawaii's Mauna Loa Observatory hit a record monthly average of 427.09 parts per million in February 2025, up from 400.55 in 2015 and 320.44 in 1965, according to NOAA and British Columbia research firm Pro Oxygen. The annual increase in CO2 in 2024 was only slightly below the modern-times record 3.36 ppm rise in 2023. In 2014, the increase was 2.2 ppm, with the lowest since 1960 being only 0.3 ppm in 1964.

"Atmospheric CO2 is rising at an unprecedented rate," Pro Oxygen reported. "Consequences are profound for earth's temperatures, climates, ecosystems and species, both on land and in the oceans." [7]

Trump return wreaks havoc

As polar bears faced extinction and king crabs invaded Antarctic waters where they've never been, the Trump administration returned in 2025 to wreak more environmental havoc than it did during its first term.

Trump pulled out of the Paris climate accords in 2025, as the U.S. became the only nation to withdraw, joining the likes of Iran, Libya, and Yemen as countries outside that agreement. Musk led the drastic gutting of important federal agencies like NOAA and EPA, as well as national parks. The Trump administration stopped clean energy programs, banned new wind projects, approved dirty energy projects, erased climate websites, and censored the words, "climate change," from materials and curriculum.

Moreover, Trump's Interior Department opened 1.6 million acres of the Coastal Plain of the Arctic National Wildlife Refuge in Alaska to maximum oil and gas leasing. With Alaska's Arctic region warming three to five times faster than the rest of the planet, the climate consequences of expanded Arctic oil and gas drilling will be disastrous, officials with environmental law organization Earthjustice said. The refuge covers about 19.3 million acres in northeast Alaska, with its habitat supporting polar bears, caribou, moose, whales, and other wildlife.

"Expanding oil drilling in the Arctic threatens irreplaceable wildlife and cultural traditions that exist nowhere else in the world," Earthjustice attorney Erik Grafe said in a statement. "It worsens the climate crisis and undermines energy security by seeking to lock in reliance on fossil fuels."

In a further nod to authoritarian regimes, Trump officials whitewashed signage at national parks and other federal land, deleting references to slavery, Japanese American detention, and other historical events they thought were negative. Many comments by visitors rejected that campaign, calling it "an embarrassment," "pathetic," and "shameful."

"Are you so insecure that you can't admit that wrongs have been committed?" wrote a visitor to Heart Mountain Interpretive Center in Wyoming, which explores the detention of Japanese Americans during World War II.

"People want signage on public lands to reflect the full, complicated truth of America's past – not a politically motivated rewrite that whitewashes history," Gerry James, deputy director for the Sierra Club's Outdoors For All campaign, said in a statement. [8]

Despite the political backsliding, scientists like Thompson, who were at least partly funded by NOAA, EPA, and others that Trump-Musk defunded, pursued their research like it mattered, like some day someone in power will listen again and understand the significance of what they were doing.

There were some positive developments, such as the hole in the ozone layer, a shield of gases that protect people and animals from the sun's harmful radiation, was closing mainly due to bans on chlorofluorocarbons. More local steps, including by businesses, were having a positive impact, though larger companies like Walmart and Amazon did little more than promote cosmetic actions.

Many were losing hope; a Pew Research Center survey in late 2024 found that 73 percent of respondents were sad about what was occurring to the planet and about 60 percent said politicians and large businesses were not doing enough.

Overwhelming majorities believed measures such as taxing corporations based on carbon emissions, requiring energy firms to seal methane gas leaks on oil wells, and home energy efficiency tax credits were necessary.

But only 45 percent were optimistic that climate change would be rectified in time. Thompson was among the more optimistic, saying that he believed serious action to really address the warming trend was "going to come from the bottom up." [9]

Climate scientist Lonnie Thompson [via remote video] and others discuss global warming during a 2024 film festival in Washington, D.C. Photo by Kevin Shay

Fossil fuel advocates keep Clinton, Gore in check

So what happened in the 1990s and 2000s to derail the environmental movement on this key issue?

For one, fossil fuel advocates were louder at opposing Clinton and Gore than the other side was in stating its case. GOP House Speaker Newt Gingrich and Sen. Bob Dole led the opposition on several issues, such as the Kyoto protocol, which sought to reduce greenhouse gas emissions. Republicans blocked that initiative by demanding that poorer nations like India, which had even fewer environmental regulations than the U.S., be included.

Another way the GOP blocked progress was by George W. Bush stealing the 2000 election, which numerous historians believed Gore would have won had the U.S. Supreme Court not stopped the Florida recount process. "Contrary to Ralph Nader's credo that there was no real difference between the major parties, it is close to inconceivable that the country and the world would not be in far better shape had Gore been allowed to assume the [presidency in 2000] that a plurality of voters wished him to have," wrote David Remnick in the New Yorker. "One can imagine him as an intelligent and decent president, capable of making serious decisions and explaining them in the language of a confident adult." [10]

Gore, who became interested in global warming in the 1960s while taking a Harvard course taught by Roger Revelle, one of the first scientists to measure carbon dioxide in the atmosphere, led a few initiatives to advance the cause as vice president. His carbon tax designed to reduce fossil fuel consumption was partially implemented. A tech-focused education program helped more students consider environmental matters. Even regional coalitions in Texas developed plans to address high ozone-pollution levels that included limiting driving and lawn mowing. Officials closed power plants that caused the most pollution. [11]

But when Bush took over the White House in 2001, one of his first actions was to ignore a campaign pledge to regulate power plants' carbon dioxide emissions. Several states, cities, and environmental organizations like the Sierra Club filed lawsuits to force the EPA to regulate carbon dioxide and other greenhouse gases as pollutants. An appeals court ruled in favor of Bush's EPA in 2005, but the Supreme Court narrowly supported regulation in 2007. Obama went further with his Clean Power Plan, which was repealed by Trump officials in 2017.

Even a Bush NOAA official admitted in 2007 that the federal government should have better addressed climate change. "It's maybe much later than we think," said Mary Glackin, then NOAA deputy under secretary. At the same Maryland conference, former Lockheed Martin CEO Norman Augustine lobbied businesses to get more involved. [12]

Thompson was among the scientists interviewed for Gore's Oscar-winning 2006 documentary, *An Inconvenient Truth*. A key part of the film depicted the change in Antarctic ice core samples over hundreds of thousands of years, as the glaciers showcased a frozen history of the planet.

"One of the reasons I like glaciers is that they have no political agenda," said Thompson, the main subject of the 2023 documentary, *Canary*. "There's no lobbyists. There's no special interest groups. They just sum up what's going on in their environment, and unfortunately, they're all speaking in one voice. Our planet is getting warmer, and it's getting to where it's actually dangerous because of how rapidly we're losing ice on land. And the rising sea level, you can think of all those implications."

Researchers retrieve an ice core sample from deep under a glacier. Photo by Lonnie Thompson, U.S. NOAA, Public Domain

Hate mail about climate change declines

There was a time when Thompson kept the right-wing hate industry busy. Regina Thompson, his daughter and former assistant director of the FBI's victim services division, said the responses included death threats. "One of the first reactions we have when we have denial is we lash out," she said. "I saw those emails, those people lashing out [against her father's work]."

But in 2024, the 70-something scientist said the hate mail has declined to almost nothing because of how obvious climate change has become.

In 2023, I journeyed to Alaska for the first time with Christy, and we hiked to a melting glacier. While some played on the dwindling ice sheet and even sacrilegiously threw ice balls, our mood contained a mixture of awe and melancholy. People I spoke with in that state – Republicans, Democrats, those who don't vote – noted the change in the disappearing glaciers in recent years. No one argued that rising temperatures were not causing the glaciers to melt. Climate change was real when you saw it right in front of you.

The government was another matter. The MAGA politicians in Washington worked against common-sense environmental policies that most Americans wanted primarily for the money and power. When the planet explodes, where do they think that money will go? Do they really think that Musk and others will take them along to Mars in their spaceships?

Rather than arguing with the MAGA forces that denied or belittled the impact of climate change, Thompson preferred to focus on reaching students, young people who will have to deal with the fallout that the previous generations left behind.

"They're going to be the voters," he noted. "They're the ones that are going to change and have to deal with all of the problems caused by our generation."

For his efforts, Thompson has won numerous awards, including the Tyler Prize for Environmental Achievement, regarded as the environmental science equivalent to the Nobel Prize. Thompson's work "provided some of the clearest evidence yet of the ever growing impact of global climate change," officials with the Tyler Prize, which is administered by the University of Southern California, wrote. "The collection of these high elevation records is a heroic mountaineering feat that requires courage, daring, and physical endurance comparable to the legendary explorers of yore." Thompson's data in particular "helped change perspectives about the contributions of tropical records to global climate change research."

His wife, Ellen Mosley-Thompson, an OSU geology professor and fellow of the American Association for the Advancement of Science, works with him at the Byrd Polar and Climate Research Center. That entity was Ohio State's first research center when it opened in 1960.

In 2012, Thompson survived a heart transplant operation. Getting him to realize back then that he had to slow down and deal with his health took a lengthy process since he didn't believe at first he had much of a heart problem, Regina Thompson said.

In a way, that health process was similar to people who deny the impact of climate change, she said. "Change is scary," Regina Thompson said. "Managing change is one of the hardest things that we do, whether it's in an organization, whether it's in a field of science, whether it's in a family."

How to get so-called Third World nations on board?

Even in 2025, as Trump opposed most solutions to global warming, two-thirds of respondents to a Yale and George Mason University study had thought at least a little about how global warming affected people's health. Wildfires that ravaged California, Canada, and other areas in 2024 and 2025 played a role in the continuing concern by individuals, if not right-wing politicians. [13]

As bad as the situation was in wealthier nations, the world's dirtiest countries were largely so-called Third World ones such as Chad, Bangladesh, Pakistan, India, and Congo, according to research platform IQAir. The cleanest ones included Australia, Iceland, and Finland. The U.S. ranked 23rd cleanest of 138 nations in particulate matter pollution in 2024. [14]

Some have tried to convince India, Pakistan, Saudi Arabia, China, and other large polluters to move away from dirtier industries like coal. "Decades of pollution-control efforts in India have foundered on a lack of political will and effective governance," research analysts at the U.S. Institute of Peace wrote. "In Pakistan, too, the lack of political will and weaknesses in governance have been the biggest roadblock to any sustainable improvements." [15]

While India passed laws against polluting, enforcement is lax. China made some improvements in power plants to lower emissions, but the policies were lacking. Some argued that poorer nations have more pressing problems than air pollution, such as hunger, building their economies, and working for democracy.

In the U.S., Democrats overwhelmingly supported alternative energy in 2025, while the large majority of Republicans older than 64 wanted to keep prioritizing the expansion of oil, coal, and natural gas. Most Republicans younger than 30 supported moving towards renewable energy.

That was in line with who Thompson was trying to reach. "Young people are enthusiastic. They are looking for direction," he said. "One of our hopes with [*Canary*] was to inspire the next generation of young people and to make the point that we can all make a difference. And if we all make a difference, we change the world."

The impact of climate change is seen by the melting remains of Byron Glacier near Girdwood, Alaska, in 2023. Photo by Kevin Shay

Natural Disasters: A Growing Threat

First published in NewsBreak and Medium, May 26, 2023; NewsBreak, June 8, 2023; and NewsBreak, March 20, 2024

A few months before Mount St. Helens blew its top in the most deadly volcanic eruption in U.S. history, federal volcanologist David A. Johnston worked night and day to alert people during a time when warning systems were virtually nonexistent.

In 1980, the lone U.S. Geological Survey volcano observatory was in Hawaii. Johnston, who narrowly escaped an eruption on an Alaskan island in 1976 during University of Washington graduate field studies, and a team of USGS scientists had to make do with a relatively primitive station they set up six miles from St. Helens' summit.

Small earthquakes that hit the volcano about 70 miles north of Portland and 140 miles south of Seattle in early 1980 turned into larger ones, indicating that a more than century-long period of volcanic dormancy was over. As the 30-year-old Johnston conducted comprehensive tests with a spectrometer and sampled gases from the 9,677-foot mountain, he warned people through radio broadcasts and media conferences to leave the area.

On March 27, the volcano erupted in an explosion that could be heard 50 miles away, spewing ash and steam, causing mud slides and a crater to form. The following day, officials began to evacuate residents close to the summit. Johnston stood in a parking lot a few miles from the blast and told science reporter Jeff Renner that a much more violent eruption was likely.

"We stand next to a keg of dynamite," said Johnston, who had joined the USGS in 1978, with duties that included improving warning systems at St. Helens. "The fuse is lit, but we don't know how long it is. If it were to explode right now, we would die." [1]

On April 3, Washington Gov. Dixy Lee Ray declared a state of emergency. Johnston and fellow scientist Jack Hyde discovered a bulge on the mountain's northern flank that was growing by more than five feet per day as the nearby crater pushed deeper. As the bulge expanded, many more earthquakes and mini-eruptions occurred that month. On April 30, state officials closed St. Helens to the public, thanks in no small part to the efforts of Johnston and his team.

In the weeks leading up to the May 18 explosion, Johnston manned the makeshift observation post. When some local business owners and residents lobbied to reopen the area, Johnston and colleagues strongly resisted. The earthquakes and eruptions increased, and another crater formed while the bulge expanded.

Still on May 17, Gov. Ray yielded to locals and allowed them to access properties in the dangerous "red zone," after signing waivers. That evening, Johnston agreed to take over the observation post from Harry Glicken, a grad student hired by the USGS as a temp to monitor the volcano. USGS geologist Don Swanson was originally slated to relieve Glicken, but Johnston ended up there after Swanson was called to another duty in Vancouver, Wash. Johnston also convinced geologist Carolyn Driedger and a volunteer to leave the area for safer ground, saving their lives.

About 8:30 a.m. on May 18, a substantial earthquake hit just below the north slope of St. Helens. Then the volcanic blast that could be heard hundreds of miles away suddenly made much of the summit's north face vanish, reducing the mountain's height by about 1,300 feet.

"Vancouver! Vancouver! This is it! This is it!" Johnston screamed into a radio with a final warning directed towards the nearest USGS unit 45 miles away.

USGS volcanologist David A. Johnston monitors conditions near the summit of Mount St. Helens about 13 hours before the eruption. His warnings to evacuate saved many lives. Johnston's remains have not been found, as of 2025.
Photo by Harry Glicken, USGS, Public Domain

Within a second, Johnston became one of the first of 57 people to perish due to the blast of hot, molten rock and other materials that traveled about 300 miles per hour. Johnston's remains were not recovered, as of 2025. In 1993, state highway workers found remnants of his trailer.

Swanson manned the U.S. Forest Service office in Vancouver that morning. As needles on seismographs shook furiously, he tried to radio Johnston with no luck. He joined a team in a fire-spotter plane that reached the south side of the volcano but couldn't continue farther north due to the heavy ash. Within the gray column of ash and gas that rose to more than 80,000 feet, they observed flashes of lightning. Glicken later joined a search plane that tried to locate Johnston and the camp without success.

"The volcano where I picnicked as a boy, and which I climbed as an adult, had turned nasty," Swanson wrote. "The science of volcanology was changed forever, and today the risks from future eruptions anywhere in the world are lessened because of what happened on that fateful day." [2]

'Own safety was compromised'

Harry R. Truman was among the few people living close to St. Helens who ignored the warnings. In the mid-1920s, he leased 50 acres from the Northern Pacific Railway on Spirit Lake, about a mile north of the volcano. He opened a gas station, grocery store, and eventually the Mount St. Helens Lodge.

As Johnston and others warned people like Truman to evacuate, the 83-year-old innkeeper told reporters the danger was exaggerated. He maintained that view even after moving his bed to the basement to keep from falling out during earthquakes that escalated in intensity. "I've walked that mountain for 50 years. I know her. If it erupts with lava, it's not going to get me at Spirit Lake," Truman told a reporter. St. Helens had not yielded a major eruption since 1857. [3]

On May 17, local law enforcement attempted to persuade Truman to leave for the final time. The following day, he and his 16 cats succumbed to the blast, likely dying of heat shock in less than a second. Spirit Lake was immediately destroyed and Truman's lodge buried under 150 feet of debris. His remains had also yet to be found, as of 2025.

Photographers Reid Blackburn and Robert Landsburg were other casualties. Blackburn took photos for National Geographic and USGS, as he ignored evacuation warnings to camp about eight miles from the volcano. He was found inside his ash-covered car. Landsburg, a commercial photographer for travel businesses, retreated to his vehicle a few miles from the summit after taking some shots of the approaching ash cloud. His body was discovered buried in ash, while film of his last photos survived.

USGS geologists Don Swanson and Jim Moore survey an ash-filled car shortly after Mount St. Helens erupted. Photo by USGS, Public Domain

Lava, mud slides, the ash clouds, and other effects of the eruption caused an estimated $1 billion in damage, including to 187 miles of roadways. The explosion deposited tons of ash and other debris across 11 states and several Canadian provinces. The volcanic clouds traveled around the world, and several smaller blasts ensued throughout that year.

In Eastern Washington some 300 miles away, Maggie Jackson Dean felt her house shake as she made cinnamon rolls for breakfast that Sunday. Then she heard an explosion and immediately thought it came from the nuclear site where she worked. She turned on the television and saw what occurred. It wasn't long before ash clouds rolled over her neighborhood. "They looked like a pinky purple pot of boiling water," Dean wrote. "It caused a lot of damage and weird diseases. But, my trees, shrubs – anything growing – were huge for years to come." [4]

In the aftermath, USGS scientists credited Johnston with saving many lives. "The volcano-monitoring effort of which [Johnston] was part helped persuade the authorities first to limit access to the area around the volcano, and then to resist heavy pressure to reopen it, thereby holding the May 18 death toll to a few tens instead of hundreds or thousands," USGS scientists Peter W. Lipman and Donal Ray Mullineaux wrote in a 1981 report. [5]

"Thousands could have perished if not for the persistence of [Johnston and] a team of scientists and law enforcement and emergency officials," wrote Melanie Holmes in *A Hero on Mount St. Helens*. "Dave would shy away from the limelight and say, 'I was doing my job.'... Dave was part of a team of geologists tasked with monitoring an active volcano at a time before the science existed to warn of an impending eruption. People with passion so deep, their own safety was compromised as they searched for answers." [6]

Mixed results on minimizing death tolls in natural disasters

Since 1980, volcanic eruptions have increased, with mixed results in minimizing death tolls. Warning systems improved dramatically, though not all heed the warnings. While no one died in smaller eruptions at U.S. volcanoes between 1981 and 2025, an estimated 23,000 people perished in a 1985 eruption in Colombia, mostly through mudflows. The 1982 explosion at Mexico's El Chichon resulted in about 1,900 casualties.

Glicken, the USGS volcanologist who was mentored by Johnston, numbered among the 43 deaths from the 1991 blast at Mount Unzen in Japan. Other deadly volcanic disasters since 1980 occurred in the Philippines [847 casualties in 1991], Indonesia [426 in 2018 and 353 in 2010], the Congo [245 in 2002], and Guatemala [at least 190 in 2018].

A large USGS photo at a Mount St. Helens visitors center shows the volcano erupting in 1980. Other area volcanoes, including Mount Hood, are in the background. Photo by Kevin Shay

While volcanoes receive much attention probably due to their explosive capabilities, other natural disasters like earthquakes and hurricanes cause more deaths. The 1976 earthquake in China resulted in more than 655,000 casualties, while the death toll of the 2010 Haiti quake was at least 100,000. The 2004 tsunami and quake in Asia led to more than 227,000 deaths. A 2025 quake in Thailand resulted in more than 5,400 deaths.

The most deadly natural disaster in the U.S. was the COVID-19 pandemic of 2020-23 with more than 1.1 million casualties, though there were debates over whether disease epidemics counted as natural disasters. Many put the 1900 Texas hurricane that saw at least 6,000 deaths as the country's worst one.

In more recent times, Hurricane Katrina caused almost 1,400 deaths in 2005, despite early warnings to residents to evacuate coastal areas. Hurricanes caused the most property harm, with the damage from Katrina and Harvey, which hit in 2017, estimated at $125 billion each.

Wildfires also caused significant property destruction, with the damage estimate of the January 2025 Southern California fires at a record $164 billion. Smoke from fires in Canada caused severe fine-particle pollution in northeastern U.S. cities in the 2020s. In Philadelphia, the pollutant level from a 2023 Canadian fire reached 447 parts per million, the highest in at least two decades. An air quality reading above 300 was in the worst range, with the tiny pollutants more easily inhaled deeper into people's lungs.

Earthquakes remained a significant threat. Alaska, California, and other far Western states were generally the most common targets of U.S. seismic activity, though other areas, including around the Mississippi River valley and Yellowstone National Park region, were susceptible, according to a 2024 USGS map. The update outlined new fault lines and computational modeling that lent more details.

States most likely to be hit with major earthquakes in the near future included not just Alaska, California, and Washington, but Nevada, Wyoming, Idaho, Montana, Missouri, Arkansas, Tennessee, and Kentucky. Eastern cities such as New York and Philadelphia could face more damaging quakes. Nearly 75 percent of the U.S. could experience significant ground shaking, USGS officials reported.

Earthquakes were still difficult to predict, but "we've made great strides," said USGS geophysicist and lead study author Mark Peterson. [7]

The 1906 San Francisco earthquake remained the most deadly in the U.S., with more than 3,000 fatalities. In more modern times, the 1964 Alaska quake, which registered a shocking 9.2 magnitude, caused 131 deaths and sent tsunamis crashing into coastal towns as far away as Hawaii and Japan. Anchorage, which had about 46,000 residents in 1964 and grew sixfold by 2024, saw some 30 blocks of downtown buildings and homes destroyed.

The last deadly earthquake in the U.S. happened in December 2022, when a 6.4-magnitude tremor struck the coast of Humboldt County in northern California. Two seniors who had medical emergencies and couldn't get services in time died, while another 17 people were injured.

Most seismic activity in the eastern U.S. was relatively mild, though a 5.8-magnitude quake centered in Virginia in 2011 damaged structures that included the Washington Monument. In 2020, a 5.1-magnitude tremor centered in the northwestern North Carolina town of Sparta caused major destruction to 60 buildings.

Oklahoma, known for tornadoes, was another state that reported more seismic events than many might think. Between 2010 and 2015, the state experienced more quakes with a magnitude of at least 3.0 than any other except Alaska. In 2016, a 5.8-magnitude one near the northern Oklahoma town of Pawnee resulted in severe building damage.

The 1964 Alaska earthquake caused streets in downtown Anchorage to collapse. This photo showed Fourth Avenue near C Street. Photo by USGS, Public Domain

Rejuvenation on some levels

Natural disasters can be hellish, particularly for those experiencing the damage. But in some ways, they spark a rejuvenation.

For instance, the area around Mount St. Helens regrew in many areas since 1980, though patches were still bare in 2025. Many aquatic creatures, insects, and animals sleeping underground during the blast benefited from the ash. Trees and plants, with some species new to the region, sprouted up.

Other volcanoes in the region could be due. Mount Rainier last erupted in 1894, Mount Hood in 1866, and Mount Adams in 950. In Hawaii, eruptions at the 4,091-foot Kilauea continued in 2025, according to the Global Volcanism Program run by the Smithsonian Institution and USGS. In 1790, Kilauea blasted the island well before it became a U.S. territory and state, killing more than 400 people. The roughly 4,000-square-mile island of Hawaii had about 200,000 residents in 2025.

The 5,710-foot Great Sitkin volcano in Alaska's Aleutian Islands and some in Central America were among others seeing eruptions in 2025. Indonesia had more volcanoes erupting in 2025 than any other country with eight, including one that killed ten people in late 2024.

At the Johnston Ridge Observatory, which opened in 1997 near the site where Johnston perished, visitors learned about events through exhibits and a film. But the main draw was the eerie summit that loomed a few miles away, its craters hiding secrets of the dead and the living and an enormous, mysterious power of nature.

Renner, who later branched out from science reporting to meteorology and environmental writing, noted in 2019 that the arguments over the proper response just before the St. Helens disaster in 1980 and the present age over climate change were similar.

"We hear the same words now that we heard in 1980. 'I don't believe it.' 'It's junk science.' Or, 'It's just a theory'," he wrote in the foreword to *A Hero on Mount St. Helens*. "I believe Mount St. Helens offers lessons today as we confront new environmental hazards, lessons we ignore at our peril." [8]

Civil Rights and the Danger of Standing Up: The 1960s Assassination Conspiracies

First published in the Richland Mandela, May 1, 1978; Richland Chronicle, January 26, 1979; SR Dallas, November 1988; Addison/North Dallas Register, December 26, 1991; Arlington News, November 24, 1994; Maryland Gazette of Politics and Business, November 22, 2013; *Death of the Rising Sun*, Random Publishers, 2017; Medium, March 12, 2022; and Democracy Guardian, June 23, 2024

When thinking of the 1960s, many people reflect on aspects such as the free love movement and rock 'n roll music. But beyond those cultural changes were political changes that involved intensive violence and more assassinations, along with failed attempts, than most realize.

The assassinations of John F. Kennedy and Medgar Evers in 1963 were just the start. The same night Evers was killed in Mississippi, civil rights leaders in Alabama and Louisiana were targeted. Shortly before JFK's killing in Dallas a few months later, plots were stymied in Chicago and Florida. The following year, Mississippi officials helped klansmen and local authorities locate three civil rights workers in a triple assassination plot. In 1965, former Nation of Islam spokesman Malcolm X was gunned down as he spoke in New York City. Other local civil rights leaders, including Vernon Dahmer, Herbert Lee, Jonathan Daniels, and Wharlest Jackson, were targeted throughout the Deep South. In 1968, bigger fish Martin Luther King Jr. and Robert Kennedy were assassinated. Then in the decade's final month, Black Panther Party leader Fred Hampton Sr. and associate Mark Clark were murdered by Chicago police as they slept in an apartment.

What did these assassinations share? Several were blamed on lone wolves, despite the targets being threatened by many enemies, public and private, organizations and individuals. Most involved authorities attempting to sow dissension among competing segments in hopes of provoking violence. In some cases, police executed the targets themselves.

Underneath the political assassinations, which involved everyone from a president to rank-and-file civil rights workers targeted to intimidate surviving black folks into not working for their rights, were waves of repression. In 1968, President Lyndon Johnson sent militarized police into low-income, mostly minority neighborhoods under the guise of a "War on Crime," similar to what

Trump did in 2025. Police tactics against lower-income Americans, racial minorities, and anti-Vietnam War protesters intensified. The crime wars of the 1960s, like those of 2025, pretty much left white-collar, financial, and political offenses alone.

Richard Nixon escalated the anti-crime campaign while hypocritically committing more serious transgressions himself. As the Nixon administration increased penalties for marijuana possession, more prisons became overcrowded with inmates found guilty of minor drug possession charges. At the same time, Nixon authorized the IRS and Justice Department to pursue political opponents and his White House approved an assassination plot against journalist Jack Anderson. Nixon's Watergate crimes involved much more than a petty burglary of Democratic National Committee headquarters. [1]

And the FBI, controlled by Nixon friend J. Edgar Hoover, worked to undermine most of these assassination targets, even as the federal agency's rank-and-file agents attempted to do their jobs.

Thanks in big part to Oliver Stone's *JFK* film, Congress passed the JFK Assassination Records Collection Act in 1992, which decreed that all assassination records should be publicly released by 2017. While that was not done, Trump authorized the release of more files in 2017 and 2025. However, many were heavily redacted and provided only a few more clues into who exactly was behind the 1960s political violence.

Evers killed, two others targeted in tri-state conspiracy

Medgar Evers should have been someone who conservatives embraced.

He was a World War II hero, having fought on Omaha Beach during the D-Day invasion. He advanced to the rank of sergeant. He went back home to Mississippi and earned a bachelor's degree in business administration. He was on the debate, football, and track teams, and was elected junior class president at Alcorn State.

He became an insurance salesman, providing for his wife and young kids. Despite all of his success, most white people in Mississippi considered him lower than the laziest, drunkest, unemployed, uneducated Caucasian. And they considered Evers an "uppity ni —-" just for trying to better himself and his community.

Simply because of his skin color, Evers had to use separate bathrooms and water fountains. He had to sit in the back of buses. He couldn't eat in most restaurants or sleep in many hotels. He couldn't shop in many stores. He couldn't enroll at major universities. His kids had to attend inferior schools. He faced intimidation at work.

So he decided to join others who were doing something to change that. He became president of the Regional Council of Negro Leadership and started organizing demonstrations and boycotts against segregation. After the U.S. Supreme Court ruled in 1954 that segregated public schools were unconstitutional, Evers applied to the University of Mississippi Law School, which rejected him based on race.

He soon became the NAACP's first field secretary for Mississippi, moving to the capital, Jackson. He aided in the integration of buses, parks, and other public facilities. He led voter registration drives and boycotts to integrate the state fair and schools. He supported the effort of fellow war vet Clyde Kennard when the latter man sought to enroll at Mississippi Southern College in 1956, 1957, and 1959. He helped James Meredith enroll at the University of Mississippi in 1962, leading to riots backed by the likes of Gov. Barnett and former Major Gen. Edwin Walker.

Because of such public legal work, Evers was a sitting duck. The White Citizens' Council, formed two months after the Supreme Court's 1954 ruling against segregated public schools, targeted him, Kennard, and others. The WCC, sometimes called the "Country Club Klan," was inspired by Mississippi Circuit Court Judge Thomas Brady, who published a book that compared black folks to chimpanzees and advocated for a separate state just for African Americans and the abolishment of public schools. The movement spread not only throughout the Deep South, but to cities such as Newark, Detroit, and Los Angeles.

Dudley Conner, the head of the WCC in Hattiesburg, where Kennard lived, reportedly offered to have his "henchmen" cause Kennard's death through bombing or an "accident." A representative of the Mississippi State Sovereignty Commission, a state agency formed in 1956 to stop integration and spy on civil rights leaders, suggested another way: Framing him for theft and sentencing him to the worst prison. There, Kennard acquired cancer and died in 1963 shortly after being released. [2]

For Evers, far-right plotters planned a more direct extermination. On the same night he was killed by a rifle shot soon after JFK's first national speech on civil rights, anti-integration racists targeted LaFayette and Rev. Cox, who had escalated their civil rights activities since the Freedom Rides.

In his last few months, Evers had steered the NAACP chapter to more aggressively confront segregation in schools and public places. He was moved by young people involved with sit-ins and Freedom Rides, even considering whether to leave the NAACP to work more directly for integration. Economic boycotts seemed to have success, but he became more vulnerable with more publicity.

Speakers discuss assassinations at far-right conference

In April 1963, as klan members stalked Evers, far-right leaders such as Walker spoke at the Congress of Freedom in New Orleans. That conference was attended by a wide range of people, from plumbers in the klan to businessmen who sought to keep their fingerprints off any dirty work.

Some speakers called for a broad-based assassination campaign against not just civil rights and political leaders they considered pro-communist, but those in business and international relations, according to government informant William Somersett. Most stopped short of specifically mentioning names, he said.

Another informant stated that someone said the Congress of Freedom "wanted to eliminate the Council on Foreign Relations through legislation, if possible; however, if not possible, the Congress of Freedom will resort to eliminating the CFR through assassination." Members of the CFR, a nonprofit think tank based in New York that dates to 1921, have included Adlai Stevenson, David Rockefeller, John McCloy, and Thomas Dewey. [3]

Walker, a Texan who had served in World War II, resigned from the U.S. Army in 1961 after calling former President Harry Truman and Eleanor Roosevelt "pink." In 1962, he ran for governor on an anti-communist platform, attracting much financial support from far-right Dallas oilman H.L. Hunt. During the campaign, Walker punched journalist Thomas Kelly after the latter asked him about being praised by an American Nazi Party leader. Walker finished last in the six-way race in the Democratic primary but compiled some 138,000 votes and was barely behind the fifth-place candidate.

That fall, he called for "violent vocal protest" against the University of Mississippi admitting Meredith. During the two-day riots, two people were killed and numerous federal marshals were shot. After joining rioters on the campus, Walker was arrested for sedition and insurrection. The charges were dropped after a grand jury declined to indict him. He was known for carrying weapons in the trunk of his car, and in April 1963, someone shot a bullet into his Dallas home that barely missed him. Some claimed alleged JFK assassin Lee Oswald fired that shot, while others thought Walker associates did the deed to help drum up support for the right-wing figure.

The attempted assassination occurred a few days after Walker spoke before the Congress of Freedom. Another speaker at that convention was retired U.S. Lt. Gen. Pedro del Valle, who also served in World War II and co-founded the anti-communist militia group Defenders of the American Constitution in 1953. Like Walker, del Valle ran for governor on an anti-communist, anti-United Nations plank, losing in the 1954 Maryland Republican primary. Both Walker and del

Valle had mentioned assassinating certain "enemies" in top government and business positions as early as 1962, author Jeffrey H. Caufield wrote.

Violence had long been employed by the white power structure to intimidate black people, especially in the Deep South. Sometimes uprisings against Jim Crow segregation and racism could be controlled by arresting a few people for offenses they usually didn't commit. Other times, lynchings, killings, and convenient accidents occurred to serve as a warning by the white power structure to anyone who pushed too hard for liberty and justice.

From 1882 to 1968, almost 5,000 lynchings occurred in the U.S., mostly in Southern states such as Mississippi, Georgia, and Texas, according to the NAACP. Black Americans were the primary victims at about 72 percent. Some whites who opposed mob rule and supported voting and civil rights for all were lynched, as were Latino and Asian immigrants. Many victims were not just hanged but were tortured, mutilated, and burned. "Lynchings were often public spectacles attended by the white community in celebration of white supremacy," the NAACP reported. "Photos of lynchings were often sold as souvenir postcards." [4]

The number of lynchings in the U.S. is believed to be significantly underreported. In a 2017 report, the Alabama-based Equal Justice Initiative documented more than 4,000 racial terror lynchings – those committed against minorities to spread white supremacy – in just a dozen Southern states between 1877 and 1950, at least 800 more than previously reported. The violence played a key role in forcing many black people to migrate to the North and West.

To this day, there is "an astonishing absence of any effort to acknowledge, discuss, or address lynching" by public officials and community leaders in places where they occurred, EJI reported. Many communities erected markers and monuments to commemorate the Confederacy and Civil War battles that honored those who fought to preserve white supremacy. But there were "very few monuments or memorials that address the history and legacy of lynching in particular or the struggle for racial equality more generally," wrote EJI, which opened the National Lynching Memorial and Legacy Museum in Montgomery, Ala., in 2018. During Black Lives Matter protests in 2020, some toppled Confederate statues, and numerous cities did more to publicly commemorate minorities' contributions and racial violence. But those efforts were met by many reversals in subsequent years. [5]

As minorities made a few gains in the mid-20th century, more traditional forms of murders were employed to attempt to discourage campaigns for civil rights. In 1951, educator Harry Moore, who founded the first NAACP branch in Brevard County, Fla., was killed after klansmen bombed his home. He had called for the indictment of the local sheriff who shot two handcuffed black men. His wife, Harriett Moore, died from injuries sustained in the bombing nine days later.

In 1955, Rev. George Lee, founder of an NAACP chapter, became one of the first black citizens in Humphreys County, Miss., to register to vote. He urged others to register, and he was soon murdered, reportedly by two members of the White Citizens' Council. The story was much the same for numerous others throughout the Deep South in the 1950s, and only escalated in the 1960s.

Two other civil rights leaders targeted on same night as Evers in tri-state conspiracy

In the months before Evers' June 1963 death, threats caused the U.S. Army combat vet to carry guns and keep weapons "in every room" of their house, Myrlie, his wife, said. "Our home was firebombed. We received threats on almost an hourly basis [at home]. We received threats through the mail. It was a life of never knowing when that bullet was going to hit," Myrlie said. [6]

Medgar talked to his three young kids, telling them to climb in the bathtub if they heard shots. He slept with a rifle next to him and carried weapons in the trunk of his car.

Evers "always had the fear, or feeling about death, but he wasn't afraid of dying," said Dave Dennis, a 1961 Freedom Rider and co-director of the Council of Federated Organizations, an umbrella entity that tried to unite the various civil rights groups. "He knew he was a marked man." They sometimes traded cars to throw off the klan and police who tracked them.

Two weeks before his death, someone threw a Molotov cocktail into his home's carport. About a week later, a car almost ran over Evers after he left his NACCP office in Jackson. The incidents caused him to ask for an FBI or police escort to his home.

But on June 11, his security disappeared. Arriving home shortly after midnight, Evers was shot in the back by a gunman who fired a high-powered rifle from about 150 feet across the street, as he walked from his car to the front door carrying t-shirts that read, "Jim Crow Must Go." He collapsed outside the door, where Myrlie and his children, who had stayed up watching John F. Kennedy's speech on civil rights, soon found him.

"We heard the car pulling into the driveway and him get out and the door slam shut," Myrlie recalled. "Then instantly loud gunfire." As the children fell to the floor and took cover, she ran to the door and turned on an outside light. She screamed when she saw him lying on the doorstep. Neighbors gathered, and when police arrived, Myrlie yelled at them that they were responsible for killing her husband.

They rushed Evers to the closest hospital, where employees initially said they could not admit him due to his race. After Myrlie told employees who he was, the hospital admitted Evers, but he died about an hour later.

Two hours earlier, LaFayette, who worked with King and became national coordinator of the Poor People's Campaign, arrived home some 200 miles east in Selma, Ala. Two white men asked him to help them start their car, then savagely beat him. As one made motions to shoot LaFayette with a gun, a neighbor reportedly pointed a rifle and chased off the assailants. On the same night, Rev. Cox eluded other assailants in New Orleans by being out of town. [7]

In Evers' case, some thought numerous parties were involved, including the Jackson police and White Citizens' Council. But authorities focused their investigation on fertilizer salesman Byron de la Beckwith, who lived in Greenwood about 90 miles north of Jackson. A rifle found by police in honeysuckle vines across the street from Evers' home on June 12 was traced to Beckwith, who was arrested and charged with murder on June 23.

Police found a fresh fingerprint on the recently-fired murder weapon, which investigators said matched Beckwith, who claimed it had been stolen a couple days before Evers' murder. Capt. Ralph Hargrove, chief identification officer for the Jackson Police Department, later testified that the print was no more than 12 hours old when he lifted it from the rifle, showing it had been made about the time Evers was shot.

Upon his arrest, Beckwith had a "circular-shaped scar" above one eye, which investigators believed likely occurred from the scope when the rifle recoiled. In addition, cab drivers said Beckwith had asked for directions to Evers' home shortly before the murder. The bullet, which passed through Evers' body, as well as a window and wall of his home, stopped on the kitchen counter. The slug was too mutilated to prove it came from Beckwith's rifle, but prosecutors thought other evidence was solid enough to pursue a trial in early 1964.

Barbara Ann Holder, a young customer and former waitress at a diner near Evers' home, was among those to testify that Beckwith waited in his car in the lot for several hours that night. She said he was still there when she left around 11:30 p.m., about an hour before Evers was shot. Lee Cockrell, the owner of the diner, testified that he did not see Beckwith's car on his lot or hear any shots. A Beckwith defense lawyer questioned Myrlie about Evers' "integration activities," and when prosecutors objected to the questions, the attorney replied they were "attempting to show others would have motive for killing Evers," according to an FBI report. [8]

Two Greenwood officers stated that they saw Beckwith in that town shortly after the killing. Some associates testified they saw Beckwith with the scar above his eye before Evers was murdered. Beckwith himself swore that he was not in Jackson that night and the scar over his eye was from previous target practice.

Beckwith appeared shook when prosecutors introduced some letters, including one to the NRA in early 1963 in which he wrote, "For the next 15 years, we here in Mississippi are going to have to do a lot of shooting to protect our wives, our children, and ourselves from bad Negroes." Asked whether he wanted to set up a shooting range in Greenwood, Beckwith replied that he had been interested in doing that for years because people should "have arms and use them." [9]

At one point, Barnett, who was Mississippi governor when Evers was murdered, interrupted the trial to approach Beckwith and shake his hand. Barnett was a member of the same White Citizens' Council as Beckwith, and the WCC paid Beckwith's legal fees. The message of official support for extreme and violent tactics was clear. "Barnett's public show of support for Beckwith spoke volumes," wrote author Reed Massengill. Another odd visitor was Major Gen. Walker, who traveled from Texas to back Beckwith. [10]

While many expected the all-white male jury would acquit Beckwith, five jurors believed he was guilty strongly enough to deadlock the panel. For the second trial, defense attorneys turned to state agency spies to secretly obtain information about more favorable potential jurors. Even so, four Caucasian men blocked an acquittal. To many, that was a victory. "A turning point seemed to have been reached in the American state most violently committed to resisting black equality," wrote author Adam Nossiter. [11]

After Beckwith, who was held in jail without bail for ten months, was released, he continued his racist activities that descended into criminal actions at times. He ran for lieutenant governor in 1967 under a segregationist platform, attracting 34,000 votes and finishing fifth in a six-way race. In 1973, Beckwith plotted to kill Adolph Botwick, regional director of the Anti-Defamation League. Police found him near New Orleans with loaded guns, a bomb, and directions to Botwick's home. In 1975, he was convicted of conspiracy to commit murder and served three years in prison.

Myrlie Evers, aided in large part by investigative articles by Jackson Clarion-Ledger reporter Jerry Mitchell, continued to pursue justice. In 1989, Mitchell discovered some secret sovereignty commission reports that outlined how in 1964, a spy referred to as "Agent Y" infiltrated civil rights organizations and stole applications and photos of Freedom Summer volunteers. The sealed reports "told the story of a state breaking the law to preserve its way of life," wrote Mitchell. [12]

Over a few months, Mitchell found sources to leak other hidden reports, including some that showed that the state had secretly worked to acquit Beckwith in 1964, even as prosecutors publicly pursued a conviction. In 1958, then-Gov. J. P. Coleman had ordered authorities to spy on Evers to catch him "in an illegal act." Spies had logged Evers' car license number, address, and other details.

Mitchell located the officers who claimed to have seen Beckwith in Greenwood near the time of Evers' murder, and they gave conflicting accounts. Former klansman Delmar Dennis said Beckwith had bragged at a rally that he killed Evers, and klan members had intimidated jurors in 1964. When Mitchell interviewed Beckwith on the phone in 1989, he denied killing anyone but added that he felt "as much compassion for the Medgar Evers family as a ni---- getting run over by a streetcar in Chicago." In a 1990 interview at Beckwith's home, the klansman suggested that Lee Oswald murdered Evers and threatened Mitchell.

The fresh details helped inspire Mississippi officials to reopen the case, resulting in a murder conviction of Beckwith in 1994. He was sentenced to life without parole and died in prison in 2001.

But others thought to be involved in killing Evers, including Greenwood klan leader Gordon Lackey, were never charged. Beckwith's son was among those who said others participated and called his father a "patsy." And no one found the assailants who attacked LaFayette and pursued Rev. Cox. [13]

Evers was assassinated as he walked from his car, parked in this driveway in Jackson, Miss. The home is now a museum and national monument. Photo by Carla Batchelor, Wikimedia Commons

More threats issued against JFK before his killing

Major Gen. Walker was among those who some consider suspects in the assassination of JFK, which occurred in Dallas a few months after Evers' murder. Most researchers agreed that Walker didn't like Kennedy, but hard evidence of

Walker executing a plot against him was scarce. He likely was one of the parties behind the "Wanted for Treason" fliers that were distributed shortly before JFK arrived in Dallas.

Walker also had ties to a full-page ad that ran in The Dallas Morning News the day Kennedy was killed that sarcastically read in bold letters, "Welcome Mr. Kennedy to Dallas." In harsh terms, it accused the president of ignoring the Constitution and giving aid to communists. Larrie Schmidt, who served in the Army under Walker and helped him organize protests against an October visit by UN Ambassador Stevenson, was a leader of that effort.

At Walker's home, American flags were positioned upside down in protest of Kennedy's visit. Walker, however, was in Louisiana that day. The following year, Oswald killer Jack Ruby inferred to the Warren Commission that Walker might have had something to do with JFK's demise. "There is a John Birch Society right now in activity, and Edwin Walker is one of the top men of this organization," Ruby said.

Former CIA director Allen Dulles was another name that surfaced throughout several 1960s assassinations. Dulles had more cause than most to plot against Kennedy since he blamed the president for the failure of the 1961 Bay of Pigs invasion of Cuba and JFK forced him to resign. The spymaster also conveniently was on the Warren Commission investigating Kennedy's death. But getting from there to involvement of a plot has proven to be difficult.

After losing his job, Dulles pursued revenge, according to author David Talbot. He acted like he was "still America's intelligence chief, targeting the president who had ended his illustrious career," Talbot wrote. "Dulles would turn his Georgetown home into the center of an anti-Kennedy government in exile." [14]

As JFK approved other steps to erode the CIA's power, such as moving the oversight of overseas agents to U.S. ambassadors, Dulles' "government in exile" took note. It wasn't long before a "clear consensus" arose among the loose network of Dulles cronies that Kennedy "was a national security threat [who] must be removed," Talbot wrote. Dulles was "the only man with the stature, connections, and decisive will to make something of this enormity [assassinating JFK] happen," claimed Talbot, adding that Dulles was skillful at covering his tracks and evidence against him was circumstantial.

Though forcing Dulles and a few other top officials to leave, Kennedy didn't go far enough to rid the CIA of Dulles loyalists and hire people more open to the changes in how he wanted the U.S. to operate in the world, director Stone said. "His problem was he didn't clean house," Stone stated. "Most of those people were Dulles people. That's why we think Dulles was involved in the assassination because of the tremendous power [he] still [had in the CIA]." [15]

As far as more people being involved in a plot against JFK, the events that occurred in early November in Chicago offered some of the most convincing details. That trip was canceled at the last moment after authorities detained three suspects who were found with weapons along the motorcade route, but there were still two at large, according to former Secret Service Agent Abraham Bolden.

One of those suspects, Thomas Vallee, had striking similarities to Oswald. Like Oswald, he had enlisted in the Marines as a teen, serving three years before taking a break and re-enlisting for a year. Like Oswald, he had been stationed at a U-2 base in Japan. Like Oswald, Vallee had apparently been recruited by CIA agents to perform discreet assignments. But instead of defecting to Russia, Vallee trained anti-Castro Cubans on Long Island. Both owned rifles and were loners, basically "perfect for a frame-up," wrote author Edwin Black. Vallee had also landed work along a future Kennedy parade route a few months before his planned visit. [16]

Vallee was five years older than Oswald and served in the Marines just before him. A John Birch Society member who claimed to be an expert marksman, he became "outspokenly opposed to President Kennedy's foreign policy," according to the House Assassinations Committee. He regularly stated anti-Kennedy remarks in public that some took as threats, to the point a Chicago police lieutenant warned him against doing that in a cafeteria.

While authorities monitored Vallee, the FBI received a tip from an informant about a four-man team targeting JFK as he rode to Soldier Field, Agent Bolden said. Agents detained two men on November 1, the day before JFK's planned visit, and could not locate the two other suspects, he said. Around 9 a.m. on November 2, just two hours before JFK was due to arrive, two Chicago police officers stopped Vallee after he made a turn without a signal near Wrigley Field. They discovered a hunting knife on the front seat and 750 rounds of ammo in the trunk. They took Vallee in for questioning, while other officers drove to his residence and found more weapons and ammo.

With two potential snipers still at large on the streets of Chicago, Kennedy's security team convinced him to cancel the trip. After he tried to blow the whistle following the killing, Bolden was arrested and imprisoned for several years for what he said was bogus charges. He was pardoned in 2022 by President Joe Biden. [17]

Vallee and the two assassination-team suspects were released. Vallee was found guilty of a weapons charge but only given probation. He continued his work with the Birchers and wrote Hoover, among others. No charges were filed against the other suspects, and their names were never released.

Following the aborted Chicago visit, threats against JFK escalated. As Kennedy prepared to fly to Florida, the Secret Service issued a memo on November 8 about a man saying he would kill JFK when he visited that state. At least two other people made threats against Kennedy, and Tampa authorities located and arrested one.

On November 9, Miami police convinced informant Somersett to secretly tape record a conversation with regional KKK leader Joseph Milteer at Somersett's apartment in Miami. On tape, Milteer, who inherited about $200,000 from his father and devoted most of his time to far-right political causes, claimed there was a plot to assassinate JFK still in the works. They discussed JFK's planned appearances on November 18 in Tampa and Miami. At one point, Somersett asked, "How in the hell do you figure would be the best way to get [Kennedy]?"

Milteer replied, "From an office building with a high-powered rifle."

"You think [Kennedy] knows he is a marked man?" queried Somersett.

"Sure he does."

"They are really going to try to kill him?"

"Oh, yeah. It is in the working," Milteer said. [18]

William Somersett, left, informed police and the FBI about plots to kill JFK and MLK in the 1960s. One reportedly involved KKK leader Joseph Milteer, right.
Photo from U.S. National Archives, Public Domain

Milteer identified Jack William Brown, a Chattanooga, Tenn., klan leader, as someone who was "just as likely to get [JFK] as anybody." He had also stalked MLK but "couldn't get close enough to him," Milteer said. Such statements show that many people actively sought to kill JFK, RFK, and King, though most plots fizzled.

Miami police provided a transcript of the recording to Secret Service agents on November 12. The Secret Service and FBI opened files on the matter and conducted an investigation of Milteer. Donning undercover plain clothes, FBI Agent Donald Adams questioned Milteer on November 16 as the extremist handed out fliers in his hometown of Quitman, Ga. Though his FBI superiors knew about Milteer's taped remarks to Somersett a week earlier, Adams did not find out about them until 1993. The information was "purposefully kept from me in total violation of the strictest Bureau rules," he later wrote. [19]

Secret Service and FBI agents took few chances in preparing for Kennedy's arrival. Advance security teams started scouting buildings and doing other work in Tampa on November 11. Scores of police and agents searched the buildings along the motorcade route for signs of trouble. The motorcade that wound through downtown streets featured cheering crowds and potential gunmen in offices above. Several hundred police from Tampa and surrounding areas manned the streets. Officers with rifles stood watch along overpasses and other potential dangerous locations. Mafia boss Santo Trafficante was reportedly involved in planning the Tampa plot, but he aborted the mission after observing the stepped-up security, according to authors Lamar Waldron and Thom Hartman.

After dealing with the Tampa threat, Kennedy flew to Miami to speak at the Inter-American Press Association dinner that evening. Authorities had received a bomb threat and a warning about a gunman with a high-powered rifle there. Some 250 police officers were added to the security force. There was only a short, relatively uneventful motorcade through Miami.

Compared to such precautions, security in Dallas a few days later was relatively shallow. On November 22, the Secret Service reportedly refused offers of aid by local police around the site where Kennedy was killed. Buildings along the route, such as the former Texas School Book Depository where Oswald worked, were not searched before the fateful motorcade arrived.

Like in Chicago, the Florida plots had a potential Oswald-like patsy, Cuba native Gilberto Policarpo Lopez who emigrated to Florida when he was 20 in 1960. He married an American woman in 1962, and they moved to Tampa in 1963, where Lopez started working for a construction company about the same time Oswald and Vallee obtained new jobs in Dallas and Chicago, respectively. Lopez attended a meeting of the Fair Play for Cuba Committee in Tampa; Oswald had tried to start a chapter of the group, which some suspected to be a CIA front organization, in New Orleans.

The day after JFK's death, Lopez made a suspicious trip from Texas into Mexico, where he took a plane to Cuba. The route Lopez took was similar to one Oswald reportedly attempted right after Kennedy's assassination. Lopez made it to Cuba; Oswald, who failed to obtain a Cuban and Soviet visa two months before, did not. The CIA kept Lopez's file until at least 1975, calling him "a subject of possible interest in the assassination investigation."

In working to destabilize leaders in Iran, Guatemala, and Cuba in the 1950s and 1960s, the CIA developed decoy plans and patsies to blame. There were other elements involved in JFK's assassination besides the CIA and military officials, authors wrote, including the mafia, oil company owners, John Birchers, and klansmen. But none had the overarching tentacles in this case as the CIA.

LBJ sends former CIA director, JFK enemy to investigate Freedom Summer murders

Some killings in the 1960s were impromptu, such as the 1965 homicide of Rev. James Reeb, a Selma march participant who was beaten to death as he walked along a downtown street. Others were generally planned – but didn't specifically target one person – like the 1963 Birmingham church bombing that killed four girls. More than a few seemed like targeted assassinations, such as the planned 1964 Freedom Summer murders of civil rights activists James Chaney, Andrew Goodman, and Michael Schwerner.

During that time, almost every civil rights organizer in the Deep South learned to live with fear, said Ivanhoe Donaldson, a Student Nonviolent Coordinating Committee field secretary in Mississippi who survived a police officer shoving a gun in his mouth in 1963. "We were constantly faced with harassment. [We] were beaten, shot at." Some learned to drive really fast. Graham Greene, an SNCC organizer in Greenwood whose father was an NAACP leader, raced at speeds up to 105 miles per hour to elude assailants who shot at his car in 1963. A few months earlier, someone shot out the windows of his house. [20]

A substantial part of the harassment came from the state of Mississippi. Mitchell unearthed sovereignty commission reports that showed the state had spied on Schwerner and his wife, Rita, three months before klansmen killed the trio. The couple had been recruited by John Lewis to leave the Northeast for Mississippi. They had worked on civil and voting rights matters in Meridian since at least January 1964, with Michael, who had the nickname, "Mickey," mockingly referred to by locals as "Goatee." They started a youth community center in Meridian, and Rita said there had been "constant threats" on her husband's life.

In May, an extreme klan group called the White Knights met, where participants talked about beating Schwerner. Rev. Edgar Killen, a Baptist minister and klan organizer, replied to leave him alone since "another unit was going to take care of him, that his elimination had been approved," according to Meridian police officer Wallace Miller, who had joined the White Knights. [21]

The commission's spies included not just those who infiltrated civil rights groups, but paid informants. Among those believed to be an MSSC spy was R.L. Bolden, a former vice president of the Mississippi NAACP. Bolden denied spying, referencing his long work in the movement.

Yet, Dawn Porter, producer of the PBS documentary Spies of Mississippi, said that Bolden gave the MSSC the car license plate and pictures of Chaney, Goodman, and Schwerner. The MSSC was full of White Citizens' Council members, who alerted klansmen and authorities to look for the trio's vehicle. "We know that [Bolden] gave this information to his handlers," Porter said. "His handlers turned that over to the Mississippi police, who were infiltrated by the klan." Others in the black community reportedly on the MSSC payroll included Percy Greene, publisher of the black newspaper Jackson Advocate; and Rev. Henry Humes, pastor of New Hope Baptist Church in Greenville. [22]

Some believe that Chaney, Goodman, and Schwerner were randomly pulled over by klansman and Deputy Sheriff Cecil Price in Philadelphia, Ms., on June 21, 1964. The trio had investigated the burning of Mount Zion Methodist Church, a black congregation a few miles east of Philadelphia that was open to having a Freedom School. They were on their way back to Meridian, where they stayed that summer.

The plot against the civil rights workers involved not just klansmen and authorities, but higher officials, Porter said. "They were being targeted by the sovereignty commission," she said. "Their every move was watched. This was quite a deliberate act to pull them over. And, you know, it results in their murders."

Price detained the trio in jail for alleged speeding and possible involvement in the church burning while reportedly planning their deaths with fellow klansmen. He released them late that evening, and they began driving southeast towards Meridian. After state highway patrol officers did not stop the trio as planned, Price raced after them and confronted them almost halfway to Meridian. He put them in his car and drove to a remote area about 10 miles southeast of Philadelphia, where klansmen following in two cars killed them. They buried the bodies 15 feet deep in an earthen dam some five miles southwest of Philadelphia and burned their car in a swamp about 15 miles northeast of town.

Price then addressed the group, reportedly saying, "You've struck a blow for the white man. Mississippi can be proud of you. You've let those agitating outsiders know where this state stands. Go home now and forget it. But before you go, I'm looking each one of you in the eye and telling you this: The first man who talks is dead. If anybody who knows anything about this ever opens his mouth to any outsider about it, then the rest of us are going to kill him just as dead as we killed those three son of bitches tonight." [23]

President Lyndon Johnson soon sent Dulles, of all people, to Mississippi. Dulles, who some thought masterminded Kennedy's death, was a strange choice as a federal investigator of the Freedom Summer murders. Some speculated that LBJ wanted to force Hoover, who was reluctant to increase the FBI's involvement, into sending more agents there, which he did.

Others thought Dulles was there to focus the investigation on a few local klansmen and law enforcement officers, and not any statewide officials or national far-right leaders. After meeting with Gov. Paul Johnson Jr., the Mississippi leader praised Dulles as a federal rep who was there "for the purpose of doing good and not destroying the state." As he left following two days of meetings with public and private officials, Dulles said he didn't know anything about the search. "I was just there to talk with a wide group of people.... about the civil rights questions," he said, dodging most questions. [24]

The burned car was found in the swamp three days after the trio's deaths. Price and Sheriff Lawrence Rainey, who was also a klan member, denied knowing anything about the killings to investigators, as well as to civil rights leaders James Farmer, Lewis, and Dick Gregory. Farmer offered to supply more than 30 volunteers to help with the search, but officials rejected that.

Federal officials also ignored requests to protect civil rights workers. The violence against Freedom Summer volunteers and black residents did not subside after the trio was declared missing. On June 23, three homes were bombed in McComb about 80 miles south of Jackson. The following day, armed white men intimidated voter registration workers in the town of Drew. Throughout the state, volunteers were shot at, beaten, and arrested, while buildings where civil rights workers met were set on fire.

While most figured the three martyrs were dead, Gov. Johnson and allies claimed they were faking it. Two weeks after they were killed, MSSC investigator A.L. Hopkins wrote, "There is still no physical evidence that these three civil rights workers have met with foul play other than the burned car [sic] which could very easily be part of a hoax." Hopkins had also secretly provided Beckwith's defense attorneys key information on prospective jurors for the second trial. [25]

As investigators and Navy sailors combed through woods and swamps, they found bodies in waterways and even on the side of roads. Those included lumber mill worker Henry Dee and college student Charles Moore, who were assassinated in May 1964 by klan members wrongly accusing them of being Black Panthers members. Moore had participated in an Alcorn State protest, while Dee was his friend. "Those deaths were [initially] forgotten," COFO leader Dennis said. "If it had just been blacks there [as part of the Freedom Summer killings], they would have forgotten again. It would have just been three black people missing." Some later pursued the Dee and Moore cases, and in 2007, klansman James Seale was convicted for the murders and sentenced to life in prison.

In early August 1964, the FBI received a tip from state highway patrol officer Maynard King, who became close with one of the FBI investigators, Mitchell reported. The bodies of Schwerner, Chaney and Goodman were unearthed on August 4, some 44 days after the murders. King's identity remained secret for four decades, as some wondered why he sat on that information so long. Mitchell reported that it took King that long to pinpoint the correct site, using another informant. [26]

Mississippi declined to prosecute the authorities and klansmen for murder, leaving it to the U.S. Justice Department to file lesser charges of violating civil rights. In 1967, seven defendants, including Price and klan leader Samuel Bowers, were found guilty. Alton Roberts, the klansman who reportedly executed Schwerner and Goodman, served six years, the longest prison sentence of that group.

In 1998, Bowers was convicted for his role in the 1966 firebombing murder of businessman and NAACP leader Vernon Dahmer. He was sentenced to life in prison and died there in 2006. Mitchell also uncovered new evidence that helped lead to the 2005 manslaughter conviction of Killen, who Bowers called the "main instigator" of the 1964 murders. He was sentenced to 60 years and died in prison in 2018. Federal and state officials declared the case closed in 2016.

Investigators examine the charred car ridden in by Mississippi civil rights martyrs James Chaney, Michael Schwerner, and Andrew Goodman in 1964.
Photo from Library of Congress, Public Domain

Hoover: 'Do something about Malcolm X'

Malcolm X faced more enmity by top government officials than King and most other black leaders. While three Nation of Islam members were convicted for Malcolm X's 1965 murder, the FBI spied on him for years. Hoover sent a telegram in 1964 to the FBI office in New York City that ordered agents to "do something about Malcolm X."

While the FBI considered him a dangerous criminal since he advocated that black people protect themselves with weapons, actor and 1963 March on Washington organizer Ossie Davis said he was used by nonviolent civil rights leaders in negotiations.

"They would say outside the door if you don't deal with us is the other brother and he ain't like us," Davis said. "It behooves white America to deal with [the nonviolent leaders]. That was the strategy, and to some degree it worked. Malcolm was always involved somewhere in the struggle."

A week before Malcolm X was killed, his home in Queens was firebombed. The police and FBI were known to have paid informants within the Nation of Islam, and some wondered if those who killed him had been paid off. [27]

King family pursues the truth in court

The King family didn't believe the official version of the civil rights leader's assassination on April 4, 1968, to the point that members pursued a lawsuit. The FBI concluded that James Earl Ray, a petty criminal and segregationist who escaped from a Missouri prison in 1967 and then volunteered with the George Wallace presidential campaign, planned and shot King by himself. Ray was convicted and sentenced to life in prison. He claimed he was framed until he died in 1998.

In 1999, a jury found that retired Memphis cafe owner Loyd Jowers was involved in King's killing, along with government agencies that included the FBI and Memphis police. The jury awarded the King family damages of $100, a token amount to show they pursued the case for justice, not money.

Jowers said in a 1993 TV interview that he was paid by mafia-connected grocer Frank Liberto to hire a Memphis police official, who the King family believed was Lt. Earl Clark, to kill King from bushes near his restaurant. The civil rights leader was shot as he stood on the second-story walkway at the Lorraine Motel, which was later converted into the National Civil Rights Museum.

The mafia, as well as local, state, and federal government agencies, were "deeply involved" in the assassination, said King's widow, Coretta Scott King, who passed away in 2006. "The jury also affirmed overwhelming evidence that identified someone else, not James Earl Ray, as the shooter, and that Mr. Ray was set up to take the blame," she said. [28]

The threats against King occurred regularly since his home was bombed by klansmen in 1955 during the Montgomery, Ala., bus boycott. In 1958, he survived being stabbed in the chest with a letter opener by a mentally ill black woman. In 1960, a Georgia judge sentenced him to four months of hard labor in prison merely for participating in an Atlanta sit-in. The Kennedys helped secure King's release within days, while GOP presidential candidate Nixon did nothing.

In May 1963, the Gaston Motel, where the civil rights leader stayed during the Birmingham, Ala., intergration campaign, was firebombed by klansmen. The Birmingham home of his brother, Alfred King, also a minister and civil rights leader, was bombed on that same night. A witness said that a uniformed police officer delivered a package to the front door that exploded after someone else threw an object through a window.

About that same time, far-right activists met at the Congress of Freedom in New Orleans to reportedly discuss killings and other topics. Jack William Brown, the klan leader in Chattanooga, Tenn., was among those stalking King. Shortly after Kennedy was assassinated in 1963, King said to his wife, "This is what is going to happen to me, also."

FBI leader Hoover long targeted black leaders. In 1919, he headed the Bureau of Investigation's intelligence division that spied on U.S. citizens thought to be "radicals," such as African-American leader Marcus Garvey. Hoover also joined with then-Attorney General A. Mitchell Palmer to crack down on free speech and dissent, a campaign that was derailed by individuals protesting and a few government officials refusing to rubber stamp the government's unconstitutional actions.

Hoover didn't let that setback stop him. In the early 1950s, he became an ally of Sen. Joseph McCarthy, whose campaign against supposed communists suppressed dissent and free speech. Hoover didn't as much as spread smears publicly as he worked behind-the-scenes. In 1956, Hoover started the COINTELPRO domestic spying program against alleged communists, targeting mostly black leaders such as King. At one point, Hoover called King "the most notorious liar in America." The FBI wiretaps did not find ties to communists, but Hoover, who remained the top dog until 1972, tried to blackmail King after discovering he had extramarital affairs. He carried out similar campaigns against the Kennedys, Malcolm X, and Hampton.

In 1966, King was hit by a brick thrown by a white counter-protester in Chicago while marching against racial discrimination in housing. In early 1968, the death and bomb threats multiplied. Government informant William Somersett told Miami police Lt. Charles Sapp about the existence of a plot against the civil rights leader in April. Sapp said he didn't relay the information to the FBI before King was shot since it was "so vague." [29]

Despite the 1999 lawsuit verdict, the many reports about far-right extremists stalking King for years before 1968 in hopes of killing him, and the FBI's campaign to discredit King, the government and many historians cling to the lone-assassin version.

Rays of sunshine reach the tombs of Martin Luther King Jr. and Coretta Scott King, which rest on a stone platform surrounded by a reflecting pool at the MLK Center in Atlanta.   Photo by Kevin Shay

More questions in assassinations of RFK, Hampton

The assassination of Robert Kennedy in 1968 at the Ambassador Hotel in Los Angeles, as he celebrated his victory in the California Democratic primary election, is riddled with more questions.

For one, did someone else besides accused assassin Sirhan Sirhan fire at RFK? Sirhan's .22-caliber gun only held eight bullets, and some witnesses said there were more shots fired at Kennedy and bystanders than eight. So why did the LA Police Department destroy door frames and ceiling panels with bullet holes, as well as photographs of the scene? And why were the two LA police officers leading the investigation connected to the CIA?

For another, how could Sirhan fire the fatal shot when the coroner told a Los Angeles grand jury that the murder weapon containing .22-caliber bullets was fired not more than three inches from behind Kennedy's right ear, while witnesses testified that Sirhan was never closer than 18 inches from the senator? [30]

And another, was Sirhan hypnotized to shoot his gun at RFK that night, as Daniel P. Brown, a psychology professor at Harvard Medical School who interviewed Sirhan for numerous hours, asserted? Sirhan said he does not remember anything about the shooting.

Finally, what exactly did Thane Cesar, a security guard hired to protect Kennedy that night, do before, during, and after the shooting? Cesar was a far-right extremist who claimed RFK would have "sold the country down the road to the commies or minorities like his brother did." He was walking directly behind Kennedy when shots rang out and said he drew a .38-caliber pistol but did not fire it. Cesar also owned a .22-caliber pistol that he claimed to have sold before RFK's killing, but it was later discovered that he lied and did not sell it until after the assassination.

Like in other cases, RFK was long targeted by far-right figures. A few weeks before Kennedy was assassinated, FBI Associate Director and alleged Hoover lover Clyde Tolson shocked a group of high-level FBI officials by blurting out, "I hope that someone shoots and kills the son of a bitch [RFK]."

"Senator Robert Kennedy was a marked man," wrote Edward J. Curtin Jr., a former sociology professor. "And he knew it. That he was nevertheless willing to stand up to the forces of hate and violence that were killing innocents at home and abroad is a testimony to his incredible courage and love of country." [31]

As for Hampton, he was shot at close range during the 1969 pre-dawn police raid, which was organized by the office of Edward Hanrahan, the Cook County state's attorney. The FBI also helped plan the raid, as it worked to disrupt and neutralize the Panthers through its secret COINTELPRO program. The FBI paid Panthers security guard William O'Neal for information that included a map of Hampton's apartment. [32]

Police fired more than 90 bullets at the occupants, also killing Panther Mark Clark as he guarded the door. Clark's shotgun fired one bullet into the ceiling as he had a reflexive death-convulsion after being shot in the heart. Hampton, an honors student who started a health clinic and free breakfast program, had reportedly been drugged and shot in the head at close range. Hanrahan claimed that Panthers fired on police as they searched for weapons, but records showed that the only round fired by Panthers was Clark's reflexive shot.

Six days after Hampton's murder, Hoover thanked FBI Agent Roy Martin Mitchell, who aided the raid, and awarded him a $200 bonus.

Others receive justice years later

In the cases of Evers and the three Freedom Summer civil rights workers, a measure of justice came years later, though some thought higher public and private officials were ultimately responsible. To the families of Black Panthers Hampton and Clark, the local and federal governments agreed in 1982 to pay $1.85 million, though none of the shooters faced prosecution. Many believe the real responsible parties also got away with the murders of the Kennedys, King, and Malcolm X.

Some justice came years after the fact in some other 1960s murders. In 1977, klansman Robert Chambliss was sentenced to life in prison for his role in planting the 1963 Birmingham church bomb that killed four girls and injured almost two dozen others. He died in prison in 1985. Fellow klansmen Thomas Blanton and Bobby Cherry received life sentences for the same crime in 2001 and 2002, respectively. Cherry perished in 2004, while Blanton died in 2020. Another suspect, Herman Cash, passed away in 1994 and was not charged.

Chambliss claimed that controversial klan informant Gary Rowe committed the bombing. Rowe, who historians believe was involved in the 1961 beatings and firebombings of Freedom Riders and the 1963 bombing of Birmingham's Gaston Motel, was never charged. Rowe told his FBI handler that Muslims bombed the motel, which many believe was a lie to cover up his involvement. [33]

In 2007, klansman James Seale was issued a life sentence for his role in the 1964 kidnapping and murders of 19-year-olds Henry Dee and Charles Moore in Mississippi. Seale died in 2011. Then in 2010, former Alabama trooper James Fowler pleaded guilty to manslaughter in the 1965 killing of civil rights worker Jimmie Jackson during the Selma marches. Fowler only served five months in prison.

Unsuccessful assassination attempts occurred against civil rights leaders James Meredith, Fannie Lou Hamer, and Fred Shuttlesworth. Four years after he integrated the University of Mississippi, Meredith embarked on a march from Memphis to Jackson encouraging black people to register to vote. As he and some friends walked along a highway about 28 miles south of Memphis just across the Mississippi border, klansman James Norvell emerged from the woods. He shouted, "I only want Meredith!"

His friends scattered and yelled at him to get on the ground. Norvell fired his 16-gauge shotgun loaded with birdshot shells, wounding Meredith before police following the march caught him. Norvell only served 18 months in prison.

As Meredith recovered in a hospital, King and others took over the march. Four days later, the FBI reportedly heard a klan leader from North Carolina saying he planned to travel to Mississippi to kill King. "I've seen too many people bungle the job of killing King," he allegedly said.

That same day, three klansmen in Natchez, about 100 miles southwest of Jackson, tried to lure King there by killing 65-year-old Ben White, who wasn't even involved in civil rights. The trio hoped to assassinate King in Natchez, according to court records. It took until 2003 to convict one klansmen charged with murdering White. He was sentenced to life in prison and died in 2004. The other two never went to trial. [34]

King went to Chicago, then returned to the Jackson march. Meredith regained strength enough to join about 12,000 participants in Jackson. Along the way, klansmen had swerved their vehicles at the marchers and attacked them. Highway patrol officers had tear-gassed them. But they registered more than 4,000 citizens to vote.

In 1962, shortly after Hamer attempted to vote in her Mississippi county, racists fired 15 shots into her home. She and her family soon moved to another county. The following year, she rode on a Greyhound bus from South Carolina in which some black riders reportedly sat in the white section. Hamer and others were arrested after the bus reached Mississippi. In jail, authorities beat and groped her, then forced prisoners to beat her nearly to death. Hamer recovered and became a statewide and national civil and voting rights leader.

Shuttlesworth faced numerous dire threats. Bethel Baptist Church, where he was minister from 1953 to 1961, and his home endured several bombings, including one on Christmas Day. In 1957, a white mob that included 16th Street Baptist Church bomber Bobby Cherry beat Shuttlesworth with bats and chains after he tried to integrate a school. Someone stabbed his wife, Ruby, during the melee. They recovered enough to lead more successful equality campaigns.

Why it's important to continue to investigate 1960s violence

Viewed singularly, the assassinations and other political violence in the 1960s seem like a series of random events. But when you start connecting the dots, you can see better how they were part of more coordinated plans involving wealthy, well-connected figures who had money and status to lose.

Many of the same violent klan and far-right organizations pursued Evers, JFK, King, RFK, and others. Beckwith, the killer of Evers, also threatened King and hated JFK. Soon after the JFK assassination, Beckwith wrote letters applauding the murder and saying the country would get straightened out now that "Adolph Kennedy" was dead.

The CIA might not have cared as much about Evers as it did the Kennedy's, but officials like the Mississippi governor sure cared about what Evers, King, and others were doing. That's why the state had its spy network. The so-called civic-minded White Citizens' Council and violent klan groups worked together in many cases, such as to publicize the whereabouts of civil rights leaders they didn't like in the hopes some of their more extreme compatriots would "take care" of them. Other Deep South states employed similar spy networks and ties between violent klan members and civic leaders, but Mississippi probably featured the most extensive such system.

James Meredith lies on the ground after being shot by a klansman during a 1966 march. The shooter is seen in the bushes at far left side.
Photo by Jack R. Thornell, The Associated Press, Public Domain

Some of the same players involved in the JFK assassination participated in the dirty business against his brother and King. The same playbook was used to blame patsies and discredit the critics. That Allen Dulles wound up in Mississippi investigating civil rights murders at the same time he was steering the Warren Commission to its lone-assassin conclusion in the JFK case seems less like a coincidence the more you study these cases.

While we have fragments of what really happened, efforts to expose the full truth about these assassinations continue to this day. It's about more than setting the historical record straight and providing justice to victims' families.

The truth can help reform the government agencies and private entities involved. If government and business agents know there are eventually real consequences for their actions, perhaps they will think twice before aiding potential extrajudicial killings these days. Perhaps when they see how long people work on discovering the truth, they will understand that participating in a scheme is not worth it. Perhaps their consciences will finally take hold, as has occurred in many instances later in the lives of key figures.

The CIA, FBI, and other federal government agencies have undergone reforms since the 1960s. Most changes were not related to assassinations, but some targeted the extrajudicial aspects. A major piece of legislation in 2004 formed a new office under the Director of National Intelligence, which helped implement more civilian control of the CIA and other intelligence agencies that had pretty much operated as loose cannons. Gone are the days when the CIA can secretly decide to work with mafia criminals to kill foreign leaders.

The wide majority of government and private agents seek to do the right thing. Some get caught up under orders from superiors. Agent Adams wrote that was what occurred to him as he pursued Milteer in 1963, and was only allowed to ask five short questions when he tracked down Milteer a few days after JFK's killing. By then, Hoover and LBJ had decided only Oswald was involved. Hoover tried hard to secure his legacy, but from what we know today, that legacy is largely negative.

Dallas Deputy Sheriff Roger Craig and CIA agent Jim Wilcott are among the insiders who have tried to unearth the truth about the JFK assassination. Café owner Jowers came forward in the MLK case. Psychology professor Brown has been relentless in pursuing new information on the RFK killing. FBI Agent M. Wesley Swearingen worked to expose the truth in the Hampton case, which led to the legal settlement and some accountability.

Author and investigative journalist Mitchell formed the nonprofit Mississippi Center for Investigative Reporting in 2018 to keep the heat on key cases and issues in that state. He is also involved with a multi-state effort called the Civil Rights Cold Case Project.

High-profile political assassinations in the U.S. have been relatively few in number since the 1960s. However, mass killings, many by white supremacists targeting blacks, Latinos, Asians, Jewish people, gays, and others, are rising significantly. The far-right MAGA movement, led by Trump, riles up its most extreme followers, leading to violence like the 2020 attacks on a Democratic bus in Texas and the January 6th mob assault on the Capitol. Some leaders continue to encourage lone wolf-types to commit violence, from which they can then distance themselves.

Perhaps by continuing to learn from the not-so-distant past we can discover a way out of this persistent nightmare.

Social Justice: Dreams Deferred

First published in the Hard Times News, later Dallas Advocate for Jobs, Peace, and Freedom, September 1983; and Medium, August 30, 2020

Kevin Shay was one of 60 Texas residents who took a 60-hour bus ride in 1983 through the Deep South to Washington, D.C., and back, attending the 20th anniversary of the March on Washington. That march was the largest of the regular commemorative marches for the original in 1963 that featured Martin Luther King Jr.'s "I Have a Dream" speech. This is an updated account of that journey.

Friday, August 26, 1983. 5 a.m.

Up late last night as usual. Somehow locate the Martin Luther King Jr. Center and see the bus from the corner of an eye. U-turn it like Starsky & Hutch before they got canned. Sleepily stumble into line. Greeted by cool, almost suspicious eyes, undoubtedly wondering why a 6–7 Caucasian man would want to attend this revival of their late civil rights hero's dream. Shay wonders why, too. It'll be interesting to find out why folks are here. To make sure their Dream Deferred doesn't become a Raisin in the Sun?

Local trip leader Gene Lantz, a 42-year-old, tall, bearded factory worker, union organizer, and civil rights activist, insists that bus riders aren't living in the past. "Sure, they still have dreams, but we're here to work towards making those dreams even more of a reality," he explains. "Just the fact they are here right now, that we got 60 people from this conservative area to go on such a bus ride, shows us that our area is not insensitive to the civil rights causes and the needs of the poor."

That number is out of a region housing well over two million people. And some people are from College Station, not just the Dallas-Fort Worth area. Still, that is better than in 1963 when only a handful from this region witnessed King's "I Have a Dream" speech.

Someone asks for volunteers to ride and help drive a 10-person van. Shay answers the call. Never could stand the crowdedness of a bus. Too many bad memories of high school and college hoops road trips in hot, putrid buses. But they were better than what the 1961 Freedom Riders faced, when participants were beaten almost to death in Deep South cities and buses set on fire.

5:30 a.m.

Only 30 minutes behind schedule, we take off. Bus driver Rocket Ricky, knowing he has a contract and schedule to keep or he won't get paid, sets the tone, pushing his crate 85 miles per hour on the highway. Elaine Lantz, partner of Gene who works in the same electronics plant, frantically tries to keep up, vainly asking Ricky through the citizens band radio to slow down.

Shay smiles in the passenger side seat, sits back and relaxes. Just another trip. If we crash, if we're stupid enough to die for this cause before we even get there, how important exactly would that cause be? Can't answer that so early in the morning.

Most of the Texas 1983 March on Washington contingent pose with in front of the bus driven by Rocket Ricky from Dallas to Washington, D.C., and back. There have been commemorative marches in other years, but the 1983 one was the largest with about 250,000 participants. Photo by Kevin Shay

9 a.m.

Over the Texas border into Louisiana, riders stir from uneasy slumber to make small talk. Fellow writer Mike McKinnon, a sharp, 20-something who once worked for a government-sponsored television show that was victimized by GOP President Ronald Reagan's budget cuts, asks why Shay's doing this.

Sits back, reflecting. "I'm a writer in search of that elusive, pot-of-gold story. This seems as good a place as any to find it." Smile. "'Course, I believe in the cause, as long as it's what it's supposed to be – one for more jobs, peace, and freedom for all. That is what it's about, isn't it?" Laughs. This is 1983, four months till 1984. Has the reality behind the American Dream ever really coincided with lofty ideals that are easily said and much harder to accomplish?

Mike nods. "I guess that's why I'm here, also. Maybe we'll find out what all this dreaming's about, how much of it is for real." He sits back, reading over notes and articles. Shay goes back to looking out the window, trying to keep tabs on Rocket Ricky's bus that's a dot on the horizon.

11 a.m.

Jennifer Eppler, an organizer from the local chapter of peace organization War Resisters League, takes wheel. Talks about how this contingent was set up. The hassles involved just in getting this small group together. The delegation of responsibility that few wanted to share. The money to raise, as more than half the people are here due to funds donated by kind souls who couldn't make the trip.

"What's the actual purpose of this trip in your view?" Shay asks more out of boredom than duty.

Jennifer is prepared. "We want people to be aware of these causes and show them there are people out there who still think about other things than making bombs and blowing up people." As if people have to be shown that. While some do, many come up with excuses to justify bomb making. They mostly come down to fear and money.

Ask if anyone on this trip was there when King spoke about his dreams two decades before. Learns that 70-year-old retired teacher Lena Hodge was. She had flown to D.C. in 1963 and at one point shook hands with King. The famed civil rights leader had spoken in early 1963 to a crowd of about 4,000 in Dallas, despite a bomb threat that delayed the speech. About 200 white protesters greeted King outside the Dallas Fair Park Music Hall, with some screaming that he was a commie.

Jimmy Robinson, member of the far-right National States Rights Party and KKK who carried a Confederate flag and rifle to intimidate blacks, told reporters that the group was not there to start trouble. In the following two years, Robinson set a burning cross on a Jewish Holocaust survivor's front lawn and physically attacked King in a Selma, Ala., hotel. Among those who stopped Robinson's attack on King was long-time civil rights advocate and Georgia Rep. John Lewis.

By then, King had faced numerous other attacks at the hands of such racists, some of which had been aborted by the FBI using KKK informants. In 1963, King urged the Dallas crowd to make sacrifices for equality and justice. The cause could cause loss of employment, even lives, he noted. "If a man has not found something worth dying for, he isn't fit to live," he maintained, before appealing for a nonviolent approach in which people could still "love the segregationist." [1]

In her brief exchange at the 1963 march, Hodge asked King to return to Dallas. He replied that he was "coming to see aaaaall of you." But he wouldn't make it back to Dallas before another plot succeeded in killing him in Memphis in 1968.

Fifteen years after that assassination, we are driving towards the belly of the beast. But not Memphis. We are taking a more southern route that is about 100 miles longer through cities where King and other civil rights advocates did much of their work. Ask Jennifer why we are taking the longer route. She shrugs, "Ricky's driving."

Maybe Ricky has a plan. Maybe he knows that the southern route with its lower elevation and fewer mountains to cross is better on gas mileage for a large bus. Maybe he figures it's fitting on this journey to drive through more Deep South sites of civil rights struggles past.

Official program for the 1983 March on Washington. Photo by Shay

Noon.

Pass through Jackson, capital of Mississippi. Over the CB radio, a device we used back in the 1970s and 1980s to communicate between vehicles before cell phones arrived, Ricky notes that Jackson was the city where NAACP leader Evers was assassinated two decades earlier. The home still has his blood stains on the driveway.

"Our schedule doesn't allow us to stop," he apologizes. "This is also the place where the Freedom Riders were forced to stop."

Jackson officials arrested several hundred riders in that 1961 action, effectively keeping them from reaching their destination of New Orleans. Many were sent to the Mississippi State Penitentiary to be placed in the Death Row unit and issued only underwear while taking away their bedding. Through such painful pursuits, they soon caused the buses and stations to be integrated.

We drive by the county jail and other drab buildings. In 2017, the Mississippi Civil Rights Museum would open here. But Jackson's downtown looks fairly empty and uninviting. In 2023, the city would suffer through the nation's highest murder rate among major cities, just ahead of Birmingham, Ala., Memphis, St. Louis, and New Orleans.

Down the road, we stop at a truck stop in Meridian. Civil rights martyr James Chaney was born here, then found dead in 1964, buried in a nearby earthen dam. Chaney and New York-born civil rights workers Michael Schwerner and Andrew Goodman, who were also killed, had organized voter registration drives, participated in various demonstrations, and investigated a nearby black church bombing.

Some two decades later, Shay asks Larry Egbert Jr., a professor of anesthesiology at the University of Texas Southwestern Medical School, how taking this journey helped keep alive the work of civil rights martyrs. The mission is "more of a way to make a statement with others and get more inspired to continue working for the causes," he says, as vehicles whiz down the highway in the background. "I really don't expect anything politically to come of the march itself. But the energy created, the awareness of those goals, can help bring them about in the future."

Egbert, a board member of Physicians for Social Responsibility and volunteer with Doctors Without Borders, would continue to go beyond such activity. He would be arrested during anti-nuclear weapons protests and cycle hundreds of miles to call an end to the Cold War arms race.

2 p.m.

Back on the road. Deep voices with unmistakable Southern accents dominate the CB, issuing racist remarks. They are angered by the sign on the bus proclaiming, "March for Jobs, Peace, & Freedom – Texas." In 2020, gun-carrying Trump supporters would attack and threaten Biden supporters who rode another bus to campaign events in Texas. No one would be arrested, but a lawsuit would be successful in holding one ringleader accountable.

One voice is particularly spiteful: "What're you nig---- and nig---lovers marching for jobs for? Why don't you go out and work like everyone else, instead of sitting around complaining about no jobs and collecting unemployment?"

Ricky has let numerous similar comments slide. But like most, he has a breaking point. You can only sit there and take abuse for so long before fighting back. "We tired of working for you, honky," I hear Ricky say in a firm voice. "We too smart for that. We want our fair share." The racist has no response. Cries of "Right on, Ricky!" erupt throughout the van and bus.

Pass through Birmingham. Old streets. Dusty houses. Black kids playing basketball on worn courts with rusty hoops and no nets in 100-degree heat. Downtown cultural center looks like it needs substantial renovations.

View the county jail where King wrote the stirring "Letter from Birmingham Jail" in April 1963 while contained therein for nonviolently protesting brutal Jim Crow segregation, bombings of black homes and churches, lynchings, and other grave injustices. King urged followers to break unjust laws through direct nonviolent action. While many called the Atlanta resident an outside agitator, he responded, "Injustice anywhere is a threat to justice everywhere." [2]

The 16th Street Baptist Church stands proudly, defiantly, its Romanesque and Byzantine design contrasting with simpler-styled surrounding structures. Dating to the 1870s, the first black church in Birmingham was the site of a horrific bombing two months before JFK's assassination that killed four young girls and injured more than a dozen others. Three of the four klansmen held responsible were ultimately found guilty, with the fourth dying by the time justice arrived. While the Birmingham Civil Rights Institute, with a museum and research center, would open in 1992, a public Confederate memorial in the city would not be removed until 2020.

Survey the bus station where in 1961, Freedom Riders were viciously beaten by KKK types wielding baseball bats, chains, and iron pipes, as law enforcement officials watched. Pass by a hospital that refused to treat injured civil rights activists. A car honks at the bus, and a clenched fist in solidarity shoots out.

The story of bloodshed for the cause was similar in Montgomery, some 90 miles to the south. Alabama's capital, where the National Lynching Memorial and Legacy Museum would open in 2018, was also the site of Rosa Parks' stand and other desegregation campaigns and marches. One would reach there from Selma after several bloody attempts in 1965, helping to pass the Voting Rights Act.

In 2024, Shay would meet Columbus Mitchell, a local teacher, historian, and tour guide, at the Edmund Pettus Bridge in Selma. Mitchell, nephew of 1965 march participant Willie Thornton, would be there most days as part of his "calling to tell people about the history of this area."

Steel rectangles hang at the National Lynching Memorial in Montgomery, Ala., representing many U.S. lynching victims. Photo by Kevin Shay

Pass through Anniston, another town where the Freedom Riders faced a bloody confrontation that included the bus being firebombed. That site would be marked by a monument in 2017.

Pondering the violence, Shay is not sure he could sit there and take being beaten. You really have to possess a higher calling to withstand that. But you can't fight back or the racists would likely kill you and others. At least that was the theory. Medgar Evers usually carried guns, but that didn't help him the night a klansman fired a rifle at him. At some point, African Americans brought rifles to certain demonstrations and meetings to protect King and others. The whole thing sickens Shay and drives him onward.

8 p.m.

Drive through Georgia's capital without stopping at the King Center for Nonviolent Social Change, the site of his tomb, the home where he lived as a boy, and Ebenezer Baptist Church where he preached. Have a schedule to keep and a long night through Georgia and the Carolina's.

Freedom Riders avoided violence for the most part in this area, though Lewis was attacked in Rock Hill, S.C. Others were arrested in various cities.

Klansmen set a Freedom Riders bus on fire in 1961 near Anniston, Ala. Photo from U.S. National Park Service, Public Domain

Saturday, August 27, 1983. 5 a.m.

A full 24 hours after we start, Shay finally gets to take the van wheel to relieve the boredom of sitting. Did get at least two hours of loose sleep. Rocket's pushing 85 again. Have to focus while trying not to doze off.

The sun rises about halfway through North Carolina. Mind gets to playing funny tricks and thinking of odd things when the body's been resting in one place for so long. Wonder what would happen if one small pothole is hit, sending this van careening to disaster. Would headlines read, "Civil Rights Activists Die Driving for Cause?" That might be a new one.

"You feel okay?" Jennifer's sleepy voice interrupts my daydream or nightmare.

"Oh yeah, sure," Shay assures her. "I could go on for hours." So, he does. Driving does relieve some boredom. Being responsible for more people's lives than just your own can be a thrilling experience. It can also be a headache.

8 a.m.

Stop for gas south of Petersburg, Va., site of a key Civil War battle. "Man, you were really slidin' and glidin' on that trip," Shay greets Ricky after he repeats his usual retort to those who tell him to slow down.

"Gotta make up for lost time," he smiles. "Gotta get y'all to the march on time."

Mike takes over for final haul to Shay's birthplace. Ricky immediately rockets outasight. Traffic heavy for early morning. Mike makes valiant effort to keep up with bus, blinking lights to get slowpokes out of his way.

"Mike, you ever drive an ambulance?" Jennifer pipes up. "This is sure a thrilling ride." Nervous laughter. Mike barely smiles, immersed in the mission.

Somehow catches up to Rocket 15 miles outside D.C. Has it made till Rocket whips over two lanes making a sudden exit. Mike has no choice but to stay on main highway. All that work catching up for naught. To see it slip away at last moment. There's a lesson, a truth, there somewhere, but most are too weary to seek it.

11 a.m.

Park and walk to subway station, after telling Ricky our plans through the CB. Mike still searching for runaway bus in dark subway tunnel. Try to cheer him up. "Damn, I came so close, all that effort for nothing," he looked away toward the pitch-blackness of the tunnel.

Away from the subway, we near the National Mall. The Washington Monument is the most visible landmark, along with the Capitol building and Smithsonian museums. Bearded activists and students representing some of the more than 700 groups here hand out leaflets on no nukes, getting out of El Salvador, boycotting GE products, and more.

A man throws a Yahweh Hebrew Israelites handbill to the ground. The volunteer picks it back up from the littered cement and hands it to someone else.

11:30 a.m.

Enter the mass confusion of the march. Not sure where we are going. People walk in all directions, stop, slow down, block each other's paths. Still, most are considerate, letting some pass before them, trying to stay in a semblance of a line.

Postal Union workers shout, "Ronald Reagan, he's no good! Send him back to Hollywood!" Many laugh. Shay stops to tell one unionist that Reagan is already near there, safely in his California retreat.

"Coward," the man snorts. "He's out only for his own kind – the rich. He wants us poor working slobs to stay in our assigned places." The ratio of CEO to average worker salaries would increase from 21 to 1 in 1965 to a whopping 344 to 1 by 2022, according to the Economic Policy Institute. [3]

Wade through mass of people, waving at Jennifer, Lawrence, social worker Pat Pomarici, and others who are holding a sign saying, "Dallas Seeks the Wisdom of MLK JR." Have to get out of crowd.

Texas advocates for civil rights join about 250,000 others for the 1983 march. Photo by Kevin Shay

Reach side of street to join photographers, some standing on fire hydrants, others climbing trees and telephone poles. Snap pictures like history is rolling by, and we need a reminder that we were there.

March stalls again. Many sing, "Amen." Some continue to chant anti-Reagan slogans. "Man, Reagan's got to hear us out, now," an African-American youth says loudly. Shay informs him that Reagan is 3,000 miles away. "Oh well, he's still going to hear from us. Someone will tell him," he retorts.

Police on horses gallop by. One stops and smiles as he talks with a demonstrator. Few in crowd seem overly fanatical. Content to shout slogans and hold signs. "Is this march going to change anything?" Shay asks a young guy with a sign saying, "Martin Luther King Jr. did not die in vain."

"Maybe not directly," he replies. "But it's better than not being here. This march is something. Just look at all these people."

Return to mass of people after discovering that the van group had reunited with the bus group. Walk along the reflecting pool leading to the Lincoln Memorial, where speakers start to assemble. Some cool off in the pool.

A man yells at those holding our sign, "Dallas, home of the Cocaine Cowboys!" More laughter.

He's probably a fan of the team with the nickname that's insensitive to Native Americans, I think.

1 p.m.

NAACP Executive Director Benjamin Hooks talks about putting Reagan on notice, even though the Republican president doesn't seem to care. In 1971, Reagan called some black United Nations delegates "monkeys" during an exchange about withdrawing from the UN with Richard Nixon, who informed others about Reagan's slur, while calling them "cannibals."

**Some participants cool off in the reflecting pond during the 1983 march.
Photo by Kevin Shay**

Hooks knows enough not to appeal directly to Reagan, but to voters. "We are not here to live in the past and leave here simply singing, 'We shall overcome.' We are here because we are committed to the elimination of Reaganism from the face of the Earth," Hooks exclaims. [4]

More speakers try to match the intensity of King's 1963 speech, falling short with phrases such as "I have a vision" and "the dream is still alive." One by one, icons Coretta Scott King, Rev. Joseph Lowery, John Lewis, Dick Gregory,

Sammy Davis Jr., Julian Bond, Andrew Young step forward to speak. "Free at last," some conclude.

Bond, co-founder of the Student Nonviolent Coordinating Committee in 1960 who left college to lead civil rights actions and was elected to the Georgia House of Representatives in 1969, later told a reporter that the 1983 event was bigger and more inclusive. Young, a close King associate who had become Atlanta mayor in 1982, added that activists have moved from the streets to City Hall. "We've been fighting police brutality," he says. "We still have those same dreams." [5]

Gregory, the comedian and civil rights champion involved in everything from finding the Meridian civil rights martyr's bodies to uncovering King's assassination plot, is more frank than most. "Don't compare this march to 20 years ago," he says. "When we came then, most of us were scared. We came to ask others to take care of our business. Now, we're here to take care of our own business."

While inspiring in parts, can only listen to so much of that. Walk through the diverse crowd, amazed that people seem calm, even when they have to wait in line for 30 minutes to buy a soft drink. A mere 25 arrests would be reported in D.C. this day, most for street vending without a license. People try to listen to the words, catch a glimpse of the utopian visions.

Come Monday morning, those who have one will return to their back-breaking jobs, usually getting someone else wealthy. The unemployment rate is at 9 percent, better than the previous year when it reached almost 11 percent. It would fall to 7 percent by late 1984 and below 6 percent in 1987. But a job is just a job. People need a passion, a mission, to rise above the mundane.

"Our day has come!" thunders Rev. Jesse Jackson, who participated in demonstrations to open public libraries and more to blacks in his native South Carolina in the early 1960s and later worked closely with King. If anyone here could come close to King's oratory skills, it is him. In 1984, he would place third in Democratic presidential primaries behind Walter Mondale and Gary Hart and rise to second in 1988, behind only Michael Dukakis, another Mondale-type uninspiring candidate. It would take the more youthful Bill Clinton – and some say a boost from Ross Perot – to win Democrats the White House again in 1992.

"We must march on, dream on, march on!" Jackson shouted. "Don't let them break your spirit! From the outhouse to the statehouse to the courthouse to the White House, we will march on!"

Many in the reported crowd of 250,000 that stretched from the Lincoln Memorial to the Washington Monument raised their fists and cheered.

3 p.m.

Try to push past security guards at press tent to get closer to speakers and maybe ask a few more questions. Guard glances at Shay's Park Cities News media pass. "Sorry, you have to have a special media pass."

"And where do I get such a pass?"

"You had to have gotten it beforehand." Walk away. Better to mix with the masses.

Stand in a drink line. Some try to butt in front, as others motion for them to get to the line's end. A few succeed. There are always those who take shortcuts. Exasperated counter workers try to maintain control, a hopeless task in the 95-degree heat and smothering humidity.

Finally get to front of line. A young black man approaches Shay to ask if he can get him some drinks. Glances at his face and the long line. Wants to help him but finally decides he cannot. "It wouldn't be fair to all those behind me. Sorry." He walks away, dejected. In the next moment, the man in front of Shay lets a guy butt in line.

5 p.m.

A black youth walks through the crowd, yelling, "I don't see no applications! Where's the jobs? Looks like I'll have to stick somebody up to get some money." The crowd steers clear, letting him pass. The African-American jobless rate has long been higher than other racial groups. Yet, many don't see a problem with that, as billionaires continue to enrich themselves.

Finds Pat under the shade of a tree. She is one of some 600 marchers treated for heat exhaustion. People offer apples, which are hungrily, eagerly, gobbled up. "That's the first thing I've had to eat all day," sighs Pat. Shay's stomach signals likewise. In the excitement and energy of the march, we had not found much to eat. We survive on something beyond food.

Inez Reyes, another Dallas marcher, joins us. She talks about retiring on a Hawaiian island as she massages Pat's feet. Barely hear the rest of speeches as we analyze why people are here. A man approaches, suggesting something rude to Inez, who tells him to get lost. Shay motions at him to do the same. "I'll see you all again," he says in leaving.

7 p.m.

Join rest of group close to the reflecting pool. Stevie Wonder hushes crowd with latest rendition, talking over the purported sound of a heartbeat about the need for people to unite in peace and brotherhood. Conciliatory statements, nothing new, but coming from a blind singing superstar, maybe they can get through to people better than preaching and long-winded speeches.

Many in the crowd join hands as the 11-hour program concludes with a tape-recording of King's 17-minute 1963 speech. The words spoken at this site that year seem revolutionary for their time in the darkest midst of Jim Crow racism. Many civil rights advocates remained captive in Deep South jails. One hundred years after President Lincoln signed the Emancipation Proclamation, "the Negro still is not free," King noted.

"We have come here today to dramatize a shameful condition," he continued. "In a sense, we have come to our nation's capital to cash a check. When the architects of our republic wrote the magnificent words of the Constitution and the Declaration of Independence, they were signing a promissory note to which every American was to fall heir. This note was a promise that all men, yes, black men as well as white men, would be guaranteed the unalienable rights of life, liberty, and the pursuit of happiness. It is obvious today that America has defaulted on this promissory note."

The crowd surrounding the Lincoln Memorial at the 1963 March on Washington was electric as King spoke. Photo from U.S. Marine Corps, Public Domain

The 1983 crowd – like the 1963 one – stands silent, hushed, straining to drink in the calls to remain nonviolent in actions. "Let us not seek to satisfy our thirst for freedom by drinking from the cup of bitterness and hatred. We must forever conduct our struggle on the high plane of dignity and discipline. We must not allow our creative protest to degenerate into physical violence. Again and again, we must rise to the majestic heights of meeting physical force with soul force."

Remaining peaceful does not mean being weak, he exclaimed. Persistence is a virtue. "There are those who are asking the devotees of civil rights, 'When will you be satisfied?' We can never be satisfied as long as the Negro is the victim of the unspeakable horrors of police brutality."

As the words parade through attendees' minds, some stifle tears, others let them fall, recalling the violent fate King faced five years after that address and the cruelty of dreams deferred.

"I have a dream that one day this nation will rise up and live out the true meaning of its creed: We hold these truths to be self-evident: that all men are created equal. I have a dream that one day on the red hills of Georgia the sons of former slaves and the sons of former slave owners will be able to sit down together at the table of brotherhood. I have a dream that my four little children will one day live in a nation where they will not be judged by the color of their skin but by the content of their character."

The speech ends, but many do not want to leave, even those who have been there with little food in the heat for almost 12 hours. For a moment, black, white, brown, red, yellow alike blend into a rainbow of hope and goodwill that illuminates over the city, making the trials and hardships to reach this place seem trivial. For a moment, you could believe in King's dream, even if it was yet to be reached.

Marchers depart the event in 1983. Photo by Kevin Shay

Shay walks alone back to the bus and van, stopping to snap pictures, as if the camera could catch lost dreams and hopes. "Aren't you glad you came?" Gene cheerfully greets marchers at the bus.

10 p.m.

Two Texas participants still missing. Mrs. Hodge is in a D.C. hospital due to heat exhaustion, while another member accompanies her. She had fainted as she strained against the Lincoln Memorial crowd to obtain a better view. "I will never forget how kind everybody was," she would later say. "I threatened to sue them if they didn't let me out. They kept me anyhow, and I'm glad they did." [6]

No one at the bus knows where she is, so Gene, Elaine, Jennifer, and some others volunteer to remain behind with the van to wait. After showering at a local church gymnasium, Texas participants get back on the bus.

Shay joins them, wanting to hear fresh reactions from participants on what they have seen. Most are too weary to think, let alone talk about the experience. Clarice Bates, a West Dallas community leader, had carried dirt here contaminated from a lead smelter, dumping it among the D.C. grounds. The lead smelters had been allowed to pollute residents' air, water, and soil since the 1940s. Officials with one would agree in 1985 to pay 370 families a total of $20 million in a legal settlement. The last smelter would not be closed until 1990.

"It is nice to see people come together in a big, large number like that, and be on one accord and agree on things," Bates says. "It was just wonderful to be in on something that should go down in history."[7]

Sunday, August 28, 1983. 12:01 a.m.

Bus is quiet, with only a few complaining about aches and hunger. Try to settle down the mind and sleep but can only doze off in spurts.

What seems like a day later, a bright sun greets us at a stop in Greensboro, N.C., where in 1960 demonstrators successfully integrated Woolworth's lunch counters. Almost two decades later, anti-klan marchers clashed with American Nazi Party members and white supremacists, who killed five and injured several others. Among the victims were union organizers and Communist Workers Party members. No one would be brought to justice, as two juries would acquit all right-wing defendants. A civil lawsuit led by the Christic Institute would find eight white supremacists liable, resulting in a $351,000 settlement. A private commission's report would conclude that klan members planned to injure protesters and the police department colluded with right wingers to allow the violence.

Over fast food, Shay discusses the march with fellow Hard Times News writer Gary Cooper and former Tennessee reporter Lee Olson. We glance at news reports that note the similar crowd size in 1963 and 1983. Gary, who grew up in mostly-white University Park, remarks how attitudes "have loosened" in recent years. "When I was going to school [in the mid-1970s], there was only one black student at Highland Park High. And he was really harassed," Gary says. "Now, more people seem to accept blacks in the community."

Shay nods, adding that there were maybe 50 black students at Lake Highlands High in northeast Dallas when he went there during the same time. "Not many white students talked with them. There was a black section in the cafeteria and a white section," he recalls. "I played basketball and befriended several black teammates. I would drive them home to their segregated neighborhood after practice. But some still called blacks the n-word. I would tell them not to say that, but I probably wasn't as forceful as I should have been." The school Latin Club back then even held slave auctions as fundraisers with some dressed in blackface.

Olson talks about his journey from mainstream reporter to socialist activist. There is good and bad in all political systems, we agree. Could there be a system that only takes the good parts out of each, or is that another pipe dream?

Noon.

More light sleep, as political talk provides a backdrop. One young Caucasian woman states that she didn't really get to meet any black people on this trip.

Shay looks around at the bus filled with African Americans, resisting the urge to ask whose fault that was. Someone has to take the initiative, the first step.

7 p.m.

Back in Birmingham for a chicken dinner. Shay breaks the ice with some African-American students around his age by discussing the Cowboys and Mavericks. That allows inroads to other topics.

Some say the trip is worthwhile, though reasons remain cloudy, which is understandable. It's hard to define a social action that just occurred in words. Time will tell its significance.

"It's something to tell my grandkids about, if we hold it together that long," one says. As of 2025, that statement remains the best one-sentence summation of the experience.

Monday, August 29, 1983. 12:30 a.m.

At Louisiana truck stop, speak with KKDA news director Marina Coker. Says numerous people seem to have gone on the march for more personal reasons, to see what it would be like. "Isn't that interesting?" she smiles.

Bus won't start. Ricky has a truck push it to get it cranked. Homeward.

6 a.m.

Wake up to familiar signs and city lights. People milling around aisles, trying to gather belongings for that final rush home and to work. Bus leader Andrea Cervantes, a strong advocate for sending economic aid, not military weapons, to Central American countries, thanks everyone for making the trip enjoyable and the march successful.

"The march strengthened jobs, peace, and freedom," she would later say. "There were more than 200,000 there, and this is certainly telling us something. If it wasn't so important, there wouldn't be this kind of numbers in Washington. People sacrificed to go so far just to be visible." She notes that many people approached her, asking if we were really from Dallas. "It made me feel very proud," she says. [8]

While the 1963 march helped pass the 1964 Civil Rights Act, a tangible victory of the 1983 march occurred two months later when the U.S. Senate joined the House to pass a veto-proof bill to make King's birthday a federal holiday. Reagan, who released a statement calling the march "a moving moment in American history," had opposed the King holiday, but he signed the bill. In 2025, Trump and allies would work to erode black history and MLK Day.

As we near the MLK Center, people seem nervous, like they don't want to come back to the scene of somewhat pain and uncertainty. They want to stay out on the road, marching, where perhaps it's easier to view some light at the end of the tunnel. A med student asks if anyone is going north so she can catch a ride. When no one volunteers, Shay does. So out of all the people on this bus, only two live north of Reunion Arena?

The trip brought home the realization that Texas and Deep South liberal and progressive types are probably the hardiest in the nation. They have to be. They fight the good fight on the front lines, overwhelmingly outnumbered, facing a potential deadly backlash with the ghosts of lynchings and firebombings never really shed. Though it's not as bad as it once was. Considered a lib in Texas, Shay would move to Maryland in 2003, where he seems closer to a moderate. And Texas and other Deep South states would descend farther into a far-right abyss.

Departing the bus, Rocket Ricky has a final present for everyone: A poster filled with notable African kings. Shake hands firmly. Not much else to say. Stay strong? Keep fighting? He knows that. He did what he said he was going to do, drive dozens of Texans in a large bus 3,000 miles over three days to attend this event. He broke speed limit laws to get us there on time, but sometimes, higher laws supersede lower ones. People like him keep the possibilities, the dreams, alive, despite all the obstacles, because they do more than talk. They follow through on their visions.

Ricky and Shay would not cross paths again. But to this day, of all the people Shay met on this journey, he stands out the most, perhaps because he was among the few advocating for these dreams while at work. Sometimes in Shay's daydreams, he hears Ricky's voice over an imaginary CB that silences another racist: "We want our fair share." That short verbal confrontation still echoes louder in Shay's consciousness than any long-winded, high-minded speech.

Ricky's message may remain as much a dream as King's, as we argue over how close to the civil rights martyr's vision we really are in 2025. While some towns reclaim Confederate names on schools and social justice advocates continue to get tear gassed, beaten, and even killed, extremists – from Donald Trump to his attempted assassins – ramp up their campaigns that lead to violence. Where will it end? Will it end?

If the ghosts of civil rights martyrs past, who advocated for liberty and justice for all in legal, nonviolent ways only to meet violent physical demises, could talk, perhaps they would say it doesn't end. At least not in our world. But you have to remain true to the visions deep within you.

Authoritarianism: Putin and the Rise of Dictators

First published in *Walking through the Wall*, 2012; Democracy Guardian, February 19, 2021; and NewsBreak, May 4, 2024

Red Square in Moscow's central district had seen executions, demonstrations attended by hundreds of thousands, riots, military parades, religious ceremonies at the landmark St. Basil's Cathedral, and more by the time I observed two Soviet soldiers standing stoically in front of Lenin's Mausoleum in late 1986. Christmas trees decorated the outside of the tomb of the first Soviet leader, whose body had rested there since 1924.

As I turned to say something to my brother, Patrick, some Russian students who recognized us as Westerners approached. One displayed a Hard Rock Cafe button from London, so I handed him one from Stockholm. After he accepted, another young man asked if I had something else to trade. I started to slip my daypack off to display the goods. "Not here," he whispered, nervously looking around. "Bridge is better."

As we started to walk away, a uniformed guard appeared and demanded to see these students' passports. He led them away amid my protests that we were "just talking." Later that evening, we met these students, who laughed about the incident, saying "KGB" and spitting on the ground. Another textile factory worker named Serg, donned in Puma sneakers, Western jeans and jacket, and a Sony walkman, explained that their little business was technically against Soviet law but "not much happens to you unless you're caught in the act quite a few times."

We discussed differences in our systems, rock groups – he had more tapes than we did – and how I looked more Russian, with my beard and dated clothing, than many natives. Though police and KGB agents swarmed around outside the modern, 21-story Hotel Intourist a block away, Serg and his friends did not seem concerned. We conversed for a good two hours on that corner.

Mikhail Gorbachev had only been General Secretary of the former Soviet Union Communist Party for a year, but it was clear that citizens like Serg were ahead of the leader's perestroika and glasnost policies that would usher in more earth-shaking changes than many Russians wanted. Gorbachev had met with U.S. President Ronald Reagan since late 1985, though they would not sign the Intermediate-Range Nuclear Forces Treaty, which banned numerous missiles, until 1987. As Eastern European nations started breaking away from the USSR in 1989, George H.W. Bush would continue meeting with Gorbachev and sign the Strategic Arms Reduction Treaty in 1991, which resulted in the removal of about 80 percent of strategic nuclear weapons.

The progress would be ruined by the rise of Vladimir Putin, a former KGB officer who became Russian president in 2000. But that seemed miles away during our 1986 visit of hope. At a café that served hot dinners for under a ruble – equal to about 60 cents in 1986 but only one cent in 2025 – Serg said his life was "OK," that the only thing he longed for was traveling in the West. "I am free to say whatever I think in my home, and I don't concern myself with party politics," he said. "Not many Russians I know do. Our basic needs are taken care of, so what do we really have to complain about?"

There weren't homeless people begging for money and scouring trash cans as in most big U.S. cities, though they were pushed to the outside fringes of the city, some living in makeshift shacks in wooded areas. Many homeless children were packed in orphanages. The city of 12.5 million people had a community, right-to-shelter housing policy in which vacant units were turned over to the state and rented out to needy families, though the waiting lists for the better apartments were lengthy. That system changed with more private industry and evictions, and Moscow would open its first overnight homeless shelter in 1992.

We had little fear of being mugged – police on almost every street corner deterred that occurrence. Factory workers sometimes made twice as much as medical doctors and technical workers, though working and living conditions were not near as comfortable for the former. What Serg lacked – cigarettes, alcohol, electronic items that were much more expensive in Russian shops than Western ones, clothing – he purchased on the black market. Patrick helped him out this evening by giving him a pack of cigarettes, which he had bought specifically for such a deal, in exchange for a red star worn by soldiers.

A couple nights later, we had a more substantial conversation with two young women we met outside our hotel. Hotel interpreters Natalya and Olga met enough foreigners to want out of their homeland. After we walked for a mile or two, Olga said she could "feel" that we wanted to go back to one of their flats for a longer chat. When I asked if that might get her in trouble if someone informed authorities, she laughed and said, "Oh no, there are too many of you who do this."

It was Natalya's "turn" to host foreigners. "If you don't mind my mother moaning in the next room, you're perfectly welcome," she said. "She's been terribly lonely since my father died a few years ago. I think she will follow him soon."

We assured her we could put up with almost anything and were soon on the subway. I gave each of them my card, which Natalya took excitedly and Olga looked at with semi-disgust. "Freelance writer? Someday I will be a more famous writer than you."

Without telling her I really was not that famous, I asked what she wrote. "Oh, just some poems," she replied. "I never tried working as a journalist because here you can't be a real journalist. You can only say what the government wants you to say."

Natalya was 28, divorced, had a 5-year-old son who was in a week-long nursery school, and looked more Italian than Russian. She engulfed our photographs and postcards, asking to keep several, particularly the ones of Texas cowboys. Olga, who was 25 and never married, did not want to see the pictures and told us to stop talking about our travels, since knowing she would probably never see such places was making her jealous. We let her complain on a chair across the room, while we sat on Natalya's bed and narrated the pictures.

The two-room flat was said to be among the best in the city for middle-class residents. The bathroom plumbing was faulty – Natalya said the landlord was "too lazy" to fix it. Rooms, particularly the kitchen, were small, compared to Western European standards. The living room was richly decorated with chandeliers, oriental rugs, and antique furniture.

After Natalya excused herself to change into a scanty, red nightshirt that barely concealed her upper thighs, she waved a diamond ring in our faces and sprung a sudden marriage proposition.

"That's something to think about," Patrick and I said almost simultaneously.

In further questioning about her motives to leave, I deduced that she did not have as much as an intense dislike for the Soviet system – at least not as much as Olga. Natalya wanted to see what other parts of the world were like and escape from some burdensome personal problems.

When we asked about political problems, their answers ranged from disgust to sarcasm. They had a good friend who was imprisoned in Siberia for allegedly working against the government. They did not know anyone in the Communist Party, which they viewed as being for the elite class and used to control the 91 percent who were not members.

"If you do not think about the situation here, if you just take what they give you, and don't look too deeply and question the system, you can live fine here," mentioned Olga at one point. "Our problem is we question. That's why we must leave."

Olga did not believe in religion or God. "How can I when I live here?" she asked. But she thought that reincarnation was an interesting theory. Natalya did not profess a belief in any of the above, saying she believed in "life and love."

They had never heard of Lee Harvey Oswald or J.R. Ewing, but they knew about the matter with U.S. journalist Nicholas Daniloff, who had been detained and falsely accused of being a spy. They laughed when Patrick said our father used to be an FBI agent. "They're the ones who are always arresting the U.S. progressive people," explained Olga. "Every time something goes wrong here, your government gets blamed."

Before we knew it, daylight cracked through the window. We had made it clear we were not presently the marrying kind, not even to help out a good cause. Nothing I said about U.S. social problems had discouraged these two from their plans to leave. "If you know someone who wants to get married for money, let us know," pleaded Natalya.

What could I say? "Yeah, sure," I whispered in the hallway.

Moscow resident Serg, second from left, criticized the KGB and supported making greater inroads with the West in 1986. Five years later, the head of the KGB led a coup against Russia's president. Photo by friend of Shay

Putin rises to power with help from Yeltsin

As Gorbachev tried to modernize the Soviet economy while maintaining the structure and many Russians protested for political rights in the streets, the economy worsened. People had to stand in long lines to buy food, medicine, and other essentials, causing more unrest. Fearing that hardliners might oust him as General Secretary, Gorbachev reformed the position as an executive president who would be much harder to remove. The Soviet Congress approved the change in early 1990.

By August 1991, hardliners had enough. The "Gang of Eight," a core group of conspirators that included the prime minister, vice president, defense minister, and KGB head, met in secret to plan a political coup. As Gorbachev spent his vacation with family at a Black Sea home, officials placed him under house arrest. KGB operators cut the phone lines to his home, and intelligence officers guarded the gates to stop anyone from leaving.

The plotters announced that Gorbachev was ill and took control of the government radio and television broadcasts. They sent several hundred tanks and thousands of military troops into Moscow and other cities. KGB officers arrested more officials. [1]

Boris Yeltsin, then a leader of the Russian legislature who supported more democratic reforms than Gorbachev, rushed to the parliament building, where he and other political leaders barricaded themselves. Yeltsin condemned the coup attempt and urged military troops not to follow the plotters' orders. Supporters distributed fliers in person to let people know what was occurring.

By that afternoon, thousands of people surrounded the legislative complex. The chief of staff of a tank battalion soon announced he would support Yeltsin, who climbed on a tank and spoke to the cheering crowd.

Led by KGB top officers in a scheme they called Operation Thunder, tanks and paratroopers moved in on the crowd around the legislative building the next day. But Yeltsin supporters held strong. The following day, the crowd blocked a tunnel near the legislature with large vehicles. Three men were killed and more injured in street fighting. The crowd set fire to at least one tank.

The violence seemed to paralyze coup leaders. Gorbachev officially fired the plotters and flew to Moscow, thanking Yeltsin and the crowd. Gorbachev then led the dissolution of the USSR.

The conspirators were immediately arrested, with one, the interior minister, reportedly committing suicide by gunshot. Most remained in custody, as trials for treason wound slowly through the Russian court system. In 1994, state legislators declared amnesty for the ones still in jail, effectively pardoning them. [2]

From his position as a KGB lieutenant colonel and deputy for St. Petersburg Mayor Anatoly Sobchak, Putin was astute enough not to openly support the attempted coup. In his time as a foreign KGB agent in Dresden, East Germany, before he returned to St. Petersburg, Putin had reportedly aided the Red Army Faction, a far-left group that engaged in bombings and other violence in West Germany to destabilize that country. Though he felt betrayed by Gorbachev, especially after the Soviet Union dissolved, Putin supported Sobchak's negotiations with the KGB and military to remain off St. Petersburg's streets during the coup attempt. He claimed to resign from the KGB shortly after hearing about the coup, but others said he remained with the agency longer. [3]

Both Putin and Sobchak, a Yeltsin ally who appeared pro-democracy while taking some anti-democratic actions such as dismantling the city council, hedged their bets based on whether the coup was successful or not, Russian journalist Masha Gessen wrote. Putin might have actively supported his fellow hardliners by agreeing to send shipments of meat paid for by St. Petersburg taxpayers to Moscow to flood store shelves if the coup was successful and make the new leaders appear better in many citizens' eyes. [4]

In late 1991, Yeltsin became the first popularly-elected leader in Russian history at the same time that the USSR dissolved. Yeltsin's economic reforms resulted in rising unemployment and inflation, as well as more contention with parliament over those reforms. In 1993, Yeltsin disbanded parliament and said he would rule by decree until new legislators were elected. Legislative leaders then impeached Yeltsin and swore in the vice president as acting president. Yeltsin ordered tanks to fire on parliament, and some 187 people died in armed conflict. A new parliament was elected and passed a constitution that expanded presidential powers. Freedom House, the organization co-founded by Eleanor Roosevelt, blamed the situation mostly on "hardliners in parliament." [5]

Putin focused on St. Petersburg politics, but after Subchak lost a re-election bid in 1996, Putin moved to Moscow to become deputy chief of the federal government's property management department. He made such an impression that Yeltsin appointed him as deputy chief of staff in 1997 and director of the FSB, the KGB's successor, in 1998. Shortly after Putin took over the FSB, Russian journalist Anatoly Levin-Utkin was beaten to death by assailants who stole documents and his briefcase. Levin-Utkin was investigating Putin's suspicious business deals as deputy mayor of St. Petersburg. [6]

By 1999, Yeltsin's popularity and health deteriorated to the point that close allies like billionaire businessman Boris Berezovsky, who Gessen wrote was among the handful of "so-called oligarchs... who had grown superrich under Yeltsin," sought a replacement. Yeltsin feared that a hardliner would take over and imprison him for corruption, while oligarchs sought a successor who would allow them to retain their wealth.

They settled on the relatively unknown Putin, who Berezovsky first met in 1990 when he sought to open a car service station in St. Petersburg. The businessman, who also owned Russia's most popular TV station and helped broker political deals for Yeltsin, said Putin was the first bureaucrat he met to "not take bribes," which made a "huge impression." Others said that Putin took as much, if not more, than the average Russian politico, somehow amassing a fortune estimated by one analyst at $40 billion by 2007. [7]

Berezovsky lobbied Putin to become Yeltsin's successor, as the political situation in Russia teetered on collapse. "Possibly the most bizarre fact about Putin's ascent to power is that the people who lifted him to the throne knew little more about him than you do," Gessen wrote. Putin ultimately sought to bring back the glory of the Soviet Union, as a stronger empire that would centralize control of all aspects, including business and the media. "His loyalty was to the KGB and to the empire it served and protected: the USSR." [8]

Thousands of citizens in Moscow surrounded the legislative building during the 1991 coup attempt. They protected Yeltsin and other officials, helping to thwart the plot. Photo by David Broad, Panoramia, Wikimedia Commons

Putin's reign marked by suspicious deaths, authoritarian moves

Yeltsin appointed Putin prime minister in 1999 shortly before Moscow was hit by ghastly apartment bombings that killed more than 300 people. Many became suspicious of FSB involvement after a witness observed some people plant what appeared to be explosives in sugar sacks at a Ryazan apartment building. After local police caught the culprits and discovered they were FSB employees, FSB officials claimed there were no explosives – contradicting their earlier statements – and the incident was a mere training exercise to see what local people would do. Later, Berezovsky said he believed the FSB was behind the bombings as a "parallel game" to get their man elected.

Meanwhile, Putin and most Russians blamed people from Chechnya, the Russian republic that fought a war for independence from 1994 to 1996. In one of his first TV addresses, Putin stated that the bombers would be hunted down and destroyed in rhetoric that differed from Yeltsin's language about bringing terrorists to justice.

"This was the language of a leader who was planning to rule with his fist," Gessen wrote. "These sorts of vulgar statements, often spiced with below-the-belt humor, would become Putin's signature oratorical device. His popularity began to soar." [9]

A Yeltsin adviser then convinced him to resign on New Year's Eve, shortening the 2000 election campaign and giving hand-picked Putin a boost as acting president. The sudden incumbent shunned rallies and debates, with his main way of reaching voters through Berezovsky's television channel and paid interviews. Putin's major slogan was one about which George Orwell warned: "The stronger the state, the freer the people."

About a month before the March 2000 election, Putin asked Sobchak, who had contradicted some statements made by Putin to his biographers, to campaign for him in the territory of Kalinigrad near Lithuania. A few days later, Sobchak died in a hotel room. The official cause was a heart attack, but the two bodyguards with him both were treated for poisoning. Writer Arkady Vaksberg discovered the poisoning link and theorized in a 2007 book that Sobchak died from a substance placed on his room's lamp bulb that vaporized when the light was turned on, a technique developed in Russia. A few months after the book was released, Vaksberg's car in his garage blew up, though he was not inside.

As president, Putin's first executive order was to grant Yeltsin immunity from future prosecution. His next decrees mostly concerned military matters, including disbanding a policy of not first using nuclear weapons. He retained former Defense Minister and Gang of Eight coup plotter Dmitry Yazov as a military adviser.

Putin spent much time working to control the media. He approved raids of media offices, where armed masked men beat up staff and stole documents. Prosecutors filed phony charges against press companies and arrested executives. Some fled the country, forfeiting their media holdings to the government. "Less than a year after Putin came to power, all three federal television networks were controlled by the state," Gessen wrote. [10]

Other Putin orders replaced elected positions in the upper house of parliament with appointed ones and called for Putin-appointed federal officials to supervise elected governors. With the orders came suspicious events that many thought were orchestrated by Putin allies to help him consolidate power.

In 2002, masked men took hostages in a Moscow theater. Russian military forces filled the building with gas from underground passages, causing everyone inside to fall asleep. Troops carelessly set sleeping hostages on their backs on outside steps, causing some to choke to death. While troops executed terrorists in their sleep, others transferred hostages to buses, where some choked en route to a hospital. Some 129 hostages died, but officials claimed at first that no hostages died.

One terrorist, who reportedly had ties to the FSB, survived by walking out shortly before the theater was gassed. In 2003, journalist Yuri Shehekochikhin died of toxin poisoning in the midst of investigating the theater incident. Among the information he unearthed was that some terrorists had been recruited from prisons, lending more evidence of FSB involvement.

In 2004, armed men took several hundred students and parents hostage in a school in the town of Beslan. The Russian military fired heavy shots from tanks and grenade launchers that destroyed the gymnasium where most hostages were, while troopers used flamethrowers as they stormed the building, After the smoke cleared, more than 300 hostages had died along with the criminals.

Putin immediately used the tragedy to announce that governors and members of the lower parliament house would no longer be elected, giving the excuse as a need to unite in the "fight against terrorism." Citizens would only be allowed to vote directly for one federal position, the presidency. In the ensuing months, chess master Garry Kasparov was among the few to publicly question why the military didn't negotiate to free hostages at Beslan. Privately, many wondered if the FSB recruited the armed terrorists from prisons, especially after details of the 2002 theater incident leaked out.

Political freedom scores drop

Putin soon dragged Russia from having a hint of democracy under Yeltsin to one of the most authoritarian regimes in the world, marked by imprisonments of political opponents, suspicious deaths, media censorship, and phony elections. In 1985, Freedom House gave the Soviet Union its worst possible scores for political freedoms and civil liberties of 7s and a rating of "not free," down with the likes of North Korea and Iraq.

By 1992, Gorbachev and Yeltsin had improved their country's rating to "partly free," with scores of 3 and 4. Russia fell back to "not free" under Putin by 2004 and remained there through 2025. Its score, which Freedom House expanded in 2014 to a 100-point system from a 7-point one, dropped to 12 in 2025 from 26 a decade earlier.

"Power in Russia's authoritarian political system is concentrated in the hands" of Putin, Freedom House wrote in 2025. "With subservient courts and security forces, a controlled media environment, and a legislature consisting of a ruling party and pliable opposition factions, the Kremlin manipulates elections and suppresses genuine opposition. Rampant corruption facilitates shifting links among state officials and organized crime groups. Since the regime launched a full-scale invasion of Ukraine in February 2022, authorities have intensified restrictions on individual rights and liberties in order to stifle domestic dissent."

Other independent watchdog groups gave Putin similar low scores. Russia's Democracy Index score, maintained by British research firm The Economist

Group, dropped from 5.02 in 2006 to 4.48 in 2008, then slid all the way to 2.03 in 2024, better than only a handful of nations. Holland-founded Transparency International also buried Russia near the bottom of countries in its Corruption Perceptions Index during those years.

The escalation of suspicious deaths didn't help Russia's international image. In 2004, journalist and critic Anna Politkovskaya was poisoned by a toxin that damaged her kidneys and liver during a flight to cover the Beslan tragedy. After recovering somewhat, she faced continual death threats. In 2006, Politkovskaya wrote about being arrested, threatened, and formally questioned by prosecutors about her sources. She described the "morality encouraged by Putin" as being, "Those who are against us must be destroyed." Two months later, she was shot to death in her Moscow apartment lobby. [11]

A month later, FSB whistleblower Alexander Litvinenko died of polonium poisoning. He had publicly claimed to be ordered to kill Berezovsky in 1998 and kidnap other prominent businessmen. He was arrested soon after those statements on excessive force charges, acquitted, then arrested on other charges. After a judge released him on bail, Litvinenko escaped, eventually settling in London. But authorities kept tabs on him. Eventually, the radioactive polonium, which was exclusively made in Russia to that point, killed him.

In 2008, Putin was forced to leave the presidency due to consecutive term limits, but his successor, Dmitry Medvedev, appointed him prime minister. Medvedev then proposed amendments to the constitution and revealed that the pair had secretly agreed to a deal to have Putin return to the presidency in 2012. Putin also won "elections" in 2018 and 2024 that international observers concluded were tainted with fraud.

Putin expanded efforts to tightly control news on the Internet by intimidating bloggers and prosecuting more journalists. The strange deaths didn't let up. In 2015, former Russia Deputy Minister Boris Nemtsov was killed by gunshots on a Moscow bridge while organizing a rally against the Ukraine invasion. Attorney Alexei Navalny, who founded the Anti-Corruption Foundation in 2011 and detailed corrupt official dealings, was reportedly poisoned by Russian agents in 2020 and imprisoned after trials described as shams by Amnesty International. Navalny died in 2024 while held in harsh prison conditions in a town near the Arctic Circle.

While no one had officially proven that Putin ordered the assassinations of political opponents and journalists, Linda Qiu wrote in PolitiFact in 2016, "Experts say the political climate in Russia is responsible for the high volume of journalist murders in the country." Added Gessen in 2012, "Putin's Russia is a country where political rivals and vocal critics are often killed, and at least sometimes the order comes directly from the president's office." [12]

Shortly after the 2006 assassination of journalist Anna Politkovskaya, Moscow residents erected a tribute in front of the apartment building where she was slain. Photo by John Martens, Public Domain

Trump-Putin ties reportedly date to 1980s

Since his 2016 campaign for the U.S. presidency, Donald Trump has harshly criticized democratic allies such as Canada and Germany while rarely saying a discouraging word against Putin and other dictators. Trump could have become a Russian asset as long ago as the late 1980s when he started meeting about business projects that included putting a Trump tower in Moscow, according to New York Magazine.

Russian intelligence worked for years to recruit Trump to aid Putin's goal of expanding into a new Russian empire, wrote former military intelligence official Malcolm Nance. "One of the greatest dreams of the old Soviet Union was to put a highly suggestible American ideologue into power who would do the bidding of the Kremlin," he said. "The idea of a Kremlin-controlled president would live on after the death of the Soviet Union [in 1991]." [13]

Individuals connected to Russia or former Soviet republics bought 86 Trump properties for $109 million in cash between 2003 and 2017, according to reports.

Eric Trump boasted in 2013 that the family operation didn't rely on American banks but had "all the funding we need out of Russia." Trump Jr. also let it slip in 2008 that Russians comprised a "pretty disproportionate cross-section of a lot of our assets. We see a lot of money pouring in from Russia." Moreover, several Trump hotels were financed from the Bayrock Group, founded by former Soviet commerce official Tevfik Arif. [14]

In the 2016 campaign, Trump copied positions taken by Putin, who disliked Obama since the latter president attempted to curb Putin's foreign excesses. Trump talked about weakening NATO, which the Russian dictator believed was in large part responsible for the old Soviet Union's fall, and the European Union, which Putin thought was heavily influenced by Muslims.

The Putin-Trump relationship was "obvious months before the election," wrote New York Times columnist Paul Krugman. The close relationship between WikiLeaks, founded by Julian Assange to release data about mostly public officials, and Russian intelligence "was also obvious, as was [WikiLeaks's] growing alignment with white nationalists. It has long been obvious – except, apparently, to the news media – that the modern GOP is a radical institution that is ready to violate democratic norms in the pursuit of power." Assange's ties to Russians dated to 2012, when he started hosting a show on Russia Today, the English-language satellite television channel funded by the Russian government.

Putin's operatives might have started helping Trump as early as 2014, hacking into email accounts of Democratic staffers and volunteers, according to the Mueller Report. They used WikiLeaks and set up phony accounts on Facebook, Twitter, and other social media to spread disinformation against the Clinton campaign. [15]

In June 2016, Trump campaign manager Paul Manafort, Don Jr., and son-in-law Jared Kushner met at Trump Tower in New York with several Russians, including lawyer Natalia Veselnitskaya. The subjects included Clinton emails from her time as secretary of state that were supposedly deleted from a server. The following month, Trump issued a public challenge to Putin and his network of hackers at a Florida press conference. "I have nothing to do with Putin," Trump said in one of many falsehoods. He then went on to say that Putin had called Obama the "n word" as a means of showing that the former KGB lieutenant colonel didn't respect the current U.S. president. Many thought that was another lie, but it wasn't.

However, how Trump knew the true racist nature of Putin in 2016 – something that didn't come out publicly until a 2018 book – was unclear, especially if he had "nothing to do" with the Russian leader. "I don't know anything about [Putin] other than he will respect me," Trump continued. "Russia, if you're listening, I hope you're able to find the 30,000 emails that are missing. I think you will probably be rewarded mightily by our press."[16]

That same day, Russian hackers worked to do just that. "On or about July 27, 2016, the conspirators attempted after hours to spear phish [attack a target through an email-spoof scheme] for the first time email accounts at a domain hosted by a third-party provider and used by Clinton's personal office," read a July 2018 federal criminal indictment against 12 Russian intelligence operatives. "At or around the same time, they also targeted 76 email addresses at the domain for the Clinton campaign." [17]

WikiLeaks, Trump aide Roger Stone, and a Russian-formed site called DC Leaks released the Democratic emails, with some showing a DNC bias against Vermont Senator Bernie Sanders to aid Clinton in the primaries. More Trump officials met with Russians, and the GOP platform was changed to support Putin's position on invading Ukraine. Trump also supported reviewing sanctions against Russia imposed by Obama for seizing Crimea in 2014 and supporting an armed uprising in Ukraine. At rallies, Trump showed little interest in international matters other than Russia, trade deals, and the proposed wall with Mexico.

Once in the White House, Trump escalated his pro-Putin campaign. At the 2018 Putin-Trump summit, Trump said he accepted Putin's denial of Russian interference in the 2016 election. Putin seemed to take advantage of his desire to impress the Russian boss, wrote Stephanie Grisham, a Trump press secretary during his first term. At the G20 Osaka summit in 2019, Putin coughed and cleared his throat numerous times. Fiona Hill, the National Security Council's senior director for Europe and Russia, said Putin probably did that on purpose as an intimidation ploy, knowing Trump's reputation as a germophobe. Trump, in turn, often messed with others' heads as he played autocrat, at one point telling Grisham that "everyone just loves you," and at other times calling her a "loser" and "useless." [18]

Other authoritarians cement power, strengthen ties with Trump

As Putin consolidated power in Russia, similar authoritarian leaders did likewise in their nations. Trump aide Steve Bannon, billionaire Elon Musk, and other far-right figures escalated their work on the international stage, helping the conservative authoritarian movement gain traction in Europe, Canada, South America, and other places.

In Hungary, Putin ally Viktor Orban became prime minister in 2010, winning re-elections that international observers concluded were fixed in 2014, 2018, and 2022. In 2011, Orban pushed through a new constitution that installed a Christian-based nationalistic system that formally discriminated against gay people and cut the number of legislative seats almost in half. Two years later, the

Fidesz Party leader strong-armed amendments that curbed the media and reduced powers by judges and legislators.

As a result, Hungary experienced a 23-point decline in Freedom House scores between 2014 and 2025, with only Turkey, El Salvador, and Nicaragua falling more. Hungary had been a shining model for democracy in 2014, scoring 88 in political rights and civil liberties, improving drastically from the Soviet Union days. "The Fidesz government has passed anti-migrant and anti-LGBT+ policies, as well as laws that hamper the operations of opposition groups, journalists, universities, and nongovernmental organizations that are critical of the ruling party or whose perspectives Fidesz otherwise finds unfavorable," Freedom House reported. [19]

Another Eastern European nation, Belarus, saw its Freedom House score slashed in half from 14 in 2014 to 7 in 2025. After the Soviet Union dissolved, Belarus declared independence in 1991, and Alexander Lukashenko won the reborn nation's first presidential election in 1994. A right-wing populist who publicly proclaimed allegiance to average people while privately serving a kind of kleptocracy, Lukashenko was a good listener at one time, but that stopped after he entered office and essentially became cruel, said 1994 campaign manager Alexander Feduta. [20]

Two years after taking over, Lukashenko pushed through changes to Belarus' constitution that reduced the parliament's powers and expanded his. One modification extended his initial term from five years to seven. In 1999, two opposition leaders mysteriously disappeared and were presumably killed. In the 2001 election, the government claimed Lukashenko won 76 percent of the vote, which was disputed by international groups, and signed a treaty with Putin that pledged greater cooperation. Succeeding Belarus elections resulted in similar charges of corruption.

In 2020, Lukashenko's regime arrested electoral opponents Sergei Tikhanovsky, a video producer and longtime critic of the dictator, and banker Viktor Babariko. Svetlana Tikhanovskaya, a teacher and the wife of Tikhanovsky, courageously campaigned against Lukashenko, attracting crowds of tens of thousands of people. But on election day, Belarus' Internet was shut down. Lukashenko claimed to have won 80 percent of votes without producing ballots, while Tikhanovskaya stated that she won by at least 60 percent.

Mass protests erupted, and security forces deployed rubber bullets, stun grenades, and water cannons against peaceful demonstrators. Many protesters were beaten and tortured in prison, the Viasna Human Rights Centre reported. They received prison sentences for relatively minor actions, such as "insulting" a Belarusian official on a YouTube video. After being threatened with arrest, Tikhanovskaya fled to Lithuania and established an oppositional government-in-exile. Her husband and Babariko received lengthy prison terms.

Meanwhile, Trump strengthened his ties with dictators besides Putin. In his first term, Trump agreed to sell $110 billion worth of weapon systems to Saudi Arabia, which carried a shockingly low 2025 Freedom House score of 9 out of 100, and refused to condemn Prince Mohammed bin Salman after the CIA concluded that he authorized the brutal execution of dissident journalist Jamal Khashoggi in 2018. Trump agreed in 2019 with Turkish President Recep Tayyip Erdogan to withdraw some U.S. troops from Syria, allowing Turkey to displace American-allied Kurds in 2019. He opened relations with North Korea dictator Kim Jong-un and lifted some sanctions on that country that had a hopelessly low Freedom House score of 3 out of 100. In 2017, Trump and his family hosted Chinese President Xi Jinping at Mar-a-Lago, the 20-acre Palm Beach, Fla., estate and club sometimes referred to as the "winter White House." China awarded White House official Ivanka Trump with trademark approvals to sell jewelry and handbags, as well as provide spa services.

The Trump Organization, run by the sons who reported to their father, who still made money from the ventures in apparent violation of the Emoluments Clause of the Constitution, pursued expansions in Dubai, among other nations, during the initial term. Representatives of at least 22 foreign governments, including authoritarians from Russia, Brazil, Afghanistan, Turkey, Saudi Arabia, China, and Iraq, likely spent money at Trump Organization businesses during his presidency, according to NBC News.

Trump "always seemed to want dictators to respect him," wrote Grisham. An underlying reason for the interest could have been that he feared getting into a nuclear war, she theorized. Mary Trump wrote that her uncle cultivated dictators because he thought they made him look strong by association. As head of his own business empire, Trump often grew bored with the democratic process of listening to others and compromising, some aides said, and sought to run the country like he ran his companies. [21]

The Freedom House scores of the U.S. fell under Trump from 89 in 2017 to 83 in 2020, due to factors like Trump eroding confidence in elections and excusing authoritarian abuses of "tyrannical leaders whom he hopes to woo diplomatically," including Putin, wrote Sarah Repucci in the 2020 Freedom House report. "Fierce rhetorical attacks on the press, the rule of law, and other pillars of democracy coming from American leaders, including the president himself, undermine the country's ability to persuade other governments to defend core human rights and freedoms, and are actively exploited by dictators and demagogues." [22]

After failing to overthrow the 2020 election, Trump further built ties with foreign dictators. He hosted Orban at Mar-a-Lago three times in 2024 alone. In addition, members of the conservative think tank Heritage Foundation who wrote the Trump administration's Project 2025 plan were aligned with Orbán's Danube

Institute, noted Boston College history professor Heather Cox Richardson. Project 2025 looked "much like [Orban's] erosion of democracy to create a dictatorship that enforces white male Christian patriarchy," Richardson wrote. The plan called for "dismantling the nonpartisan civil service and replacing it with officers loyal to an extraordinarily strong executive" and "that strong executive to take control of the Department of Justice and the military.... to impose Christian nationalism on the country," Richardson wrote. Hartmann added that the Heritage Foundation has been funded for years by the Koch brothers, with Project 2025 being "a 21st century cleaned-up version of Koch's 1980 Libertarian Party platform." [23]

After polls showed Americans didn't like most of Project 2025's goals, Trump tried to distance himself from the plan during the 2024 campaign. Musk became a major campaign official after donating millions of dollars. The South African billionaire not only turned the former Twitter into the far-right machine X, with tens of millions of bots and Russian troll farm accounts repeating right-wing lies, but he held $1 million lotteries for voters in Pennsylvania, spurring a federal bribery investigation.

Some also raised questions about Musk's Starlink satellite-based Internet communications system having a role in tabulating votes. Then there were Musk's regular conversations with Putin, which had occurred at least since 2022, according to media reports. In one, Putin reportedly asked Musk not to activate his Starlink satellites over Taiwan as a favor to China leader Xi. [24]

On election day, more than 60 bomb threats were called into Democratic precincts, most of them from Russian sources. Journalist Greg Palast blamed mostly GOP vote suppression campaigns, including organizing thousands of volunteers to visit polling places and get Democratic votes tossed, for Trump's slim electoral victory. Despite the GOP vote suppression laws, bomb threats, and thrown-out ballots, most Democrats didn't protest and Freedom House termed the election "free, fair, and credible."

Upon retaking the White House, Trump ruled like a corporate boss. He and Musk started the anti-government entity DOGE, which some called the Department of Greedy Egomaniacs. He allowed Musk to take over the U.S. Treasury Department and federal financial system, closing down departments, firing tens of thousands of employees, and gaining access to most citizens' financial data. He installed loyalists at the top of departments and in the workforce. He threatened universities and other institutions with loss of federal funding, while using federal resources to prosecute and intimidate the media, Democrats, administration critics, and protesters. He ignored judges' rulings that he didn't like.

As Trump publicly called to take over Greenland, Canada, Mexico, and the Panama Canal, his cabinet choices made Putin proud. "What stands out about them is something that transcends even their total incompetence: their notorious positions in favor of destroying international and domestic legal order," Yale University history professor Timothy Snyder wrote. Musk and other extremists like Deputy Chief of Staff Stephen Miller are likely leading the Trump forces in many matters. "Who do we think told Trump that Greenland and Canada had valuable mineral resources? Is this something that Trump read about on his own?" Snyder asked. "Musk's own rhetoric on Canada, though it has received less attention, has been even sharper than Trump's." [25]

Democracy Forward and others helped hand Trump his first big loss in 2025, when he caved in and rescinded his federal funding freeze order. Many average Americans continued to protest in the streets and at public meetings in large cities and smaller towns in 2025. But Republicans and even some Democrats in Congress caved in to most demagogic demands, putting the U.S. on the road to becoming another Hungary.

By 2025, the percentage of countries worldwide that Freedom House considered free fell to 41 percent from 45 percent a decade earlier, while those designated not free rose to 33 percent from 25 percent. The average country's score of The Economist Group's Democracy Index declined to a record low 5.17 in 2024. In Ecuador, criminal organizations killed political candidates, while incumbents in Guatemala, Thailand, and Zimbabwe pulled a card from Trump by attempting to reverse election results they didn't like.

On the brighter side, Bangladesh, Bhutan, Sri Lanka, and Syria improved their freedom scores the most in 2025. Fiji's score rose more between 2014 and 2025 than any other nation at 32 points. Finland scored a perfect 100, while nine other countries, including Sweden, New Zealand, Norway, Denmark, and Canada, hit 97 or above in 2025.

The U.S. score – lower in 2025 than 53 nations, including Argentina, Chile, Taiwan, and Greece – will likely slide even farther in the near future. In 2025, the U.S. callously sided with dictatorships such as Russia, Belarus, Syria, North Korea, Nicaragua, Haiti, and Sudan in opposing a United Nations resolution that condemned Russia for invading Ukraine.

Over the past decade, the U.S. and many other democracies have failed to condemn coups and prevent repression in nations such as China, Iran, and Russia from growing worse, Freedom House reported. "Only sustained and coordinated action can reverse the nearly two decades of decline in global freedom," the authors wrote. [26]

While the steps taken by the German dictator in the 1930s and Project 2025 were likely factors behind Trump's actions after he took over the White House in January 2025, pure pettiness, revenge for past impeachments and prosecutions, and the Putin influence seem to be greater components.

Democracy: The Valor of Vigils and Marches

First published in *Walking through the Wall*, 2012; and Democracy Guardian, September 23, 2025

I'm standing in a line with some 300 other democracy advocates in Woodside Urban Park in Silver Spring, Md., at 8 a.m., preparing to hike into the nation's capital for the final day of the We Are America March. Though the sun hasn't appeared for long, most are already sweating.

It's September 19, 2025, nine days after the killing of conservative activist and Donald Trump ally Charles Kirk. MAGA has already made this guy – who in 2023 said on his podcast that the sitting president of the United States, Joe Biden, should be "given the death penalty" – a martyr. Even Wikipedia, which strives more than most for political impartiality, wrote that since Kirk's death, he "has been considered an icon of modern American conservatism." [1]

The right-wing machine had also turned the narrative of his alleged killer around from a far-right Groyper to a supposed leftist with a transgender roommate, even though Wikipedia noted that no evidence had surfaced connecting the suspect to left-wing groups. Few media voices point out that libertarians and many independents support gay/transgender rights, while the Groypers apparently have their own views that include shunning women and allowing certain men to dress as women. Anyways, the mainstream media helps the Trump forces blame political violence on the left, which numerous studies conclude is more prevalent on the right. [2]

I try not to think of potential repercussions of us being the first group since Kirk's death to address the Trump regime's many constitutional violations in the belly of the D.C. beast. Others, including rally speakers U.S. Rep. Al Green of Texas and former Capitol Police officer Harry Dunn, will do that for me. And I'm sure the vigil keepers for Kirk have to confront their fears of potential more gunmen at their prayer vigils.

At the moment, march partner Lynn issues some instructions that clarifies at least one of the risks involved.

"Make sure you write a contact number on your arm," she says, matter-of-factly. Lynn, who has not only walked significant miles but provided support from a vehicle and helped with march logistics and details like meals, hands me a black sharpie and shows me immaculately-written numbers along the inside of her forearm. "And this number of the National Lawyers Guild legal defense hotline."

For the past six days, I've been getting up earlier than usual during my retirement years and walking as many as 15 miles through humidity, heat, storms, vehicle exhaust, mostly supportive cheers and waves. It's too early for me to grasp certain realities that I really don't want to confront.

"Write it *where*?" I ask.

"On your arm. In case there are arrests."

I look around and see others either writing on their arms with sharpies or already sporting the numbers. I'm not a protest novice, having participated in many during the 1980s end-the-Cold-War times. I was among the D.C. crowd of 250,000 at the 20th anniversary of Martin Luther King's epic "Dream" speech in 1983, when civil rights leaders Coretta Scott King, Rev. Joseph Lowery, John Lewis, and Jesse Jackson spoke. I joined the longest group walk in modern times, covering about 5,000 of the Cold War project's 7,000 miles across the U.S. and Europe in 1984-85. The route included retracing the Selma to Montgomery, Ala., "Bloody Sunday" march and walking through occupied Belfast. I participated in Black Lives Matter marches in 2020. I couldn't count the number of Indivisible and 50501 rallies I had attended in the D.C. area following my retirement.

But this is the first time I have written phone numbers on my arm before an action. I have, though, carried an old Monopoly "Get Out of Jail Free" card among some expired media passes since it helped me out of a jam in the former Yugoslavia in 1985. I often assumed the press passes would help, especially when they weren't expired. But maybe I'm wrong. Maybe, as MAGA likes to say, it is a new era, the kind where only the side in power can call for and celebrate violence against political foes, where Trump, whose knowledge of the arts is limited to the inside of a strip joint, can head the Kennedy Center board as he plays the role of dictator, where JD Vance, one of the whitest guys on the planet, can order around the National African American History Museum as he sucks up to the man he once compared to Hitler.

I take the pen and scribble some numbers on my arm. I'm trained to write so only I can interpret the scrawling, and they don't look nearly as neat as Lynn's. "That's the best I can do this early," I shrug.

As it turns out, being arrested is not the gravest risk for us this day. Being the target of a crazed MAGA sniper intent on avenging Kirk is not out of the realm of possibility, though rally speakers are more likely targets than march participants.

Welcome to Trump's America, Project 2025 Version.

'This is the time we needed to do something'

Soon, march co-founder Margaret Bohara, a community organizer from suburban Philly, addresses us through a bullhorn. She describes the project as a nonpartisan one calling for greater constitutional accountability and checks and balances. She requests that signs with Trump on them be left in the park. More than a few are left behind, but there will be a number of them at the National Mall rally near the Capitol in a few hours.

Five days before this march left Philly, I took a sign that read, "No Turd Reich" on one side and "Stop the Grand Old Putin Party" on the other, to the White House for a protest. For this march, I simply wrote, "Stand Up for The Constitution, Checks & Balances, Due Process." On the other side, I finally settled with "We Are America, Not a Dictatorship."

Bohara, like numerous people marching, is fairly new to activism. Soon after Trump took over in January 2025, she started attending rallies in Philly organized by the Indivisible and 50501 movements. In March 2025, she helped organize 300 people for a protest of Trump's visit to Philadelphia for the NCAA wrestling championships. They set up skits that mocked wrestling to make it more entertaining. It was fun and interactive, MJ Tune, another suburban Philly organizer who later helped Bohara form the We Are America March, told a reporter with the Delaware County [Pa.] Daily Times. [3]

Margaret Bohara, left, and MJ Tune, right, co-founded a march from Philadelphia that reached D.C. in September 2025. WAAM Facebook page

Then, Bohara came up with the idea for the march, and Tune soon got onboard. "There's been famous marches in history, and this seemed like this is the time we needed to do something," Bohara told the Times.

When they first contacted groups and individuals, they didn't get much response. But they persevered, and people from 15 states – as far as California, Wyoming, Texas, and South Carolina – signed up to march from Independence Hall in Philadelphia, the birthplace of America as the nation's first capital in 1776 that served in that role four other times until D.C. took over in 1800. In a support van, they carried a large copy of the Constitution hand-written by children and signed by people met en route.

People also wrote messages to Congress that decorated a large trojan horse named Farcie that Jaxy Lagrome of Perry Hall, Md., towed. "I have a lot of Republicans who come up to me and ask questions, and when I tell them that this is really just to be funny, light hearted, keep everything positive and to bring community together, they're open to it, too," Lagrome told a reporter with Capital News Service. "It's hard to be mad at the purple horse." [4]

Jaxy Lagrome drives a vehicle towing a large trojan horse named Farcie covered in messages for Congress alongside marchers in a Baltimore suburb. Photo by Kevin Shay

The kickoff rally featured speakers such as Brita Filter from RuPaul's Drag Race, as well as balloon artists and bubble machines to lighten the environment and make it more kid-friendly. They were ferried across the Susquehanna River in Maryland. They mostly stayed in churches with organizers from Indivisible, 50501, and other groups providing support in cities. Community potlucks and meetings featuring bands and speakers were organized at most stops, helping to create a network of community democracy advocates for what many believed would be a lengthy period of resistance against the Trump regime.

By the time they reached the Baltimore burb of Towson, where Rev. Robert Turner praised them and detailed his monthly one-day, 43-mile marches from Baltimore to D.C. to support causes such as reparations and preserving black history, they had grown to more than 50 core marchers. Many others joined for a few hours, a day, even a week. They were "normal people" taking an extraordinary stand, as the group's Facebook intro says. They came from all walks of life – the young, old, middle-aged, health care workers, teachers, tech analysts, librarians, administrators, retirees, students.

Debbie from Kentucky, right, and Tammi from Illinois lead the march through a Baltimore street. Photo by Shay

Judy Shatkin, center, and other participants cross a highway bridge in Laurel, Md. Shatkin founded Democracy 12, which organized another Philly-to-D.C. march in June 2025. Photo by Shay

'This is what resistance looks like'

On its final day in Silver Spring, Bohara continues to relay instructions and tips to the largest group of marchers on the project. About 300 people, many from the local Methodist and Episcopal churches that hosted the marchers, join us in the park to walk about eight miles to the U.S. Capitol. "Show me what democracy looks like," Bohara exclaims.

"This is what democracy looks like," marchers reply.

"Show me what community looks like."

"This is what community looks like."

"Show me what resistance looks like."

"This is what resistance looks like."

Such slogans and chants have a purpose, to remind participants why they are there, to relay messages to onlookers, to cement a bond, to energize marchers during what can become repetitive doldrums. Most younger participants require fewer energy jolts, and Carly and others employ a bullhorn as they walk all day to lead chants such as "When Democracy [immigrants, the Constitution, Social Security, science, libraries, etc.] Is Under Attack, What Do We Do? Stand Up, Fight Back" and "From Philly to D.C., To Keep America Free."

During one stop at a Chipotle near the always-crowded D.C. Beltway in Silver Spring, with the sun bearing down and thermometers rising to near 90 degrees Fahrenheit, one young marcher started a modified chant, "Tell me what democracy *smells* like." So chants are not always stuck in concrete during such projects.

On the 1984 walk, songs – some with alternative words – were utilized more than chants. At times, Buddhist monks chanted a prayer for peace, "Namu Myoho Renge Kyo," which translates to "Devotion to the Mystic Dharma of the Lotus Flower Sutra." During a 1982 walk in the Deep South, a low-IQ Ku Klux Klan member thought that prayer chant was an anti-American slogan and drove his pickup truck through the line, injuring one marcher.

No one had driven a vehicle through this march's line, though some revved up their cars, flashed middle fingers, and yelled, "Trump 2028." The overwhelming majority of responses had been supportive waves and honks.

We start the last leg of the project to the sound of a portable speaker on a handcart pulled by core marcher Judy Shatkin, a retired pediatrician and musician who founded a June 2025 Philly to D.C. march, blasting Tom Petty's "I Won't Back Down." The 1989 resistance anthem sets a defiant mood, propelling us forward to who knows what.

Jimmy, in vest in front, helps marchers navigate the streets and sidewalks of D.C. Photo by Shay

During the previous 150-plus miles, walk monitors, or "peacekeepers," clad in yellow vests worked hard as they walked to keep us together and stopped traffic at crosswalks so we could proceed in relative safety. The jobs of Susan, Jimmy, Justin, Ashley, Jim, and others intensify with the larger crowd. It takes several rounds of stoplight changes to get everyone over a single street, which adds to the wait times. Still, having many more participants is fully worthwhile when you are trying to speak truth to power.

We reach 16th Street, then the D.C. border, where a group standing on a street corner holds "Free DC" signs. Another chant breaks out. "Free DC! Free DC!" Onward to Rock Creek Park and a short lunch and bathroom break, where we rendezvous with Teddy and others who do the often thankless behind-the-scenes work like find enough meals for the group and transport marchers' personal belongings.

Metro D.C. police are visible, but National Guard troops will remain out of sight until we hit the National Mall. On one side street, what looks like a modernized paddy wagon sits, just in case things get out of hand. Bohara speaks with officers, then we are allowed to use the entire right lane of 16th Street as police cars provide escorts. The transformation from a sidewalk march to street march sends an energetic jolt. Chants become louder, the mood more joyful, less apprehensive.

Susan and other "peacekeepers" navigate a Maryland street. Photo by Shay

'Enough is enough!'

We pass the First Baptist Church on 16th Street, which still sports its "Black Lives Matter" sign from 2020. Soon, the granite obelisk Washington Monument – the tallest building in D.C. at 555 feet – comes into view. We proceed through a tunnel to bypass a busy roundabout, then walk along the 16th Street pavement that featured a mural with "Black Lives Matter" painted in 35-foot-tall yellow letters from K Street to H Street. After the work was completed following massive protests in 2020, conservative groups filed lawsuits against the city, saying they wanted to see other messages such as "All Lives Matter" and "Blue Lives Matter."

While the lawsuits were dismissed, workers removed the mural in 2025 after pressure from Trump and Congress allies such as Rep. Andrew Clyde of Georgia.

Clyde was among the GOP Congress members who hid in fear from the January 6 attackers, then later claimed they were merely tourists. When Metro D.C. officer Michael Fanone tracked down Clyde to tell him how bad January 6 was, Clyde refused to shake the officer's hand. In 2022, Clyde was one of three members to vote against a law that made lynching a federal hate crime.

Marchers approach Lafayette Square and the White House along 16th Street, where Trump and GOP allies forced the removal in 2025 of the Black Lives Matter street mural that had been there since 2020. Photo by Shay

Finally, we reach Lafayette Square, the park just north of the White House that houses the longest continuous protest in U.S. history, a 24-hour vigil for world peace begun in 1981. A day after the We Are America March left Philly, workers under Trump's orders removed a tent stationed here to guard protesters from the elements, but the vigil continued without a tent. In 2020, BLM demonstrators attempted to tear down a statue here of slavery-supporting President Andrew Jackson. Their efforts failed, unlike in other areas of D.C. and other cities like Baltimore, but the park was closed for almost a year.

As we walk along the northern edge of the square, the relatively-new DC Activist Street Band joins as it plays the *Rocky* theme song, "Gonna Fly Now." Band member Dylan Laird later tells a reporter that their role is to provide an inspirational boost, to make the cause "attractive, bring people in, raise energy." [5]

A nice-sized crowd at the square cheers and waves. Others start walking with us. I get caught up in the moment. Seeing the White House, I yell at the occupants, "Enough is enough!" I'm not the only one to yell something towards that building. They don't hear us, but that's not the point.

Then I observe a vendor stand with its "Trump 2028" hats and flags. Fanatical supporters often carry large "Trump for King" flags here as well. "Stand up for the Constitution!" I yell at them, holding my sign high. Since I'm 6–7 tall, the sign reaches fairly high. "The First Amendment! Free Speech! Due Process! Due Process!" The vendors look away.

Passing the National African American History Museum, I yell, "Free the museum from JD Vance! Free the Kennedy Center from Trump!" There are bigger issues than those, what with people being kidnapped in the streets by unidentified agents, federal troops in U.S. cities, the FCC, DOJ, FBI, CIA, IRS, and other agencies used against political opponents and the media, the defunding of agencies by the billionaire-run DOGE. But pointing out the more obvious, ludicrous excesses can wake up people who are on the fence more quickly that something is terribly amiss.

On the mall, some children wave and slap us high-fives. The band plays "Down By the Riverside" as we approach the U.S. Capitol steps. Supporters cheer as we reach the end, led by organizers. Among those near the front are Debbie from Kentucky, who has carried the U.S. flag in front practically the entire way from Philly, and Tammi from Illinois, who displays her sign reading, "When Injustice Becomes Law, Resistance Becomes Duty." A man holds up a t-shirt. "It's a Philly thing!" he yells. Some laugh. Some are too thirsty and weary to laugh.

Marchers approach the U.S. Capitol along the National Mall, the end of their 160-mile trek. Photo by Shay

The Montgomery County Indivisible group had contacted numerous media about the rally, and there are reporters and broadcast cameras waiting. Articles by The Associated Press, German broadcast station Deutsche Welle, as well as local television, radio, and print media, result.

'Edmund Pettus Bridge moment'

Rally speakers congratulate us and detail the abuses that need rectifying. "In America, we do not bow down to kings and dictators," says U.S. Senator Chris Van Hollen of Maryland. "We have a president who claims to stand up for free speech but locks up students for exercising it and is using government coercion to try to silence his critics."

Rep. Green compares the march to the 1965 Bloody Sunday march when civil rights activists were beaten by authorities and local thugs on the Edmund Pettus Bridge in Selma, Ala. The marchers knew they would be beaten but continued anyway, and that resulted in the Voting Rights Act, which helped Green become a Congress member, he adds.

"Every generation has an Edmund Pettus Bridge moment," Green says. "You are a part of an Edmund Pettus Bridge moment. You knew before you got here that there might be some danger associated with what you were doing, but you marched on. You knew that because of current events [associated with the Kirk killing] that there are threats that are being made, threats that some people are allowing to cause them to change their course. But you didn't change your course. You didn't change your direction. ... You marched on 160 miles, and for this, you are now bringing the Edmund Pettus Bridge moment to Washington, D.C. You're bringing it to fruition."

This moment is about "ensuring all that we will not allow democracy to devolve into a dictatorship in the United States of America," Green continues. "We will not allow ourselves to be intimidated.... We are people who take to heart the Constitution of the United States of America.... This is a free speech moment."

Security guards are near the stage to "ensure you are protected and provide me some degree of comfort," Green adds. "Do not approach the stage while I'm speaking."

Dunn, who ran for Congress in 2024, admits that he had second thoughts about speaking in person at this rally. He thought about whether to send a video message or do it virtually. "Courage is contagious," he says. "Because all of you showing up gives me the courage to show up. We feed off of each other."

Marchers and rally attendees listen to former Capitol Police officer Harry Dunn speak. Photo by Shay

Conversely, the government cracking down on free speech, as in the Jimmy Kimmel case, "scares people into being silent when we need to be the loudest," Dunn adds. Kimmel's show would be reinstated by September 23, but numerous stations, led by conservative-owned Sinclair Broadcast Group and Nexstar Media Group, declined to air the show. Some wonder about the effect of the FCC's involvement, which seems to directly violate the First Amendment, on people publicly criticizing Trump and conservatives in the future.

Jessica Denson, founder of the Removal Coalition that is working to impeach and remove Trump, says she is happy to speak at the rally, but she notes that it is "disgusting" that Americans "have to walk 160 miles on foot to get these people in their air-conditioned, comfortable offices, in suits, to simply honor their oath, to simply file an article of impeachment." She reminds Congress members that they "cannot give an inch," as most have been doing, to help "this illegal administration to sabotage our democracy." She remains positive about the effort to impeach Trump again and says support is growing.

The previous evening at the Silver Spring Methodist church, U.S. Rep. Jamie Raskin of Maryland, a Constitutional scholar, noted that "everything in the Constitution is under attack." "We've got to play defense, too," he said, lending examples such as football and chess.

Bohara thanks organizers, marchers, and supporters for their help and dedication. Along the miles, participants found that the country is "united, resilient, and yearning for connection and community," she says. "People who value education, equality, diversity, freedom of speech, science, bodily autonomy, climate science, we are everywhere. If anything, this march has shown that we are not alone. We are a community larger than you can imagine, and our resistance runs deep."

D.C.'s bittersweet nature

It's a great reception and rally, but as I record videos near the large Constitution copy, my mind wanders to recalling something about the days when I lived in this area after being born at a hospital near the U.S. Capitol. I recall playing on swings and slides, neighborhood tag and baseball games, typical normal childhood stuff. Then there is the funeral of John F. Kennedy, which I attended at age four-and-a-half. I recall that day as a grainy, black-and-white, confusing nightmare. And nothing was ever the same after that.

Right after JFK died, numerous conservatives openly celebrated. At the D.C. home of Charles Cabell, the former CIA deputy director and brother of then-Dallas Mayor Earle Cabell reportedly toasted Kennedy's death with high-ranking military officials in a celebratory party. At oilman Clint Murchison's Dallas mansion, champagne and caviar flowed in celebration for an entire week, according to an employee. Deep South Klan leader Joseph Milteer was "very jubilant" about JFK's assassination, according to an informant. Milteer soon circulated propaganda fliers that blamed Kennedy's death on Jewish people.

In Dallas, grown men cheered and threw their hats in the air upon hearing the news. Students cheered in schools. Soldiers cheered at military bases. Those hateful reactions weren't confined to Texas; many also applauded the news in other states. In Oklahoma City, a physician told a visitor, "Good, I hope they got Jackie." [6]

And none of them were fired from jobs or faced repercussions, as Kimmel and others who pointed out that Kirk wasn't such a saint faced. And Kirk wasn't even a local elected leader. None of the people, including Trump and Utah Sen. Mike Lee, who mocked violence against Melissa Hortman, Josh Shapiro, Gretchen Whitmer, Paul Pelosi, and other Democrats faced repercussions.

D.C. has always been a bittersweet place for me. It's a beautiful city in certain ways, designed by French architect Pierre L'Enfant, with wide avenues, roundabouts, inspiring memorials and public art, and canals. There are no real skyscrapers to block out the sun. The Potomac River provides scenic areas. The National Mall is memorable. The Smithsonian museums and zoo are largely impressive and free to enter. It's *the* place to protest the federal government.

Still, I can't go by the White House without remembering the nightmarish JFK funeral. I can't go by nearby Arlington National Cemetery without remembering how my older sister died of Reye's syndrome when she was nine. She is buried there with my dad, who lived a full life until he passed at age 84.

I can't walk the streets of D.C. without feeling that we are letting down those who lived before us and those who will survive all this bullshit, by allowing this menace to control our country. The ghosts in D.C.-area cemeteries whisper of catastrophes we should avoid, but we careen on, ignoring the grave warnings. This is not Barack Obama vs. John McCain. This is potentially the modern version of FDR vs. Hitler. I might not have said that in 2024, but in late 2025, the U.S. appears more and more on the road that Germany took in the 1930s. Perhaps we will avoid the worst of it, perhaps not have as many concentration camps and huge fascist-supporting rallies, but it could become a form of that on a smaller scale.

After the We Are America March, many of us continued to do weekly sign brigades and other protests in our communities. In October, a Trump ICE thug sent to Portland for political intimidation purposes pepper-sprayed a guy in a costumed frog. He, as well as others like the chicken with his "Portland Will Outlive Him" sign, found the resolve to keep protesting against Trump's policies, and the situation became immortalized on Stephen Colbert's *Late Show*.

A week later, more than seven million Americans hit the streets for No Kings Day, the largest mass political protest in U.S. history. Then in early November, Democrats won every notable election, including ones in red states. The tide seemed to be turning, but that can change in an instant.

That's why we must walk the streets of D.C. and continue to protest with all our might, because certain spineless leaders seem to always undercut progress. We must continue to confront the regime, to stand up for free speech, for truth, for justice, for due process, for press freedom, for the right to peaceably assemble, for the right to petition the government to redress grievances. We can't afford to succumb to fear and intimidation to the point we become more like 1930s Germany or 2000s Russia, not less.

Some ask what a project like the We Are America March does. Some think it's better to focus on organizing larger rallies attended by hundreds of thousands of people like the one on October 18, 2025, organized by the No Kings movement and other groups.

My view is it's all important. Marches can impact people on a personal level to get more involved. The participants work harder. Communities that are often overlooked become engaged. New people are attracted to the movement. They can reach people on the other side of the aisle.

But they are by no means the only way to stand up. They are just one part of the recipe that has been used to topple authoritarians throughout history. While some credit the 1965 Selma march for largely bringing about the Voting Rights Act, the civil rights movement employed a wide variety of tactics, including prayer vigils for those who died or were injured, registering to vote, public rallies and demonstrations, boycotts, strikes, and asking questions at public meetings. By being persistent, by not quitting, by taking actions large and small, the battle was won, at least for a certain time period.

As for vigils, they can be highly effective, especially in places where marches and rallies are more risky. They are often religious-based, with participants praying for a person and/or cause. On the long walk, we often stopped at military bases and nuclear power facilities to witness for peace and ending the Cold War arms race. In 1984, Andy Zipser, then a writer for the Phoenix New Times, summed up a Walk of the People vigil at an Arizona nuclear power utility aptly, "We all have fears, and we usually succumb to them through silence, hostility or by preferring to be ignorant. [The vigilers] are proclaiming another response, one of affirmation…. They aren't 'accomplishing' anything in the conventional sense, but their message of pride and dignity would have been understood easily in a more distant, anachronistic time." [7]

Before I joined the We Are America March, I hadn't walked as many as ten miles in a day in years. Besides learning I could still do that in my 60s, I saw how people as old as 80, such as Dianne Shaw-Cummins, who walked with her son, Ted Regnaud, from Minnesota, were still willing to put themselves out there. I saw how students and parents with young children were still willing to do more despite the risk of repercussions to their careers. I saw how many people across large cities and small towns were willing to stand up for the rights in our Constitution.

This isn't the retirement I envisioned, but that's fine. I once thought I would spend these years focused more on traveling, spending time with relatives and friends, pursuing hobbies, while still writing and engaging in political activism at times. I see now that I have to do more for liberty and justice at this moment.

People in my generation have a duty to stand up for our Constitution against a regime that is violating it on a daily basis. We don't carry the repercussion risks to our jobs that younger people do, though Social Security and Medicare are among the potential casualties of the Project 2025 crowd. I advise anyone who is not retired and wants to make a controversial social media post to do so under a pseudonym or burner account, which means refraining from doing that on Facebook since that platform requires participants to use real names. And don't give your phone number to a social media platform. Only give an email address that doesn't include your real name.

My generation mostly caused this mess, though many have tried to improve society. We should be out in the streets in greater numbers, out there more often.

It's said that history is written by the winners, which on the surface, in late 2025, still appear to be the Trump and Stephen Miller gang. However, that is only on a temporary basis. Eventually, the truth prevails.

The protests today to support democracy and oppose Trump authoritarianism are more important than anything I have stood up for in my life. For the future of democracy, for the future of our children, for liberty and justice for all, we have no choice but to march on.

The Afterlife: Exploring What Happens After Death

First published in the Eternal Flame, January 1982; Maryland Gazette of Politics and Business, October 27, 2006; Medium, October 31, 2018; and NewsBreak, January 16, 2024

Before a fateful day in early 2023, Lauren Canaday lived a fairly normal life, while dealing with epilepsy. But that changed as she suffered a grand mal seizure that sent her into sudden cardiac arrest.

Her husband was across the hall in their home in Page County, Virginia, and heard her say, "Oh, shit," as she fell to the floor. He found her unconscious, not breathing, her face blue. He immediately called 911 and performed CPR. "My body was starting to shut down vital organs very quickly," Canaday wrote in a Substack post. [1]

Paramedics arrived four minutes later. They worked on her for 20 more minutes, using several defibrillator shocks before her heart resumed beating. The CPR kept her alive since without it, cardiac arrest is fatal within minutes.

In that vegetative state, Canaday wrote that she experienced "extreme peace" and lost her fear of death. "That isn't the same as wanting to die and leave my husband," she said. Her memory of the experience remained spotty. She had a "gut feeling that it was friendly and peaceful even though I can't report any shapes or personas or visions of that time. I feel like I dissolved, and it was just really nice."

At a Winchester, Virginia, medical center near the Blue Ridge Mountains, Canaday, just 38 years old, was wheeled to the intensive care unit. She tested positive for COVID-19 and was diagnosed with myocarditis, a condition that can cause reduction in the heart's pumping action. She descended into a coma for two days, then miraculously recovered enough to be released about a week later.

Canaday was declared "cognitively intact," with a normal EEG and no brain damage noticed on MRI scans. Two years later, she had experienced setbacks, including a post-traumatic stress disorder diagnosis, cancer scare, heart racing episodes, and medication problems. But even amid personal difficulties, not to mention the political and social chaos of 2025, she found some refuge through meditation and yoga. "As those of us who have experienced near-death or temporary-death experiences find, it is precisely in our most dire moments that we discover new realms of inner peace," she wrote. [2]

Canaday's experience was relatively rare, but probably occurred more often than many think. As much as five percent of the population has experienced a near-death experience, in which a person's heart stopped, according to studies in the U.S. and Europe. Many reported sensations of peace, traveling through tunnels, and seeing parents, children, and other relatives. [3]

Some 20 percent of people who survived cardiopulmonary resuscitation after cardiac arrest described lucid experiences of death, according to a 2022 study led by researchers at the New York University Grossman School of Medicine. They analyzed 567 men and women whose hearts stopped beating while hospitalized in the U.S. and United Kingdom between 2017 and 2020. Fewer than 10 percent recovered and were discharged from the hospital.

Patients said they observed events that occurred during their lives and experienced a life evaluation. Researchers found that brain activity such as gamma, delta, theta, alpha, and beta waves increased during these sessions.

"These recalled experiences and brain wave changes may be the first signs of the so-called near-death experience, and we have captured them for the first time in a large study," Sam Parnia, an intensive care physician and associate professor in the Department of Medicine at NYU Langone Medical Center, said in a statement. "Our results offer evidence that while on the brink of death and in a coma, people undergo a unique inner conscious experience, including awareness without distress." [4]

The experiences as the brain shuts down and releases "braking systems" weren't tricks that might occur as a person dies, he said. A person's consciousness can store memories and even thoughts from long ago. The studies have not been able to "absolutely prove" the existence of near-death experiences, but they have shown that they cannot be disclaimed entirely, Parnia said.

Psychiatrist: Near-death experiences typically make people 'more spiritual'

While researchers need to differentiate genuine near-death experiences from psychotic hallucinations, the real experiences can "totally transform someone's attitudes, values, beliefs, and behavior," Bruce Greyson, professor emeritus of psychiatry and neurobehavioral sciences at the University of Virginia, told Newsweek in 2021. "They typically make people more spiritual if I can use that word. They make them more compassionate, more caring, more altruistic, and they become much less interested in physical things, in material goods, in power, prestige, fame, competition." [5]

When Greyson started looking into near-death experiences in the 1970s shortly after completing his residency in psychiatry at UVA, he was one of the few with a doctorate or medical degree at various conferences on the topic. In the 2020s, it was not unusual for a substantial number of medical doctors and other scientific researchers to attend life-after-death meetings.

"The attitude among doctors has changed dramatically in the decades that I've been doing this work," said Greyson, author of *After: A Doctor Explores What Near-Death Experiences Reveal about Life and Beyond.* He said he originally started researching the subject "unwillingly" after various encounters with patients.

Rick Komotar, a neurosurgeon and professor of neurological surgery with the University of Miami Health System, admitted that Greyson gave him more to consider during a 2023 interview.

"As a neurosurgeon, I operate on the brain over 800 times per year," Komotar said during a 2023 segment of his podcast, *The Brain Surgeon's Take.* "The brain is the most complex entity known to us, and we have so much more to learn about it. During the interview, I started to wonder, where is the soul? Does our being enter an afterlife when we die?.... Bruce helps approach these difficult-to-answer questions with real science and moves us closer to understanding what the meaning of life is." [6]

Kubler-Ross, Moody pioneer field

The near-death experience field can be traced to Swiss-American psychiatrist Elizabeth Kübler-Ross and American psychiatrist Raymond Moody. After earning a medical degree at the University of Zurich, Kubler-Ross started teaching at the University of Chicago's Pritzker School of Medicine. Her classes included controversial interviews of terminally ill patients, and she developed her studies into a best-selling book, *On Death and Dying*, that was published in 1969.

The outpouring of response to a Life magazine article on her in 1969 led her to focus mostly on that topic. She championed the hospice movement and became interested in spirit guides, as well as mediumship and other ways to contact the dead. Following a Virginia house fire in 1994, she relocated to Scottsdale, Ariz. After suffering a stroke in 1995, she had to be confined to a wheelchair and talked about wanting to determine her time of death. She entered a nursing home under hospice care in 2002, passing away in 2004.

Moody also started to study the phenomena in the 1960s while an undergraduate at the University of Virginia. He was fascinated with the account of

Virginia psychiatrist George Ritchie, who claimed to have been dead for almost nine minutes after becoming sick with pneumonia as an army recruit in Texas in 1943. A medical officer reported him dead and covered his face with a sheet. But then an attendant thought Ritchie was still moving and convinced the doctor to inject his heart with adrenaline.

After Ritchie regained consciousness, he reported that his spirit had flown outside the state to Vicksburg, Miss., where he tried to talk with some residents at a café. He then visited "other realms in the presence of a Being of Light whom he identified as Christ," researchers Robert and Suzanne Mays reported. They said his description of the scenery and café, which he had never visited in person, were accurate. [7]

Moody documented other incidents, publishing them in a best-selling book, *Life After Life*, in 1975. After obtaining a medical degree from the Medical College of Georgia, he constructed a psychomanteum, based on the ancient Greek practice of consulting dead spirits. He also said he had a near-death experience himself in 1991 when he attempted suicide due to a thyroid condition that impacted his mental health.

Other scientists and researcher worked to prove the existence of other paranormal experiences, such as telepathy and clairvoyance, decades before Kubler-Ross and Moody. Duke University botanist J.B. Rhine was among the first to conduct experiments on telepathy involving students and others in the 1930s. He published his research in a 1934 book titled *Extra-Sensory Perception* and became known as the founder of parapsychology, founding a parapsychology lab at Duke in 1935. The lab still existed as of 2025, having been renamed the Rhine Research Center.

Ruth Montgomery wrote about near-death experiences and life after death in books such as *A Search for the Truth*, published in 1967. She transitioned from a journalist and syndicated columnist in Washington, D.C., to a psychic who contacted spirit guides through writing. She said she could communicate with popular medium Arthur Ford after he died in 1971. Montgomery advanced numerous theories, such as a person's soul being able to depart a body and be replaced by a "walk-in."

In 1981, I befriended Texas psychic Frances Baskerville. Two years earlier, she developed chronic bronchitis and diabetes to the point she had to use a breathing machine. She prayed to God to change her life and began attending a hypnosis clinic, learning a self-hypnosis, meditative technique. She lost weight and soon the diseases lessened.

"I relaxed my mind and concentrated on filling it with positive thoughts instead of negative, old ones," Baskerville said. Then she found she could read people's minds at times and move objects with her mind, something she had started to do around age five before repressing that urge. She began doing psychic readings, which developed into media appearances, law enforcement agency sessions to find missing kids, a cable television show, and even records as "The Singing Psychic." [8]

Shortly before Baskerville passed in 2009, her daughter, Anna, said her mom told her she saw "a golden tower" in the afterlife where she would be with relatives and friends who were "so happy."

Confronting some spirits

While relatively few people have had near-death experiences, more have reported paranormal encounters like feeling an odd presence or seeing lights turn off and on without explanation. Only 19 percent said they saw an actual spirit or ghost, though 37 percent admitted to feeling an unknown presence, according to a 2022 YouGov survey. [9]

Some otherworldly sightings have occurred at famous landmarks, such as the White House and Alcatraz, and sites of historic occurrences like the battlefields at Gettysburg, Pa., and Dealey Plaza in Dallas, where JFK was assassinated in 1963. Writer R.D. Whitaker detailed numerous sightings at Dealey Plaza in a 2015 Amazon Kindle ebook. For instance, Bill Hinton and Jewel Marshall reported in separate incidents seeing the ghostly image of a woman in 1969 at the grassy knoll in Dealey Plaza, before she vanished. They identified the woman as actress Karyn Kupcinet. Hinton and Marshall said they viewed the apparition while taking breaks during a work training meeting, Whitaker wrote. [10]

Kupcinet was killed just six days after Kennedy; her body was found at her home in West Hollywood, Calif. Officials ruled the cause of death strangulation, with a bone in her throat fractured. Researcher Penn Jones wrote about how a woman believed to be Kupcinet called someone in Dallas about 20 minutes before JFK was shot to warn him. Irv Kupcinet, her father, was a popular talk-show host who reportedly knew Mafia figures, but he said he did not have advance knowledge of Kennedy's assassination and did not believe his daughter made that call.

In the early 1990s, retail sales manager Nibor Noals started walking towards the back of a Bowling Green, Ky., store when "it seemed like time had stood still," he wrote. Noals and a fellow employee near him both observed an elderly man walk towards them. They recognized him as JFK but at an older age in his 70s. He had a massive scar on the side of his head. "He looked right at me and continued walking until he got out of sight," Noals wrote. [11]

The pair stared at each other. "Did you just see what I saw?" Noals asked his coworker.

"Yes, but I'm sure not going to tell anybody about it," he replied.

Noals wrote that he kept quiet for years but then decided to write about it. He described himself as a "Christian" who placed importance on honor and dignity.

Investigative medium Laine Crosby started communicating with ghosts after moving to Maryland from Atlanta in 2004. A former marketing executive for The Weather Channel, she and Mark Nesbitt, a former National Park Service historian, hosted the podcast, *Ghost Talkers*, and were featured in the Travel Channel's series *Mysterious Journeys*. Many of their investigations dealt with hotels and other buildings believed to be haunted in Gettysburg. [12]

"When I was a child, ghosts would talk to me," Crosby said. "I shut that down because it kind of frightened me." After moving to a former plantation home in 2004, the experiences awakened. She'd wake to find all of her kitchen cabinet doors open. Doors would lock and unlock by themselves. A Bob the Builder toy of one of her child's would proclaim, "I am in control." That toy soon exited the house, but it was just the beginning of many paranormal encounters, as well as efforts to find missing children and explain the sometimes unexplainable, during the next two-plus decades.

Laine Crosby tried to rid herself of psychic abilities but eventually accepted the gifts. Photo of news clipping by Shay, Fair Use

Crosby said she wanted to rid herself of psychic abilities at first but eventually accepted the gifts. She prayed to learn how to control the situation as much as possible and continued to meditate to help her make sense of what occurred.

"Many people who contact me have ghosts that won't leave, or who frighten them," she wrote in a blog post. "You can't get rid of a ghost by asking it to leave if it is convenient for them. You must take control and tell the ghosts in a courteous, yet stern manner, they are not allowed to frighten you and that they have to leave, if this is a problem for you or your children. Remember, ghosts were people too, and you wouldn't just let anyone in your house to hang out during dinner. Ghosts are not pets either, and most of the time, they get the message and move on." [13]

Personal tales

My mother was particularly interested in the paranormal, having had unexplained otherworldly experiences. After my sister, Sharon, died at the age of nine in 1965 of Reye's syndrome, mom said she saw her floating above her grave at Arlington National Cemetery during a visit. "Her face was smiling," she said.

I remembered the time I found my sister's grave during one visit after some new headstones had made it hard to locate. We were about to give up searching for it, when I suddenly took off, as if guided by an unseen force, walked with head down hurriedly past some rows away from everyone else, then along a row past more graves. I looked up, and there was Sharon's headstone.

Then, the morning an uncle died, our old landline phone in the kitchen rang at 3 a.m. "I remember being awake because we only had one phone in the kitchen, and I had to walk all the way from the bedroom to answer it," mom recalled. "There was just a voice on it, a strange voice, that said, 'Uncle Al is dead.' The next morning, I got the call from a relative that Uncle Al had died that very morning."

Mom was nothing if not practical, not the type to engage in wild goose tales. But she saw what she saw and heard what she heard. I believed there was something to those incidents.

One of my earliest memories was attending John F. Kennedy's funeral in D.C. when I was four. Right after my older sister died, my five-year-old self thought I would die when I turned Sharon's age of nine. I had nightmares of dying and a fear of hospitals and doctors. After one nightmare, I woke up suddenly and observed what looked like hooded, faceless apparitions in the middle of my room standing in a circular huddle. None looked straight at me. I closed my eyes, turned away, and tried to go back to sleep. After that incident, I made sure not to open my eyes when facing the middle of the room; if I awakened at night, I would feel for the wall.

I have written in a journal off and on since I was ten. In 1837, transcendentalist leader and writer Ralph Waldo Emerson encouraged 20-year-old Henry David Thoreau to write a journal. I was ahead of Thoreau's timeline, though my first journal only lasted four days. But at times since then, the habit stuck for a few weeks. We didn't have Twitter or Instagram or Reddit to vent and broadcast our inner-most thoughts to the universe until I was in my 30s. We had to put them down on paper. And then hope no one found them.

Death still consumed my thoughts at age 14, as I wrote, "I often think of what will happen after I die. I don't want to just lay in [the] ground forever and ever. I believe in reincarnation kind of. I think God takes our dead spirit and places it in a new-born babies' body."

I left the Catholic Church in middle school, then returned briefly in high school. I soon researched other religions and spiritual studies, from New Age thought, Buddhism, and Hinduism to Protestantism, Islam, and Judaism. I visited an ashram in my college town, where followers stared into a leader's eyes during a meditation. After college, I joined some spiritual meditation groups that were more free-form in which you could sit or lay down and just listen to hypnotic music and voices. Frances' readings were interesting, but I never really saw any proof of otherworldly existence beyond some strange sounds and photos.

That is, until after I married.

Ghosts at Texas restaurant

For almost four decades, the Catfish Plantation fed visitors and locals in Waxahachie, a town of some 30,000 about 30 miles south of Dallas where movies such as *Tender Mercies* and *Places in the Heart* were filmed. The restaurant, converted from a Victorian house built in 1895 where former Major League Baseball manager and player Paul Richards, among others, was born, served a wide variety of Southern Cajun-style cuisine. The blackened catfish, chicken fried steak, sweet potato fries, fried dill pickles, and bread pudding were popular.

The eatery became a backdrop for some wild tales of the paranormal, some of which were chronicled by the likes of the Travel Channel and Dallas television programs. In 2022, the business closed and was up for sale. [14]

The building's history as a restaurant dated to 1984 when Tom and Melissa Baker converted the empty house. Weird things happened as workers disturbed the cobwebs.

Strange incidents occurred at the Catfish Plantation restaurant in Texas.

Photo by Kevin Shay

One morning, Melissa arrived to find a large steel tea urn in the middle of the floor, well away from where it had been the previous evening. Another time, she smelled coffee brewing as she unlocked the door and discovered a fresh pot waiting for her in the kitchen.

Employees also reported a can of chives flying off the shelf, a fry basket levitating in the kitchen, a glowing blue light illuminating an empty room, and the ghostly figure of a bride by a front window. Paranormal investigators concluded there were several friendly but mischievous spirits haunting the building. One named Elizabeth Anderson reportedly appeared during a séance conducted by a local psychic. She had allegedly been strangled by a jealous ex-lover in the dwelling on the day of her wedding around 1920 and is believed to be the ghostly bride looking out the bay window. She was also known to follow some customers to their home or lodging. [15]

A farmer named Will Anderson, the father of Elizabeth, died there in the 1930s. Some said they spotted his figure on the front porch dressed in overalls before vanishing. Caroline Mooney, who lived in the house from 1953 until 1970, is another presence cited. Some have witnessed a fourth spirit, Lola Roller, who was reportedly murdered nearby in 1929.

The place burned in 2003 but was rebuilt. During renovations, workers said tools disappeared or were moved. As one worker put up a pane of glass, he noticed writing in dust on the window that read, "Don't be scared."

In 2007, the Bakers sold the restaurant to family friends, including Ann and Richard Landis. They invited researchers with the Association for the Study of Unexplained Phenomenon, who employed high-tech equipment to confirm some ghostly presences. While filming a segment for the Travel Channel, several people observed an apparition behind an investigator that had seemed to materialize from a nearby restroom. It reportedly vanished when someone pointed out its existence.

Customers continued to report instances of silverware moving, strange voices, restroom lights going on and off by themselves, and more. Workers did as well, including plates knocked out of their hands and ovens turned off. "When something raises up into the air in front of your face, it doesn't register in your mind," Shawn Sparks, an executive chef there, told a CBS television affiliate in 2016. "You think, 'Wait, no, that's not supposed to happen.' And then you look at the person next to you, and they're like, 'Yes. We saw it, too.' And you're like, 'Thank God! I don't need a CAT scan!'" [16]

Growing up in Dallas and working for newspapers such as The Dallas Morning News, I was curious enough to visit the Catfish Plantation several times. I never experienced anything out of the ordinary there, but did so in a bed and breakfast about a block away.

In October 1996, I visited Waxahachie to write a Halloween-themed article about how cities used haunted attractions to draw visitors. My then-wife, Michelle, and I visited several haunted attractions, including Screams Halloween Theme Park. We slept one night at the Chaska House, a Victorian Revival-style bed and breakfast converted from a 1900 home down the street from the Catfish Plantation.

We went to sleep before midnight not expecting anything unusual. But around 2 a.m., I woke up, hearing laughter. I first glanced over at Michelle. To my horror and surprise, her eyes were wide open. A look of fear dominated her face as she fixed her gaze above the bed.

Then I heard the distinct sound of laughter again. It was high-pitched like an adolescent. I heard a voice say something like, "Look, she's scared," and then laugh.

I looked up and observed some ghostly figures flying in a figure-eight motion above the bed near the ceiling, a mere few feet away. There were at least two, maybe three. They looked like wisps of light for their bodies, with detailed faces. One had the face of a young woman with gentle, laughing eyes and straight hair that she wore close to her head. She appeared to be in a frock decorated with embroidery and lace. Could that have been Elizabeth, the Catfish Plantation spirit who reportedly liked to travel around town?

Needless to say, I was surprised, but only slightly frightened. I wondered if I was dreaming for a moment. I was fascinated and sat up, trying to look closer to make sure I was really seeing this. Before I could form any questions, I glanced again at Michelle, who seemed frozen in fear. I told our visitors to leave in a fairly loud, firm voice. They did, seemingly vanishing in the air.

I arose, looked outside the bedroom, and didn't see anything. The following morning, Michelle and I told the Chaska House host what we had seen and asked if others had ever reported any similar incidents. He said they had, but unlike the Catfish Plantation, they didn't like to publicize their ghostly visits. He said similar reports came from several other century-old homes in the Waxahachie area.

As of 2025, I had yet to hear or see anything like that myself since 1996 – at least nothing that clear. While some said it could have been joint imagination figments, it seemed real to me at the time. And it seemed real to Michelle as well. We weren't trying to provoke a paranormal experience when it occurred. Neither of us had been drinking or taking prescribed or illicit drugs. I wished I had thought to grab my camera and snap some photos before telling those otherworldly visitors to leave.

Strange sightings and occurrences in that town and many other cities worldwide continued to be reported on blogs and in media reports, and investigated by researchers. While no one knew for sure what occurred after death, one thing was sure: We will all find out one day.

More Societal Ills

Race and Class: Why was Ruben Triplett Murdered?

First published in the North Texas Daily, University of North Texas, Denton, January, 1981; and Medium, February 23, 2018

The couple standing in the North Dallas movie theater line to see newly-released *The Empire Strikes Back* stood out for several reasons that warm May evening.

For one thing, they were playing Yahtzee as they waited. Who does that in a movie line? They were attractive and well-dressed. The man was extremely tall at 6-foot-7.

And he happened to be black, she white.

While that last characteristic might not be notable in 2025, this was 1980 in Dallas, not New York. Until 1969, "segregation of the races" had been written into the North Texas city's charter. Interracial marriage, mostly defined as between "negroes" and whites, was not officially legalized in predominantly Southern states, including Texas, until a 1967 Supreme Court decision that was vehemently opposed by most Americans. At least Texas was not like two defiant states that held onto bans long after the high court's ruling; South Carolina did not remove the clause until 1998, Alabama until 2000. In the latter state, some 546,000 voters – 40.5 percent – still wanted to keep the ban. In 2000.

Such marriages grew slowly. In 1970, only 65,000 couples nationwide were black-and-white. That more than doubled to 167,000 by 1980, but mixed marriages still only comprised 0.3 percent. By 2015, the number expanded to about 600,000 – still less than 1 percent of the total. A study released in 2014 found that only 26 percent of white Americans favored a close relative marrying an African American, compared with 54 percent of blacks supporting a family member marrying a white. Even in 2015, there were many more marriages between whites and Hispanics [42 percent of the total] than whites and blacks [11 percent] and slightly more among whites and Asians [15 percent]. [1]

In Southern cities like Dallas, black-and-white dating was still frowned upon by many for decades after the 1967 ruling. Even black members of the adored Dallas Cowboys had to live in segregated housing developments much farther away from the team's practice facilities until lawsuits forced change in the 1970s.

During those years, the KKK regularly marched through downtown without inciting a riot.

Interracial dating was such a taboo around that time, so rebellious of the established social order, that members of the Richland College basketball team and cheerleaders decided one evening in 1978 to walk arm-in-arm into a small North Texas town diner as black-and-white couples. That was their Rosa Parks' moment of social protest, their revolutionary act. They received icy stares but no incidents.

Deflecting icy stares and worse was part of everyday life for Ruben Triplett and Nancy Patrick for at least a few months in 1980. Triplett was used to breaking color barriers. In Galesburg, Ill., he easily made friends with kids from all backgrounds at an early age. Former Texas Rangers catcher and executive Jim Sundberg was among Triplett's childhood friends; both played on Galesburg High's baseball and basketball teams and made that school's Athletics Hall of Fame. They remained in touch in Dallas to the point that Sundberg got his friend autographed baseballs to give to children. [2]

At SMU, Triplett became the first African American to earn a basketball scholarship in 1971 with the aid of Galesburg High coach John Thiel, whose son, Zack, also signed with the Dallas-area private university that same year. Triplett continued to date outside his race, even after having a daughter with a common-law spouse.

"He was a nice guy to me," said Patty Hines, a gymnast and former Richland student who lived in the same North Dallas condominium complex as Triplett that was then called The Lofts. "He would talk to everybody. But he was also the cocky, jock-type. That rubbed some people the wrong way."

On that May evening, Triplett was in a jovial mood before seeing the latest Star Wars movie. Intrigued by their board game, I asked who was winning at Yahtzee. He laughed and replied, "She is, as usual."

We engaged in more friendly, small talk until making it inside the theater when he left to purchase some movie food. The woman with Triplett asked how tall I was since I was the same height as her date. She said he used to play basketball for SMU. I had been a Mustangs fan during his time – the Ponies were more successful in the early 1970s than the ABA's Dallas Chaparrals, which only won one playoff series in six years – and immediately recognized his name. When he returned, we discussed SMU basketball until the movie began.

Two months later, Triplett and Patrick would be dead. I couldn't be sure that the woman with Triplett that night was Nancy Patrick, though she seemed to match the photos. But I knew for sure that had been Triplett. That link alone was enough to make me – then a college journalist at the University of North Texas – pursue an independent investigation of the case and learn more than I wanted to about the ugly nature of racism and classism and jealousy.

Newspaper coverage of a white banker killing a black athlete dodged the race question. Photo of front page of Dallas Times Herald, July 28, 1980, Fair Use

'Straight-arrow' killer?

Don Fountain Patrick grew up in the conservative four-square-mile hamlet of University Park, home to SMU and one of the richest burbs in the country. Bordered by Dallas and the even wealthier burb Highland Park, University Park was about 95 percent white in 1980, and that would not decline much in ensuing decades. More than 90 percent of minorities were Asian or Hispanic, mostly SMU students. Its population of some 24,000 in 1950 remained about the same through 2025. Some 80 percent of housing was single-family with an average value of about $2 million.

To say that University Park resisted change was an understatement.

Patrick shunned the local college to attend an even more conservative private university, Baylor in Waco. Working his way through the First National Bank ladders, Patrick became vice president of the large banking institution's trust department in 1977. An active Baylor booster, he regularly took his stepson, Shane, to Baylor football games. He introduced Shane to players such as Neal

Jeffrey, an All-American quarterback who led the Bears to their first Southwest Conference title in 1974 and briefly played in the NFL.

Gerald Bennett, First National Bank vice president for community relations, described Patrick in 1980 as a "straight-arrow guy." Some neighbors said he appeared glum, which could have been in part due to marital difficulties with Nancy Patrick. Around May 1980, he moved out of their house near University Park into an apartment. [3]

Doing so was almost the end of the world to him, said Brenda Cox, a family friend. "Don was raised in a strict Christian family, and the idea of separation or divorce was horrible to him," she told the Dallas Times Herald. [4]

Despite his Christian upbringing, Patrick did not attend church with Nancy and Shane at Wilshire Baptist near their house, said Rev. Bruce McIver. Nancy was more outgoing and involved in church ministries, including befriending a child who had cystic fibrosis, he said.

Nancy and Triplett could have met through sports – she regularly played tennis and he remained active in basketball and softball leagues. Both outgoing extroverts, they could have also met through social functions. Triplett drove a delivery route for Julius Schepps Wholesale Liquors, and neighbors saw him with numerous women, black and white. Nancy kept her romantic interests more private.

An executive assistant to then Trammell Crow Co. President Don Williams, Nancy attended college in the evenings to work on a bachelor's degree. She was a model person and employee, said Williams, a mover and shaker who was involved in efforts to revitalize minority neighborhoods and decrepit schools. Supervisors lent similar compliments about Triplett's job performance, saying he was "pleasant, well-dressed and never missed a day" of work, according to news reports. [5]

But Nancy had another side that remained hidden from work colleagues, neighbors, and her pastor. She and Triplett became intimate enough for her to possess a key to his condo. While Texas law considers couples to still be married even if they live in separate residences, Triplett did not view Nancy Patrick as still being Don Patrick's spouse. To him, living in separate places meant being single, and he was reportedly smitten enough with Nancy to tell her he loved her.

By early July 1980, Patrick's apparent glumness turned violent. He reportedly held a gun to his estranged wife's head for 30 minutes, demanding she stop seeing Triplett. At some point, he forced her to hand over her key to the condo.

About two weeks later, Patrick visited his parents' house. He asked his mother, who taught Sunday school for preschoolers at a prominent Baptist church, and father, who was a deacon at the same church, to pray for him and his marriage.

"Nancy wouldn't pray," Ruth Patrick told me. "She loved that black man."

And more and more, her son blamed "that black man" – Ruben Triplett – for his problems. The bank exec also had another side. "He was real jealous by his nature," his mother said. "He loved Nancy so much."

Triple killing on a Sunday afternoon

Patrick's other side led him to venture to Triplett's condo wearing a fake beard, mustache, and wig around July 20. A police officer found him peering into Triplett's window. Upon questioning Patrick, his fake mustache fell off. Still, no arrest was made.

On July 27, Nancy visited Triplett, and they swam at the complex pool. She left around 3 p.m. to pick up Shane, who returned from a church-sponsored camping trip about 4 p.m.

That was when Don Patrick entered Triplett's condo with the key he took from Nancy, carrying a .38-caliber pistol. Somehow, Patrick knew right when to enter when Triplett's German shepherd, Thor, was behind a closed door in an upstairs bedroom.

As Triplett spoke on the phone to friend Maurice Grover, he heard a noise at the door like a knock or someone trying to open it. Some accounts claimed Triplett opened the door, while others reported that Patrick used the key.

"Oh," Grover heard Triplett say into the phone.

Patrick fired at least one shot. A bullet passed through Triplett's throat and lodged in his head, as Thor barked ferociously from upstairs. The bank executive left a note saying he killed Triplett because he "still loved" Nancy. He then exited the way he came, locking the door.

No one saw Patrick come. No one saw him leave. One woman, a neighbor in a condo about 20 yards away, heard some shots but didn't think anything of them until two-and-a-half hours later when the area swarmed with police and reporters.

Grover knew something was wrong. He called Triplett back, but no one answered. No one heard Thor barking wildly in the upstairs bedroom. By the time Grover and another friend knocked on Triplett's door, two hours had passed.

Triplett was killed in 1980 at this Dallas condo in the middle of a Sunday afternoon. Photo by Kevin Shay

They observed blood running under Triplett's door and couldn't get the locked door open. After running to a neighboring apartment to call police, officers had to summon animal control to remove Thor from the condo. [6]

After Patrick committed his first murder, he drove to Nancy's house, where she had taken Shane. Patrick informed his estranged wife of Triplett's sudden death. He emphasized that he had killed him to save their marriage and that it was wrong for Nancy to have a boyfriend, particularly a black boyfriend. [7]

An argument followed, and Patrick ran out to his car to get another .25-caliber pistol. Nancy informed Shane of what his stepdad planned to do, then ran out the back door in her bare feet screaming, "Help me! Help me! He's trying to shoot me!" At least two neighbors heard the cries and laid low while Patrick ran after his wife with the pistol. Shane scurried after them.

Nancy cut through a yard and ran down the street. The owner of the yard was watching a golf tournament and in the corner of his eye saw a man and boy run past the window. He glanced out to see the 12-year-old boy jump on the man and attempt to drag him to the ground. The boy fell off, and the man kept running.

The owner of the house walked from the window to the bedroom to tell his wife. He heard a popping sound like firecrackers. He stayed in the room. "The man had a gun," he later said. "I knew that was no place for me."

Meanwhile, Nancy ran through another yard and across an alley to Lovers Lane, a six-lane busy street with a median separating the two sides. Some young men were across the street playing basketball in the parking lot of Zion Lutheran Church.

They stopped playing as they heard the women's screams and saw the man running after her with a gun. One of them later said he first thought it was all a "joke." [8]

Patrick got close enough to Nancy to fire a shot or two. A witness observed Nancy on her knees in the middle of the busy street, "pleading for her life." As she fell over, Patrick walked up to her and pumped at least four shots into her back. Police found six empty .25-caliber shells at the scene of the crime. [9]

Motorists stopped their cars. People rushed to the aid of Nancy, and a guy ran to a neighbor's house to call police. Shane lay face-down, pounding the sidewalk, crying. "My daddy killed my mother!" he told a witness. Shane had been the only one in the neighborhood to try to stop the killing. He finally turned to a man and said, "Please, mister, see that [his stepdad] goes to jail." [10]

No one paid much attention to the murderer. Amidst the confusion, he just quietly drifted away. No one tried to stop him. He had a gun. But, what no one except maybe Patrick knew was that his gun was empty. One passing motorist later said Patrick had stood there looking at his gun after the shooting "like he couldn't believe what was happening."

Nancy Patrick was shot and killed in 1980 in the middle of this Dallas street on a Sunday afternoon. Photo by Kevin Shay

The double-murderer ran to his silver Datsun 280Z parked in front of the Patricks' house and drove to his parents' house. He told them what he had done and what he planned to do – finish off his own version of justice. He took his .38-caliber pistol with him and walked out the back door into the backyard.

Ruth Patrick followed, pleading with him not to pull the trigger. But, he knew he couldn't live with what he had just done. He put the gun to his head and fired his final shot in front of his mother.

A University Park police officer, who had come to the house to inform the elder Patrick's of their daughter-in-law's death, reached the scene seconds after the suicide shot. Don Patrick, 39, died in the ambulance on the way to the hospital. Nancy Patrick, 33, and Triplett, 29, died almost immediately after he shot them.

'He just did what he felt he had to do'

Two weeks after Don Patrick ended three lives, I found myself in front of the scene of the final crime. A short, elderly woman answered my tentative knock on the door of Ruth and James Patrick's small-but-well-kept residence in University Park.

"Mrs. Patrick?"

"Yes. Can I help you?"

I explained I was a journalist "looking into that triple killing" and wanted to ask some questions. I all-but turned to leave, expecting another slammed door, which I had become used to in the previous few days.

But to my surprise, this lady looked at me curiously. "Well, I guess so. What do you want to know?" Apparently, I was the first journalist bold enough to knock on her door. I sure hadn't seen her quoted anywhere.

Surprised, I immediately cut to the chase. "Why did your son do it?" That was the million-dollar question that ran through my mind.

She detailed how her son had come to her house and asked her to pray for him. She seemed disdainful that Nancy declined to pray, mentioning with no small measure of disgust that she "loved that black man." Even though I grew up knowing how to decode racist code words, her refusal to refer to Triplett by name shook me for a few moments. But I didn't want to make her stop talking by questioning her about that.

After saying how her son's jealousy caused him to go off the deep end because he "loved Nancy so much," Ruth Patrick gazed at me and asked, "Are you a Christian?"

Again, I resisted the urge to question her query. "Keep the subject talking" was an axiom drummed into me by numerous journalism professors. "Yes, ma'am," I answered, having had a religious reawakening that summer.

"Then you pray for him," she urged. "You pray for us. You pray for Shane. You pray for that black man's family and kin. Don's gone now, and I pray that the Lord will forgive him. I think He will."

She was silent for a moment, then said in a lowered voice, "He just did what he felt he had to do."

I almost didn't catch that last sentence. *Did what he felt he had to do?* My mind reeling, I blurted out a question about Shane.

"He's at Nancy's parents' house. I just hope he finds some way to deal with this."

I then mistakenly followed that up by asking where Nancy's parents' lived.

"No way I'll tell you that," she stated, her voice getting louder. "You stay away from that boy. I've told you too much already."

Slam.

An attorney for the Patrick's denied she tried to justify her son's actions. "I would drop this matter if I were you," he said. The Patrick's later declined to comment further during a second visit to their house that was less cordial than the first.

Others tried to convince me to let things lie. Carlos Gonzales, the 23-year-old eyewitness to the murder of Nancy who told a reporter that at first he thought the chase scene was a "joke," claimed he was misquoted. "How were you misquoted?" I asked.

"I don't want to say," he replied. "I think you should just drop the whole thing. The people are dead, and nothing's going to bring them back."

A neighbor of the Patrick's told me I should "find out who shot J.R. [Ewing]" after completing an investigation of this case. But at least he wasn't among those who slammed the door in my face.

Several neighbors denied knowing the Patrick's. That included Triplett's old SMU coach, Bob Prewitt, who ironically lived right across the street from the Patrick's. "I saw him and his wife out a few times, but we didn't socialize or anything like that," Prewitt said. He added that he was out-of-town that fateful day and hadn't talked with Triplett in more than a year.

Prewitt, who played for SMU himself back in the 1940s, became an assistant basketball coach in 1949 and was promoted to head coach in 1967, taking over for the legendary Doc Hayes. Through eight seasons, his teams lost more than they won, with an overall record of 88–115. His best year came in 1972, when Triplett scored 18 points and grabbed 11 rebounds a game to lead SMU to a share of the regular-season Southwest Conference championship with a record of 10–4. Triplett earned first-team All-SWC honors that season.

Prewitt was replaced in 1975 by Sonny Allen, who happened to coach a former Richland teammate of mine with the most appropriate basketball name in the world, Ollie Hoops. The Mustangs would not win another SWC title until 1988. Triplett wouldn't advance to the NBA like teammate Ira Terrell, but he would play on international pro squads in Europe and South America.

A 1973 story on Prewitt called him "the tall, gentlemanly basketball coach at Southern Methodist, [who] shuns controversy in the same manner he would likely shun a mountain lion who had missed his lunch." [11]

Prewitt, who lived close to the guy who murdered one of the best players he coached, didn't seem interested in picking my brain on what I had learned about how his former star player had died. Perhaps it was too controversial for him. The situation was weird, but I didn't find anything sinister with that residential coincidence.

Happier times for Ruben Triplett, far left, middle row, and Coach Prewitt, third from left, front row, as co-SWC champs in 1972. Photo from SMU Basketball Twitter post, May 29, 2013

'Truth will come out in the end'

Working full-time as a security guard in a warehouse for former department store chain Sanger-Harris that summer cut into my investigation time. But the job also introduced me to some people with heart-tugging stories. Fellow guard J.C.

West said he had served three years in prison for manslaughter on what he called "trumped-up charges."

"Three white guys jumped me outside a bar in Seattle," stated West, an African American who knew karate. "I was just defending myself. One had a knife, and one ended up dying."

He expressed remorse for that tragedy but added that he really had no choice when it was three-on-one. He had to use all of his training to survive. "All the judge and the jury saw was a black guy killing a white guy, even though they started it," West said.

I tried to use my present occupation and my father's former one as an FBI agent to my advantage in getting information from Dallas and University Park police about the triple killing. But on those visits, I gave them more than they shared with me. Some tried to claim that public police reports were confidential; at times, I wondered if they were trying to keep a lid on the case so it didn't fester into a racism-infused controversy or legal battle.

For several nights, I got off work around 8 p.m. and drove to The Lofts still in my security uniform. On one occasion, resident Mike Greaves detailed other crimes at the complex, including robberies and shootings. "I've complained to management and security guards ten or 12 times about punks hanging all over my car late at night," he said. "Nothing is ever done. I finally took a gun out there myself and waved it at the kids until they left."

"That sounds like a dangerous situation," I noted. Not to mention probably illegal, especially if the gun happened to go off. "Why don't you leave here if it's the way you say?"

Greaves shrugged. "Somebody's got to stay and fight this thing. I've always believed in meeting a problem head-on. I've never been one to run away from anything."

Dick Thomas, a manager with the complex, said he had hired a full-time, night security guard. Before that, including on the day Triplett was shot, a company patrolled the complex and numerous others by car. Greaves was "a troublemaker," Thomas said. "If he doesn't like the way the place is run, he can just leave."

The killing was a tragedy, but one that "happens everywhere," Thomas claimed. "Whose fault is it that the woman got shot on Lovers Lane? Is it the Dallas police department's fault?"

A guard for the patrolling company said he had just gone on duty at 7 p.m. the day Triplett was murdered. Another guard had been on duty since 5 p.m. but hadn't noticed anything until police carried Triplett's body away.

Joe Clark, the full-time guard Thomas had hired, told me that no one had informed him someone had been killed in those condos. He found out about it one night while doing foot patrols from a resident working out in the complex exercise room.

"I was glad he informed me of that," Clark said. "If someone's killed in the place where I work, I want to know about it." When Clark confronted his boss over that matter, he had laughed. "It's no laughing matter to me. When a man's killed at a place I work, I want to find out the details and take measures to see it don't happen again."

The other guard wasn't impressed. "You gotta remember that we're here for the manager's sake, not the people's sake," he said. Then he had to leave to patrol another area – in his car.

Clark didn't respond to that statement. But I could tell he didn't agree with the younger guard. "He only comes through here about every two hours or so," he said. "Before they hired me, that's all the security this place had. And that's not good enough because you can't protect anything just driving around in a car."

At his former job at a hospital, the African-American Clark said he was fired about a week before he would have qualified for a pension for supposedly "cussing" at another employee. He told me about his son dying of a knife wound, his brother-in-law being killed supposedly over a football bet, and a young daughter dying of meningitis. Such tragic events could easily make people bitter and take shortcuts. Yet, that didn't seem like Clark's style.

The following day, I ventured by Triplett's old condo and knocked on the door. A young woman answered and said she had just moved in from Mississippi two days earlier.

"Oh yeah? So what do you think about living in a place where a man was murdered a month ago?"

Her face turned pale. "A man was murdered here!?" she shrieked. "No one told me anything about that. The owner said a murder had taken place around here, but he didn't say it was in this place."

"Well, the killer can't bother you. He killed himself." I tried to change the subject, asking how she liked Dallas. She still seemed shocked.

"I have to go. I'm going to go get a bolt for my door."

After working later than usual, I ended up at The Lofts again, finding Clark near the pool. He sought more details about the Triplett case – he also thought there was more to it than jealousy. "A man doesn't shoot another without some deep-felt rage," Clark said. "Then to go and kill his wife in front of his son and himself in front of his mother. Something doesn't add up…. Racism, psychological problems. There is something else there."

We talked about many subjects – the mafia, Olympic boycott, presidential election, gun control, lost ideals – as I walked with him around the complex. He never asked why I spent so much time there; I guess a strange guy in security garb hanging out at a murder scene, asking questions about a case the authorities classified as solved, made as much sense as anything.

Numerous security lights were turned off or burned out. Four model condos were left unlocked, likely by careless salespeople. More than half of the condos were unoccupied, Clark said. One had its door wide open and didn't have a doorknob. "I've reported that door having no lock or doorknob ever since I started working here," he said. "They're slow here."

Suddenly, Clark motioned for me to be quiet and pointed to a second-floor window that had been removed. A light was on in the condo. He quietly climbed the stairs and peered in the window. He then pulled his gun and disappeared through the unlocked door. After what seemed like an eternity, he emerged.

"I have to chase out people from these empty condos all the time," Clark said. "The guy in this one must have moved in. There was a frying pan in there and some food. I'll have to come back and chase him out when he comes back."

Some squatters offered him money to let them stay in the empty rooms. But he never accepted it. He always made them leave. The man who risked his life here for $4.50 an hour – as much as I made at Sanger-Harris guarding clothes and workers – didn't look the other way.

We discussed whether guns were too easy to obtain. In 1980, surveys found that about half of the households in the United States had firearms, a trend that would decline to 39 percent by 2013 before rising again. "Damn right, they're too easy to get," Clark said. "Too many kids get them. And drugs, too. Guards like me need them for this job. But kids and those with prior criminal records? No."

I nodded. "I had a good friend in high school who kept a rifle in his room. He was really smart and played basketball on my team. One day, he found out he wasn't accepted to a university where he had applied. That night, he drank too much. He ended up in his room with his rifle there.... It was too easy to pull that trigger during one weak moment." I shook my head. "I can't help thinking to this day that had that gun not been so handy, he'd still be alive."

Clark let the story – one that was all-too common – sink into the early-morning mist. "There are too many stories like that. Such a waste," he finally said. While the rate of gun deaths would decline in the U.S. from some 7 per 100,000 people in 1980 to about 4 in 2020, incidents of multiple shootings by assailants in schools, shopping centers, and other public places would rocket. The number of shootings involving at least four people in the U.S. more than doubled between 2014 and 2023 to 659, before declining some in 2024, according to Gun Violence Archive. The U.S. gun-death rate remained way higher than other wealthier nations. El Salvador, Brazil, and Mexico were among the only nations with higher rates. [12]

The conversation turned to Jim Jones and his cult that had resulted in almost 1,000 deaths in 1978, mostly by mass poisoning. "He started out with a good idea, trying to build a community that had people's interests at heart," noted Clark. Jones had supported integration and equal rights for African Americans earlier than most, and his church initially attracted praise from civil rights leaders. "But he went power-crazy. That always seems to happen."

Still, Clark wasn't ready to give up on a similar dream. "I wish I had about a million dollars or so. I'd purchase me a piece of land out West or somewhere that no one was around. I'd start my own town with decent, honest people who cared about others," he said, his eyes getting a bit misty. "I'd build a general store, a bank, a hotel, maybe even a bar – you gotta have someplace to go to get a little crazy. I'd have one of those old-fashioned towns like in the Wild West. On Saturdays, we'd have picnics like the kind I went to as a boy where everyone would just come and eat and drink and have a good time."

I stood there listening to Clark describe his Utopian town, steps away from the place where a month earlier one of SMU's top hoopsters was gunned down. Crickets chirped in the grass near the pool. A cool breeze swept over us, contrasting with another steamy-hot day that would start in a few hours. Nearby, someone committed a crime. Others cried over losing a home, a job, a loved one. But in those wee morning hours, I remained focused on listening to this middle-aged security guard – who had seen more heartache in his life than most – holding fast to a childhood vision.

It was weird. I barely knew this man who was at least twice my age. But we had bonded quickly over something more than our security badges. Stifling a yawn, I wondered what would happen if Clark somehow scraped together the money to pursue his dream. Would it become compromised, like Eden, Brook Farm, La Reunion, Oneida, Jonestown? Or would it survive in a substantially different form, like many towns and cities that outgrew their founders' vision?

Clark must have read my thoughts. "But all that's pretty foolish. Someone would come in and mess it up somehow."

I looked at my watch. 3 a.m. I had been there five hours. "Well, Joe, I wish I could stay longer. I have to get up early in the morning."

"You better get going." He shook my hand as firmly as the day we met. "Thanks for keeping me company out here for awhile. And thanks… for listening to an old man."

"Sure, it was great." I smiled. "You're not so old." I wanted to tell him not to change, to keep working honestly against adversity, to hold fast to his dreams. I wanted to say he was doing God's work as much as any preacher or missionary. I wanted to tell him he had restored my faith a bit, made the hours on this search worthwhile during the last summer of my youth. I wanted to say that I'd rather be out here walking and looking around, helping him keep the place where Triplett died a little safer, than drinking and chasing women in some bar.

But I didn't tell him. Perhaps on some other level, he knew what I wanted to say. I started to open the drivers' door of my 1972 Pontiac LeMans. "Hey!" Clark yelled at me from across the parking lot. "Don't let go of your quest. I'll keep asking around. The truth will come out in the end."

I stood there for a few moments, trying to think of an appropriate response. "Thanks, Joe," I finally managed. I crawled into the car and drove away.

Playing Yahtzee against an opponent who always wins

That was the last time I would see Joe Clark. I soon moved back to Denton for my senior year of college and confronted new mysteries and challenges.

In the more than four decades since that triple killing, I would continue to raise tough questions, to write about tragedies and triumphs, disasters and heart-warming stories. I would meet presidents and homeless folks, celebrities and people who shunned the spotlight, yahoos who yelled at me and kinder souls who stopped to help, cynical criminals and adults who still believed in Santa Claus.

But I would get no closer to figuring out why senseless tragedies like the 1980 one involving Triplett and the Patrick's continue to occur. I would get no closer to figuring out how to prevent them, other than to live your life in a bubble, which is not really living. I didn't want to give up on finding answers. But perhaps one's survival ultimately came down to something as random as luck. Maybe the most important concept in life is to live each moment like it's your last.

Perhaps that was what I was doing during those few weeks when I investigated that triple killing, which culminated with helping Joe Clark get through another graveyard shift at the complex where Don Patrick gunned down Ruben Triplett in a fit of rage, insanity, racism, and jealousy the previous month. I lived without fear, knocking on doors in pursuit of answers, of truth. As a lowly college student, I chased the story longer and farther than anyone else, doing so while working full-time at another job and trying to have some fun. That the pursuit culminated with more questions than answers wasn't the point.

When I first read about the triple killing, I immediately thought it was tied to race and class. The stories I read largely ignored these factors, at least openly. Many assumed Triplett was engaging in an affair with another man's wife, which was not really the case since they were separated. If a middle-aged, white executive had been dating the estranged Nancy Patrick, I doubt Don Patrick would have gunned him down on a Sunday afternoon. He might have reported him to the IRS to trigger an audit or let the air out of the tires to his Mercedes-Benz.

But killing him in cold blood in his own condo and calmly leaving a note as his dog went wild upstairs, then murdering his own wife in front of numerous witnesses who included his stepson, then killing himself in front of his mother? Would jealousy alone drive a respected banker to do all that?

When Patrick was born in the 1940s, white bankers and businessmen ruled Dallas and most American cities with iron grips after they took down the more outwardly racist tyrant Hitler. Between the late 19th century and 1970, Texas led the nation in the number of white people lynched and was third behind Georgia and Mississippi in blacks lynched. Many black victims were accused, but not tried, of sexually assaulting white women, while some white people were targeted for being sympathetic to, or intimately involved with, African Americans. [13]

"Whites' fear of sexual contact between black men and white women was pervasive and led to many lynchings," reported Equal Justice Initiative in 2017. "Charges of rape, while common, were 'routinely fabricated' and often extrapolated from minor violations of the social code, such as 'paying a compliment' to a white woman, expressing romantic interest in a white woman, or cohabitating interracially." The mobs often stripped and castrated victims before further torturing, hacking, hanging, burning or boiling them until they died. [14]

The Dallas of Patrick's and his parent's time was different in numerous ways from the one today. Dallas did not have an African-American city council or school board member until the late 1960s. The city did not choose a minority manager until 1986, while the school district did not hire a minority superintendent until 1988. The large civil rights demonstrations seen in Birmingham and Atlanta and Montgomery and other Southern cities largely bypassed Dallas, thanks in no small part to deals made between black preachers and the city's white power elite that wanted to maintain political and economic control. The remnants of slavery and Jim Crow racism would long remain entrenched in this city. The statue of Confederate leader Robert E. Lee wouldn't come down until 2017. Black officials would continue to be targeted by federal investigations of alleged transgressions that white officials executed in their sleep, mostly without prosecution. [15]

In 1980, an attitude that whites were inherently better than blacks remained ingrained in many longtime white Dallas residents, especially older ones. No one I interviewed came out and said Patrick was a racist, but more than a few surmised that race and class were factors that drove him to do what he did. The reports that Patrick told his estranged wife it was particularly bad having a "black boyfriend," Patrick's mother referring to the celebrated SMU athlete who her son ruthlessly struck down only as "that black man," and other clues lent some hints of confirmation. Were there elements of racism and classism in the Dallas police choosing not to arrest or detain white banking exec Patrick for peering into a black working man's place wearing a disguise? Had a suspicious black man peeped into a white-owned home, it's likely he would be arrested. Especially in 1980 Dallas.

Some psychologists might conclude that Patrick's temporary madness, insane jealousy, and deep-seated rage came from a subconscious, triggered reaction to the racist code words and symbols of his conservative upbringing. Patrick was successful in his education, successful in his career, but the one person – in his mind – standing between him being successful in his family life was a brash, womanizing, athletic, young black man, who symbolized the "uppity n-words" who the outstanding citizens from Patrick's parents days lynched.

Sexism also likely played a role. Patrick expected his wife to come crawling back to him, and when she didn't and dared to continue seeing Triplett, that likely added to his rage. Did this banker really need to pump four more shots into his wife, not caring who was observing, once he already felled her with a bullet? Such actions go beyond mere jealousy.

So does it matter that race and class played roles in killing Ruben Triplett – and Nancy Patrick – more than four decades ago? Dead is dead, some will argue. Why dredge up the past and open sore wounds?

As for resurrecting the past, that continues to regularly be done by SMU and Galesburg High School since Triplett was a significant contributor to their basketball programs. In 2007, members of the 1972 basketball team – one of just 13 SMU men's hoops teams in 76 seasons to win a Southwest Conference title – were recognized during a football game between the Mustangs and North Texas as part of the university's Lettermen's Reunion Weekend. Triplett, the only SMU player to earn first-team All-SWC honors that year, not being there left a major hole.

Galesburg High has honored the two-time All-State Triplett several times posthumously, including with the Hall of Fame induction in 2009. In 2018, the 1968 team that, led by Triplett, finished second in the Illinois playoffs was recognized at a game. "Ruben was the only team member who had died," noted Tom Wilson, who broadcast Galesburg games for more than four decades and wrote for the Galesburg Register-Mail.

Triplett, who had eight siblings, is buried in a Galesburg cemetery near relatives' homes. Nancy Patrick and Don Patrick are buried in Dallas.

Ultimately, it's our responsibility to see that the truth is not buried with them. If we really believe that the truth will set you free in a society that seeks to protect concepts like "liberty and justice for all," we must have the guts to pursue that truth and set the historical record straight whenever possible, damn the consequences.

And we must take steps to address and fix whatever issues that truth unearths.

Otherwise, we are merely playing Yahtzee against an opponent who always wins.

Funeral service is set for Reuben F. Triplett

Reuben F. Triplett, 29, Dallas, Texas, a former Galesburg High School basketball star, died Sunday in Dallas as a result of gunshot wounds.

Funeral will be at Hinchliff-Pearson West Chapel Friday at 1:30 p.m., with Rev. Raymond Floyd, pastor of Allen Park A.M.E. Church, officiating. Friends may call at the funeral home Thursday from 7-8:30 p.m. Burial will be in East Linwood Cemetery.

Mr. Triplett was born in Peoria Feb. 25, 1951.

He was graduated in 1969 from Galesburg High School, where he was a member of the varsity basketball team. He was graduated from Southern Methodist University in 1973. Since then, he had played and coached basketball in the Dallas area as well as traveling to many foreign countries, playing on basketball teams there.

He worked for Julius Schepps Wholesale Inc., Dallas.

He was a member of Allen Chapel A.M.E. Church in Galesburg.

Surviving are his parents, Mr. and Mrs. Elbert Chukes, Galesburg; a daughter, McKenzie Dawn Triplett, Dallas; seven brothers, Lewis LaViolette, Galesburg, Larry LaViolette in California, Bruce LaViolette, St. Paul, Minn., Ronald Triplett, Waterloo, Iowa, and Joseph, Charles and Everett Chukes, all of Galesburg, and a sister, Mrs. Angela Wood, Waterloo, Iowa.

COYT O. CARLSON

LYNN CENTER — Coyt O. Carlson, 60, of near Lynn Center, died Tuesday in University Hospital, Iowa City, Iowa.

He was born March 21, 1920, in New Windsor. He married Stella DeNess Oct. 5, 1946, in Moline.

Surviving are his widow; his father, C. Oscar Carlson, New Windsor; three sons, Ronald of Coal Valley, Alan of Alpha and Dean at home, and five grandchildren.

He was reared and educated in New Windsor. An army veteran of World War II, he was employed at the John Deere Plow and Planter Works, Moline.

He was a member of Bethany Lutheran Church, Woodhull, Woodhull Masonic Lodge and Woodhull American Legion Post.

Funeral will be Friday at 11 a.m. in Bethany Lutheran Church, with Rev.

Triplett's obituary in the Galesburg Register-Mail gave details about his family but little about the circumstances of his death. Fair Use

Education: The Religious Right's Long Campaign to Destroy Public Education

First published in Democracy Guardian, September 27, 2023, and May 18, 2024

A week before GOP front and extremist group Moms for Liberty invaded Maryland in 2023 with a school protest and conference, I visited my daughter at her college apartment not far from the meeting site. She was in the last semester of her senior year, working busily on a grad school application to study for a masters of library science.

We hadn't discussed her future plans too much lately in any depth. I have a fairly hands-off parenting philosophy, believing my kids can figure out their career paths at their young adult stages better without much interference from me. But this time, I queried her about what type of position she wanted to pursue in the field. "Are you interested in working at a university library or in research?" I asked.

"No, I think I'd like it better at a regular community library," she said. Back in 2018, when she was 15, she started working as a community library aide. That was three years before the January 6th Capitol attack, three years before Moms for Liberty and similar groups formed to continue their pursuit of an arch-conservative republic ruled by force and intimidation by the likes of Donald Trump, Elon Musk, and Steve Bannon.

"I remember how much you liked working at that library," I said. It seemed like innocent times then, much longer than three years ago. I'd usually drive her to work and hang out, reading in the library until she was done with her relatively short shift. When I was her age, the Audelia Road branch library in North Dallas was my refuge, opening up avenues of thinking I didn't consciously realize back then among the Mad Magazines, sports bios, *Catch-22* novels. Those sessions, more than anything, lifted me out of the stifling, conservative suburban thinking of that neighborhood, and made me understand there were greater parts of life out there than mowing a lawn and going to church.

That, of course, was long before Al Gore invented the Internet. If teens wanted to broaden their minds or relieve boredom before then, we couldn't merely look at our phones. We had to drink, take drugs, join a church or community group that tried to ram Jesus down your throat, or spend time reading in a library. Until my latter high school days, I preferred the library, not that I was a saint. It was there my eyes were open to the tough early lives and racism experienced by favorite athletes Wilt Chamberlain, Bob Hayes, and Bob Gibson. I gravitated to the adult section of the library at a fairly young age. It was there I discovered that things were rarely what they seemed. Though I was too young in the '60s to understand the catchphrase, "Don't trust anyone over 30," in the '70s, I learned to not trust anyone over 21.

"But things have really changed," I told my daughter, as if she didn't know. "More bully-type Republicans are getting on these school boards and firing people they don't like and attacking librarians in the process. Many aren't content with wrecking the schools; they are also going after community public libraries."

She wasn't convinced. "Yeah, but every place has problems."

"Maybe. But right now it's really bad at public libraries.... I'd also consider university libraries and research. The Library of Congress would be good."

As we spoke, a 224-year-old community library in Front Royal, Va., faced closure, with petty officials cutting off most funding because a few conservatives didn't like it having some books on gay themes. It would survive, but conservative leaders would push for more control on what books were offered. Residents of Jamestown, Mich., voted twice to defund that town's public library over a similar issue, though the third election resulted in some funding after public outcry. Arkansas Gov. Sarah Huckabee Sanders signed a bill that would force city libraries to move books on gay issues out of children's sections and provide criminal penalties against librarians, which was blocked by a judge. Arkansas lawmakers would then pass a law in 2025 to fire all members of the state library board because they wouldn't censor books, which Sanders signed. Louisiana Attorney General Jeff Landry joined efforts in that state to ban books at local libraries. City officials in Billings, Mont., considered a request to place labels on LGBTQ books, which was denied after a hearing.

Librarians nationwide faced nasty online and in-person attacks, being accused of being pedophiles and "groomers" for merely doing their jobs. GOP politicians called for them to be prosecuted for violating obscenity laws and forced states to leave the American Library Association just because then-president Emily Drabinski tweeted about being a "Marxist lesbian." Some librarians quit; others were forced to resign. A visitor to the Rochester Hills, Mich., branch physically threw part of a Gay Pride display at a librarian. Some conservatives fantasized about shooting librarians.

School board meetings throughout the country seemed like they were overrun by far-right cultists/zombies in a nightmarish video game controlled by dark GOP overlords. Bannon, who in the midst of Trump's 2020 coup attempt called for beheading Dr. Anthony Fauci and other officials, summed up the GOP's plan soon after the smoke from the January 6 Capitol attack cleared: "The path to save the nation is very simple: It's going to go through the school boards."

On Bannon's podcast, Moms for Liberty co-founder Tiffany Justice stated, "We're going to take over the school boards, but that's not enough. Once we replace the school boards, what we need to do is we need to have search firms, that are conservative search firms, that help us to find new educational leaders, because parents are going to get in there and they're going to want to fire everyone." She claimed that being a school board member was only a "part-time job" that "anyone can do. You do not need to have a background in education." [1]

Justice added that the group would endorse "at the state board level." Of course, it would not stop there. The group would be essential to getting Trump back in the White House in early 2025. And library-hater Trump would work tirelessly to defund public libraries and kill institutions that supported them. Through it all, M4L members would openly engage in partisan politics despite being part of a nonprofit organization that is forbidden to engage in partisan activities to keep its charitable status.

Schools and libraries become Ground Zero in GOP Culture War

For decades, school boards have tried to appear nonpartisan, while appeasing non-mainstream views on the right and left. Public libraries have long held a wide range of books, magazines, and other materials, though they have undergone almost continual debates over content and values, some more vehement than others.

The integration battles of the 1950s and 1960s were among the more intense struggles for control of school boards and information between left and right factions in the 20th century. The U.S. Supreme Court's landmark public school desegregation order in 1954 resulted in newspapers such as the Jackson Daily News in Mississippi claiming it would lead to the "mongrelization of the human race." White radicals bombed the homes of black families that moved into their neighborhoods. Many parents angrily protested at schools and colleges as black students were bused there.

In Dallas, one of the most conservative cities in the nation, school lawyers fought the 1954 order so fiercely that initial desegregation efforts were not made until 1961. Other Texas school districts responded more quickly, with those in Austin, El Paso, and San Antonio starting integration in 1955.

Lawsuits filed by the NAACP first forced the issue in the Dallas area when a federal judge ordered the mostly white burb of Mansfield to allow a few students to enroll at the high school in 1956. White mobs prevented students from entering the school by blocking the doors. A local assistant district attorney was reportedly roughed up by the crowd. No one was ever arrested for disorderly conduct or another offense.

The Mansfield protest was the nation's first failure to enforce a federal school desegregation court order, wrote historian George N. Green. The incident "possibly inspired" Arkansas Gov. Orval Faubus' resistance to school integration efforts there in 1957 that were countered by the Eisenhower administration, Green said. In 1965, faced with the loss of federal funds, Mansfield High finally allowed a black student. [2]

Some states like Missouri and West Virginia integrated much faster than ones such as Alabama and Mississippi. Boston was one of the last major cities to fully desegregate schools in 1988, with ugly protests that turned violent. Many white families fled to the burbs. Eventually, school textbooks were changed to remove passages that praised slavery. Minority leaders gained some mention.

In the 1960s, federal courts struck down evolution teaching bans and school prayer. Many public schools continued prayer at sporting events. Many white families enrolled students at private schools. Meanwhile, public libraries became havens for students, especially those from lower-income families that couldn't afford organized after-school programs.

Fueled by the ideas of libertarian economist Milton Friedman, who first proposed public schools granting parents vouchers to use for private education in 1955, the school choice movement blossomed in the 1990s. Minnesota became the first state to approve a charter school law, where public funds were allowed to prop up private institutions, in 1991. Eighteen other states followed suit by 1995. By 2025, there were some 8,150 charter schools in 45 states, according to the National Alliance for Public Charter Schools.

In 1996, Christian Right leader Ralph Reed stated that he "would rather have a thousand school board members than one president and no school board members." By controlling schools, social conservatives knew they could oversee curriculum to limit teaching on evolution, sex education, slavery, civil rights, LGBTQ issues, and more, while pushing through school prayer. Reed didn't seem to think a lot about libraries, though many conservative officials cut public library budgets and tried to get them to use more private funding sources.

Groups such as Moms for America, which dates to 2004, soon formed to help the conservative school cause. Catholic, evangelical, and other religious groups became more involved. Members ran for school boards, aided by funds from conservative political action committees funded by the Koch family and other far-right big donors.

In the 2000s and 2010s, social cons' goal of controlling school boards remained out of reach. Most officials strived for a nonpartisan stance and resisted the hard-right minority of loudmouth bullies. Public libraries survived conservative budget axes for the most part.

Teenager Joseph Rakes assaults lawyer Ted Landsmark with a flagpole during an anti-busing protest in Boston in 1976. Photo by Stanley Forman, Boston Herald American, Wikimedia Commons, Fair Use

More aggressive Moms for Liberty emerges

Then came Moms for Liberty. In 2020, public relations consultant and Trump backer Tina Descovich lost a school board race in Brevard County, Fla., to speech pathologist Jennifer Jenkins, who was supported by Democrats and more moderate Republicans.

Descovich, who claimed on her Facebook and Twitter pages to be the "daughter of God," and supporters did not take defeat well. Some protested in front of Jenkins' home, where "F-U" letters were burned into her lawn. Jenkins said that protesters carried weapons, almost hit her with a flag, vandalized plants and trees, and harassed neighbors. She was followed by private investigators and stalked online by state Rep. Randy Fine. The Florida Ethics Commission found probable cause that Fine violated ethics rules by threatening to veto funding to the town of West Melbourne due to his personal dispute with Jenkins. [3]

Another Moms for Liberty member filed a false child abuse report with the county against Jenkins. One sent her a message saying, "We're coming at you like a freight train! We are going to make you beg for mercy. If you thought January 6 was bad, wait until you see what we have for you!" Jenkins would leave the board in 2024 to form an education PAC and run for U.S. Senate.

Meanwhile, Descovich took the group's aggressive version to more communities. Bridget Ziegler and Tiffany Justice were among those to join Moms for Liberty as founders. During her four years as a school board member in Indian River County, Fla., Justice did little besides waste "too much of everyone's time squabbling childishly with then-chair Laura Zorc," wrote the Vero News. "Justice regularly provoked conflict and stirred controversy with petty antics and snarky remarks that antagonized Zorc and too often dragged the board into crippling dysfunction." After former Indian River Shores Mayor Brian Barefoot announced he would run for the board in 2020, Justice declined to seek re-election. [4]

In its first 18 months, Moms for Liberty grew to almost 100,000 members with chapters in almost every state. Contributions totaled more than $500,000, mostly from large donors who include Koch and Walton family members, in the first year alone. Descovich and Justice appeared on major right-wing TV shows, including those hosted by Rush Limbaugh, Tucker Carlson, Glenn Beck, and Steve Bannon. M4L leaders were trained by the Leadership Institute, which had worked with conservative activists since 1979. In 2023, Gov. Ron DeSantis named Descovich to the Florida Ethics Commission. At the same time, M4L leaders claimed they were merely Facebook moms selling t-shirts.

Besides Moms for Liberty, new groups that cropped up included Parents Defending Education, No Left Turn in Education, and Jamestown [Mich.] Conservatives. The "sudden proliferation of parents and moms groups has signaled a new and more virulent turn," wrote Maurice T. Cunningham, a retired University of Massachusetts political science professor, in a 2023 report on dark money. [5]

Nicole Neily, president of Parents Defending Education, was a veteran operative for the Koch family. PDE, M4L, and NLTE were incorporated into a right-wing network that includes the Koch's, the Council for National Policy, and Julie Fancelli, who helped to underwrite the January 6th rally that turned violent.

Ziegler, the wife of Florida Republican Party chairman Christian Ziegler, provided many of the initial political contacts for the group. A member of the Sarasota County School Board since 2014, she and other M4L-backed members voted to terminate the contract of Superintendent Brennen Asplen in 2022 with little cause or warning. The move came shortly after the election gave M4L members a board majority, causing numerous residents to say they regretted voting for the M4L slate.

In Orange County, N.Y., M4L members – some of whom won board seats – harassed gay Superintendent Larry Leaven so much that he resigned in 2022. Many of the online attacks against him were overtly homophobic, with some wrongly accusing him of sexually abusing boys, according to media reports.

In Berkeley County, S.C., a new slate of M4L board members immediately fired the school district's first black superintendent without cause, chose a M4L-supported member as chairman, and banned critical race theory, a concept that was not taught. Other superintendents were fired in California, Colorado, and other states soon after conservative groups with similar messages and donors helped elect a majority of board members.

In Charleston County, S.C., Ed Kelley, a Moms for Liberty-backed school board member, told a M4L group in 2023 that if a teacher had told his child she was transgender he "would have shown up at the teacher's house with a gun," according to one attendee. Kelley also "threatened to immediately fire the superintendent if the teacher showed up at the school the following Monday." The board later voted to censure Kelley, who claimed he never made a direct threat, and remove him from leadership positions. [6]

Kelley and four other M4L-backed members then voted to place the district's superintendent, who had just been hired four months before, on administrative leave without stating why. They also approved a policy censoring classroom discussions about gender and sexual orientation. In addition, the M4L-majority slate violated the state open meetings law by holding "unannounced meetings" that were not attended by the public, according to Jace Woodrum, executive director of the ACLU of South Carolina. The ACLU helped publicize candidates' positions for 2024 school board races, in which Kelley was defeated.

In Arkansas, M4L member Melissa Bosch spoke about shooting school librarians at a 2022 meeting that was taped, according to a police report. A reporter with the Arkansas Times quoted Bosch being upset about a librarian supposedly making $85,000 annually and saying, "I'm telling you, if I had any mental issues, they would all be plowed down by a freaking gun right now." [7]

A police investigation confirmed the statement but claimed it "was not made in the context of a threat." After the school district banned her from campuses for making the threat, she sued the district, saying her statement was not directed at librarians as much as "the school board and superintendent." A judge dismissed the lawsuit in 2024.

In Tennessee, M4L members targeted an opposing group, Moms for Social Justice, threatening to report them for supposed pornography distribution and child abuse. They called them "groomers" and "pedophile sympathizers." In New Hampshire, M4L leaders offered a $500 bounty for anyone to "catch" a teacher violating a controversial law restricting discussions on race.

In California, M4L member Kaylee Campbell Layton advocated on social media in 2023 for the "public execution" of Biden. Her husband was a U.S. Marine.

In Hamilton County, Ind., a M4L chapter quoted Hitler in its newsletter in 2023. At the group's 2023 national conference, Christian Ziegler advised attendees to not apologize for anything, not even quoting Hitler, since that supposedly shows weakness. Lending more proof that M4L is a GOP front, Ziegler gushed that the group had finally allowed Republicans inroads into the 20-year-old to 30-year-old female demographic.

In another conference speech, Tiffany Justice stated, "One of our moms in a newsletter quotes Hitler. I stand with that mom!"

The crowd cheered.

'Book Nazis' challenge more books for removal at city libraries than school

While Moms for Liberty largely focused on schools and their libraries, it provided lists of banned books for other conservative groups to challenge in community libraries. Numerous activists challenged more than 100 books at a time.

In 2023, members targeted city and county libraries even more than school libraries. The number of books challenged by conservative users, who some termed "Book Nazis" in reference to the Soup Nazi on *Seinfeld*, increased by 92 percent at public community libraries over 2022, according to the American Library Association. School libraries saw an 11 percent rise. Almost half of the books challenged related to LGBTQ or people of color themes, while few targeted books with gratuitous violence and horror. Challenges declined some in 2024, but they were still well above the level of 2020.

Few communities were spared the wrath of the "Book Nazis." In 2021, the Williamson County, Tenn., M4L chapter was the first to file a complaint under a new law banning the teaching of critical race theory in high schools and lower ones. The chapter took issue with teachers recommending and reading from books about Martin Luther King Jr. and civil rights advocate Ruby Bridges. They especially objected to passages about firemen turning powerful hoses against black children and a white mob yelling at Bridges as she walked to school in Louisiana during integration battles in 1960.

Instead, Moms for Liberty recommended using *The Making of America*, a 1985 volume by John Birch Society supporter W. Cleon Skousen. That book calls black children "pickaninnies" and claims that slave owners were the "worst victims of slavery." Most slaves were "woefully unprepared for a life of competitive independence," while abolitionists "did much to perpetuate slavery" by taking a "too militant" approach, Skousen claimed.

CatholicVote, a Wisconsin-based conservative group formed by Catholic laity in 2008, unveiled a "Hide the Pride" campaign in June 2022, where activists were encouraged to check out multiple LGBTQ books they didn't like from public libraries to keep them from being read by others. The group advised participants to write a letter to the library board about their actions and keep them "until the library agrees to remove the inappropriate content from the shelves." They also demanded that libraries "immediately take down" Pride Month displays in June.

CatholicVote spokesman Joshua Mercer said the plan to essentially steal taxpayer-owned books was implemented to "prevent kids from being exposed to smut." Calling the books "nasty," he recommended that one person in the scheme remained "ready to film" in case a staff member sniffed out the ploy. CatholicVote advised activists to lie that they were merely "local residents with library cards checking out books." The participants then were supposed to place the books "out of reach" of children at home. [8]

Some advocated moving books they deemed offensive to other sections of the library themselves, which added to library staff aides' workload. Donna Jorgenson Farrell, a Colorado Republican, argued that giving minimum-wage aides more work by intentionally moving books to their wrong locations did not hurt them. "Keep them busy," she wrote.

In San Diego, two women who checked out many books they objected to at a public library kept them over multiple renewal periods. In response, some 180 people donated $15,000 to the city's public library system to restock the shelves and fund other programs. But Hide the Pride continued to grow. The 2024 campaign saw more participants than the previous two years, CatholicVote officials said.

Some "Book Nazis" turned their efforts to Little Free Libraries, a book-sharing project started in 2009 that has grown to encompass more than 175,000 boxes in some 128 countries. The activists remove books they don't like and replace them with a Bible or another religious volume. The free libraries are individually designed, with many resembling bird houses, crafted of wood, metal, and other materials. They are usually erected on private residents' lawns and sometimes public places, where people can peruse books, take some that interest them, and leave some at essentially anytime. The concept particularly became popular during the pandemic, when many public libraries were closed or limited borrowing books.

Greig Metzger, executive director of the St. Paul, Minn.-based organization, told Newsweek that other areas have experienced people removing books on gay and minority topics that they didn't like from the boxes. "Sadly, this kind of behavior overwhelmingly targets BIPOC and LGBTQ+ authors," Metzger said. [9]

Conservatives even target Little Free Libraries, book-sharing boxes that became popular during the COVID-19 pandemic, with banning campaigns. Photo by Shay

Mixed results

The plan to overtake school boards had mixed results. Groups like Stop Moms for Liberty effectively countered the right-wing noise at many public meetings. States such as Illinois, California, and New Jersey passed laws to restrict book bans.

M4L candidates lost races in 2022, 2023, and 2024 more often than they won. Still, enough won to keep their misleading campaigns alive. In Sarasota and Broward County, Fla., upstate New York, South Carolina, Orange County, Calif., and Douglas County, Colo., candidates endorsed by Moms for Liberty gained majorities of school board seats and immediately fired superintendents and other officials without cause.

"They created this kind of environment of threats and division, and people are saying to them that we want nothing of it," Randi Weingarten, president of the American Federation of Teachers, told USA Today. Candidates "might find being associated with M4L brings out more votes for the opposing candidate than for themselves," the Brookings Institution reported. [10]

By 2024, leaders claimed membership was up to 130,000 members with 310 chapters in 48 states. But that year, political candidates decided to publicly distance themselves from the toxic group, while planning to reunite after the elections. Some refused to submit questionnaires about their views to local media, keeping their links to M4L hidden.

In Maryland, conservatives funded the 1776 Project PAC, which helped several right-wing candidates win school board seats. Jaime Brennan, founder of the local chapter of Moms For Liberty, made a show about resigning as chair of the group after she filed for an open Board of Education seat. In forums, she mostly refrained from talking about banning books and changing curriculum to just issue broad catch phrases like "school choice" and "parental rights" that meant little on the surface.

She and fellow M4L-backed candidate Colt Black were among those who won seats in 2024. Along with Nancy Allen, a M4L-supported candidate who was elected in 2022 and passed around a photo of genitals at a candidates forum that she claimed was in a school library book, they lobbied against a transgender identity policy. Former state Del. Trent Kittleman, who helped form a M4L chapter in central Maryland, also won election to a school board seat in 2024.

In Florida, which saw probably the strongest M4L influence with the GOP controlling some 82 percent of the state's 67 school boards in 2024, school officials funneled so much tax money to private and charter schools that they targeted public schools for closure. Led by Gov. DeSantis, officials not only banned books and CRT, but required teachers to sign loyalty oaths and post a syllabus online, according to scholar Henry A Giroux. Students were allowed to video classes without consent.

"Florida is inexorably moving away from traditional public schools," Nate Monroe, a columnist for the Florida Times-Union who became executive editor of nonprofit The Tributary, wrote in 2024. "Proposed school closures are not limited to Black or low-income neighborhoods, as shocked residents of Atlantic Beach learned in recent weeks when they saw their eponymous A-rated art deco neighborhood elementary school on the list. Forcing the district into this Hobson's choice can only be the end-result of a desire to cancel traditional public education." [11]

The closures included a technology and career magnet school. Funds were siphoned off to Jacksonville Classical Academy, a charter school founded by GOP donor John Rood. The state and city provided the school with $6.4 million to build a gym, according to Monroe. Many charter schools used public funds for rent payments to private landlords, rather than infrastructure improvements.

April Carney, a M4L supporter on the Jacksonville area school board, also helped funnel money to private Cornerstone Classical Academy. That helped put Atlantic Beach Elementary on the shutdown list, though that school was later saved after public outcry from wealthier families. Officials then targeted schools in poorer minority neighborhoods for closure, instead.

Numerous professional officials were leaving Florida school districts. "To be superintendent of a Florida school district today is to manage decline and to do so while standing mute – because outspokenness is off limits in the Free State of Florida," Monroe wrote. "Vindictive state officials, vindictive school board members, vindictive right-wing activists who want to ban books and micromanage the curriculum: they are ghouls, all, that a superintendent must wrestle with. The turmoil in Duval is a harbinger of Florida's dark future."

School choice grows immensely

To no surprise, the charter school alliance sung the praises of private schools funded by public money, claiming they helped students raise test scores and improve attendance and behavior. While studies showed that test scores among students in urban charter schools were generally higher than enrollees at regular public schools in those cities, students in suburban schools fared about the same in charters and public institutions.

In a study released in 2022 in the American Economic Journal, author Kirsten Slungaard Mumma concluded that there was "no impact" on student achievement in charter schools in Massachusetts and North Carolina compared with regular public schools. She also found "no effects on attendance or suspensions." [12]

Charter schools did reduce public school enrollment by about five percent in those states, with a particular effect on white student enrollment in North Carolina, wrote Mumma, an economics and education professor at Teachers College, which is part of Columbia University.

More states, including Arizona, West Virginia, Arkansas, Iowa, Utah, Indiana, Ohio, and Oklahoma. expanded voucher programs that funnel tax money to the families of students to attend private and charter schools. Some passed school choice tax credit allowances. Once mostly used by lower-income families to transfer students to better schools in tough neighborhoods, those programs were widened to allow wealthier families to take advantage as they sent their kids to existing private institutes, not just charter schools.

In numerous states, high-income families benefited the most. Arizona, the state with the nation's first universal choice program, saw families making a median income greater than $114,968 with the highest choice participation rate in private school programs, according to a study released in 2024 by the Brookings Institution.

"More advantaged communities are securing a highly disproportionate share of these [private school] scholarships," wrote researchers. "Nothing in the analysis above even remotely suggests that this program is addressing inequities in school access by students' socioeconomic status." [13]

Participation levels were higher in suburbs and cities than small towns, which often do not have private and charter schools. The lack of transportation and not knowing about the program in rural areas likely factored into that trend, researchers said. Tuition and other costs at private schools were often greater than the program funds.

The rise of school choice programs coincides with funding by mostly wealthy conservatives. The Koch family and American Federation for Children, founded by the billionaire family of former Trump Education Secretary Betsy DeVos, long bankrolled organizations that advocate for private school programs.

Billionaire Jeff Yass, co-founder of Philadelphia-based trading and technology firm Susquehanna International Group and a major investor in the controversial TikTok app, gave millions of dollars to school choice groups. Yass was also a major donor to Republicans who advocated for private schools, such as Texas Gov. Greg Abbott.

Courtney Gore, a school board member who won a seat in Granbury, Tx., in 2021 and once championed book bans, told ProPublica that conservative candidates were recruited to lobby for school choice and "cause as much disruption and chaos as possible" in local public districts. Former state representative Mike Lang and political consultant Nate Criswell, who hosted a Granbury political podcast, were among those who stirred up people over false claims about books with sexual content in school libraries and teaching of critical race theory, Gore said. The pair also lobbied against bond elections for needed infrastructure improvements to school buildings. [14]

Gore, who joined Lang and Criswell on the podcast before a falling out after she didn't find any evidence of sexual content and CRT in the schools, said she was "threatened" at board meetings by opponents. The campaigns of Lang, a Republican who represented Granbury for four years, were heavily funded by wealthy businessmen such as billionaire oilman Tim Dunn.

In 2005, Dunn wrote about his support for private school vouchers, saying they would "create a system of public education that serves all children equally well." A longtime board member of the conservative Texas Public Policy Foundation, he founded the private Midland Classical Academy in Texas, which provided a "classical education from a Biblical worldview," according to its website.

Some 29 states and Washington, D.C., had at least one private school choice program in 2025, according to Education Week. Ten states had voucher programs and seven tax-credit allowances. [15]

Trump-Musk takes out U.S. Department of Education

The biggest impact to public education since perhaps the 1954 Supreme Court ruling came in 2025, after Donald Trump regained the White House and allowed unelected billionaire Elon Musk to raid the federal treasury, fire thousands of employees, and slash billions of dollars in funding for education and other programs. Trump also signed a flurry of executive orders related to transgender policies, book bans, educational funding, and school choice that sounded like they were written by his most extreme aides, such as Stephen Miller.

Trump campaigned on abolishing the U.S. Department of Education, claiming it was responsible for diversity, equity, and inclusion programs and the teaching of critical race theory and LGBTQ issues. Some officials noted that curriculum decisions were controlled by state departments of education, and abolishing the DOE had to be approved by Congress. So slashing funds and firing employees became the way for Trump and Musk to essentially kill the department.

A large part of the unit's work was to oversee the FAFSA program, which awards more than $120 billion annually to some 13 million college students in grants, work-study employment, and low-interest loans. If that program was not moved to another agency, universities across the country faced drastically lower revenue and potential staff and program reductions.

As far as K-12 schools, the DOE only provided about 10 percent of funding, with most picked up by local and state governments, according to Education Week. Much funding was in special programs aiding disabled students. The DOE also provided research and ensured compliance with federal laws protecting civil rights.

Student mental health programs were a substantial component of the DOE's mission, wrote Dilice Robertson, a professor at New York University. "Abolishing the department risks dismantling a crucial safety net that supports our youth during formative years," Robertson said. "Rather than leaving the responsibility solely to states, we must recognize the essential role the federal government plays in ensuring equitable access to mental health support for all students." [16]

Republicans long attempted to kill the DOE since it was established as a cabinet-level agency in 1979. Project 2025, Trump's blueprint written by the conservative Heritage Foundation and many former Trump aides, joined Trump's call to abolish the DOE and change K-12 funding programs. In Trump's shorter platform, Agenda 47, he pledged to "cut federal funding for any school pushing critical race theory, radical gender ideology, and other inappropriate racial, sexual, or political content on our children."

Some noted that Hitler engaged in a similar campaign to destroy public education and blame social problems on educators, while most stopped short of comparing Trump and other GOP officials to 1930s German leaders.

"This GOP attack on education is part of a larger war on the very ability to think, question, and engage in politics from the vantage point of being critical, informed, and willing to hold power accountable," wrote Giroux, who has held positions at Boston University, Penn State, Miami of Ohio, and McMaster University and earned a doctorate in history from Carnegie Mellon University. [17]

DeSantis and others justified educational repression by claiming that schools, especially universities, have transformed into "socialism factories," he noted. The goal was to turn schools into "propaganda factories and components of the security-surveillance state," Giroux said. "In many ways, the GOP and DeSantis approach to education is not unlike what Putin is doing in Russia… [The GOP] model of politics and reactionary education are closely related to the attacks on education and history that took place in Nazi Germany."

The ties were seen in the elimination of the history of oppressed groups from school curricula, book bans, and the assault on educators and librarians "who do not agree with the transformation of American education into right-wing propaganda factories," Giroux wrote. "As historical consciousness and critical knowledge and skills disappear in schools…. young people are not merely misinformed, they are powerless to recognize in the realm of popular culture how supremacists are using history for their own toxic purposes."

Press Freedom: The Last Great Texas Newspaper War

First published in Medium, June 7, 2018

Four hostile newspapers are more to be feared than a thousand bayonets.
— **NAPOLEON BONAPARTE**, 1769-1821

It is the duty of a newspaper to comfort the afflicted and afflict the comfortable.
— **GENE KELLY**, Stanley Kramer's *Inherit the Wind*, 1960

"You got that story sent over yet, Doc?" Lawrence's formidable presence dominated my shoulder, as he gazed at the archaic computer screen in a confused fashion. When Lawrence requested something – which could seem like a demand – everyone in the building knew it.

Another attempt failed to electronically send the first story of the fledgling Arlington Morning News from a nondescript office building near Six Flags Over Texas and the Texas Rangers' Ballpark in Arlington to The Dallas Morning News about 15 miles away. It was the day after April Fool's Day, 1996. I wondered whether someone was continuing to play tricks.

"Shit! When was this machine built – 1880?" I asked. Complaining about your plight using sarcasm and profanity was a journalist's right – or rite. It not only helped ease the stress of the relentless deadline pressure that hung over the dense newsroom like fog on the Golden Gate Bridge, but it deflected blame outwardly, to somewhere else other than the obvious guilty party.

Lawrence let out his distinctive, nervous, baritone laugh. Just about everything AMN Managing Editor Lawrence E. Young did was larger than life. He possessed one of those high-energy, boisterous personalities that filled the room. Like most everything in Texas, such personalities in this state seemed somehow bigger and more numerous than other places. "God-damned bozos downtown, sending us this shit! How are we supposed to put out a newspaper with this fucking crap?"

By that time, a crowd had gathered behind me. "Do we have our first story sent over yet?" Publisher and Editor Gary Jacobson bellowed, chomping on his trademark cigar.

"Almost," I replied, trying to act like I knew what I was doing.

City editor Tracy Staton and assistant city editor Christopher Ave attempted to make helpful suggestions. Veteran reporters and assistant editors Chris Payne and Darrin Schlegel thumbed through a manual, searching for clues. "This thing is not in English," Chris noted.

"I hear you," I said. "I tried to read it. It's in another language."

A message came over from our head copy chief, Marc Gilbert, who was stationed in the News' downtown Dallas offices to oversee the production process. Back then, it took three or four copy editors what one copy editor with a decent iMac can now do. It was towards the end of what some called the good ol' days and others called the archaic times, when newspapering was a little more fun, yet inefficient.

Newspapering's real heydays were more in the Watergate era of the early 1970s, when reporters kept liquor bottles in their desks and openly fought with enemy government officials and button-down executives. There was no Google, no Twitter, no Facebook, to make reporting easier, but what journalists lacked in technology, they made up for in perseverance and ingenuity. Papers then were viewed by many in newsrooms as more of a sacred mission than a bottom line-driven venture, though a good number of media executives still made out like bandits.

That was slightly before I broke into the business by freelancing a story for the Texas Singles News in 1978 about skydiving while I was the sports editor of the Richland College student paper. I was paid all of $25 for the piece. I was in Heaven. From there, it was all downhill along a slow, rocky descent into Hell.

After re-reading parts of the manual and attempting a few times to send the AMN's first story, something clicked. "I think it went through," I stated. "At least I hope it did."

Soon, Marc confirmed it. Some cheered and slapped my back.

"We have liftoff!" Lawrence announced. "The Arlington Morning News is on our way." To what, who knew?

A newspaper war is born

For decades, the competition between the Fort Worth Star-Telegram and Dallas papers pretty much abided by an unwritten agreement to not significantly cross into each other's base. The Morning News was more preoccupied with its battle against the former Dallas Times Herald, a war it won in 1991 when the latter paper closed after a heated, sometimes nasty conflict. Some say the DMN, which bought much of the Herald's assets, directly killed the Herald; others say Herald execs agreed to shut down in a backroom deal. After that, the DMN increased its print dominance of Dallas County and the fast-growing, affluent northern burbs in Collin County.

A.H. Belo Corp., the parent of the News, traced its roots to the Galveston Daily News, formed when Texas was still a republic in 1842. Alfred Horatio Belo, a former Confederate colonel, became publisher and majority owner of the Daily News in 1865. After the old Dallas Herald shunned Belo's acquisition overtures, he sent George B. Dealey to Dallas to start a sister paper in 1885, namely The Dallas Morning News. Like it did more than a century later, the DMN soon swallowed the Herald and had only to compete with outside papers such as some from St. Louis. [1]

Dealey rose to president of the company in 1920 and renamed it A.H. Belo Corp. six years later. The business purchased what became WFAA-TV, the largest television station in the region, in 1950 and continued to grow its holdings. Acquisitions in the 1960s included News-Texan Inc., later called Dallas-Fort Worth Suburban Newspapers, publisher of what became the Arlington News and other community papers. After closing the Times Herald, Belo aggressively pursued television stations, newspapers, and other media properties, and saw annual revenues increase from $628 million in 1994 to $1.4 billion in 1998. The Morning News' daily circulation increased substantially through the decades, from 86,000 in 1928 to 150,000 in 1950; 239,000 in 1970; and 527,000 in 1994.

The Star-Telegram, then owned by the Walt Disney Co., kept its home turf in Tarrant County, while venturing out to Denton and other nearby counties. Formed in 1906, the Fort Worth Star became that county's chief paper in 1909 when Amon G. Carter led efforts to purchase competitor Fort Worth Telegram. For many years, the Star-Telegram touted itself as having the largest circulation of any paper in the South, venturing as far as New Mexico. In 1952, the paper had morning and evening circulation of 243,000, more than 50,000 beyond both the DMN and Houston Chronicle. [2]

The Star-Telegram, like Belo's group, expanded into other media, creating radio station WBAP in 1922 and the first TV station in the state, WBAP-TV, now an NBC affiliate, in 1948. Execs also ventured online into an ASCII service in 1982, earlier than most competitors. The Carter family sold the Star-Telegram for a reported $80 million to Capital Cities Communications in 1973, and Disney bought Cap Cities in 1996 for $19 billion, before selling the Star-Telegram and other papers to publishing chain Knight Ridder in 1997.

Throughout the 1980s and early 1990s, the DMN and Star-Telegram kept a few token reporters in the other's home territory. The DMN even formed a short-lived zoned section in Fort Worth in the 1980s. Then in the mid-1990s, Belo execs, seeking a wider regional net, decided to make a bigger play for Arlington. That city of some 300,000 residents between Dallas and Fort Worth – the home of Six Flags, the Rangers, a major General Motors assembly plant, and seemingly a subdivision and shopping mall on every corner – had the kind of upscale demographics advertising execs craved, often not found in cities of its size.

On average, Arlington's residents were younger, better educated, and wealthier than its counterparts in Fort Worth as well as most cities in the country. The average household income in 1995 was $46,500 – 50 percent higher than the national average – while 65 percent of adults had attended college compared with 45 percent nationally. The population was growing at an annual rate of 5.2 percent, almost double the national rate.

While some observers thought that Belo's play for Arlington was motivated mostly by ego, execs disavowed such notions, claiming they were performing a public service. "People in the Mid-Cities area between Dallas and Fort Worth, particularly in Arlington, tell us that they want an identity for their own," The New York Times quoted Burl Osborne, publisher and editor of the Morning News, in an April 1996 story. [3]

Belo execs were not satisfied with the DMN's small bureau in Arlington or the twice-a-week Arlington News, where I was news editor. That paper was once a daily, but revenue declines resulted in downsizing. With a small staff and little resources, we had not cut much into the Star-Telegram's home turf.

In January 1996, Gary, then the DMN business editor, first heard about the new venture in a meeting with Osborne, who told him to keep the project under wraps. It didn't take long for Gary to accept the challenge, and June DeRousse, a ten-year DMN advertising manager, agreed to be the paper's advertising director. In an AMN video celebrating its first year, Gary recalled that he spent two hours trying to recruit the first DMN staffer he approached only to be turned down. He knew he couldn't afford to spend that much time on each potential candidate. "I gave my best pitch in five minutes, and if I didn't see a spark, then that was it," he said. [4]

Others recognized the challenge. The Dallas Observer reported about a month before our launch that some staffers "hired to work for America's eighth-largest daily have expressed reluctance to accept a transfer to a new 20,000-circulation suburban operation." The story described execs as "hastily trying to assemble a reporting staff for the new paper." [5]

Gary soon had some success, coaxing Lawrence from his position as DMN assistant national editor and Tracy from being editor of Texas Business magazine. Christopher, Marc, Chris, and Valerie Fields were recruited from the Star-Telegram. Darrin came from the Houston Business Journal. Eric Garcia, who had also worked for the Times Herald, was recruited from the DMN Metro operation.

Cliff Schexnayder was a clerk and reporter for the DMN, while Larry Hartstein and Rosa Maria Santana had written for the Chicago Tribune and Tamara Chuang for the Philadelphia Inquirer. Photog Tom Fox transferred from the Corpus Christi Caller-Times, while Mark Kegans' previous positions included being a DMN intern who took a famed photo of Dallas Cowboys owner Jerry Jones speaking with potential new coach Jimmy Johnson in a Tex-Mex restaurant. April Washington worked at the Denton Record-Chronicle, which later became part of the Belo empire, and Nancy Calaway at the Plano Star Courier.

Most former Arlington News staffers were hired and given good raises, though we did not have quite the same jobs. Editor Russ Rian became editorial page editor, while I became a copy editor. Reporters Tra Clough, Kelly Patterson, Amy Norris, and Jennifer Rankin gained similar positions at the new venture. Some sports reporters, such as Mark Goodson and Ken and Keven Costlow, took on similar jobs.

Some with the Grand Prairie News and other editions, fearing the end of their publications and sensing an interesting opportunity, joined the expanded Arlington outfit. Pennie Boyett, news and lifestyle editor at the Grand Prairie operation, signed on as lifestyles editor. That paper's editor, Herb Booth, and Brad Loper, a photographer with the Mid-Cities News, also made the move. Others, such as Irving News editor Miles Moffeit, who eventually landed at the DMN, jumped over to the Star-Telegram, instead.

Even with a much larger staff than the old Arlington News had, we found filling up 16 pages five days a week to be challenging. Top Belo execs seemed pleased with our first few issues, which contained stories on the city hiring a consultant to work on large-scale improvements to a creek that officials wanted to try to turn into a San Antonio-style River Walk, minority hiring policies at the growing University of Texas at Arlington, and the Amber Hagerman Child Protection Act, a law named for a slain Arlington 9-year-old girl that resulted in a popular nationwide system to catch sex offenders. I even found time between designing pages and proofing copy to pen a story on Arlington's political system of electing council members, which ran on the front of our second issue. Osborne wrote a letter addressed to our staff, saying, "The first week of publication has demonstrated the validity of the notion that Arlington wants its own nameplate.... I am very proud and you also should be very proud." [6]

DMN editor Ralph Langer voiced similar sentiments: "The AMN is instantly a credible newspaper with a competitive opportunity to establish itself as Arlington's favorite local newspaper.... All of you should be praised for the planning and obstacles overcome.... Take a bow." [7]

Others did not think we should take a bow. The Times described our product that first month as "a scrawny foe, with a scant 16 pages of color and local news and more self-promotional ads some days than the paid kind." The Observer poked fun at our front-page weather report and apparently thought we did not cover enough hard news, noting there was a "chance of scattered drivel" today and "mostly fluffy, chance of pandering" the following day. In a story under the headline, "A.H. Belo here to rescue Arlington," the Observer jokingly claimed we only published Wednesday through Sunday because "Arlingtonians may not be accustomed to prolonged bouts of reading." [8]

That weekly also took shots at the FWST's coverage in Arlington, joking that the paper would invite Arlington civic and business leaders to submit stories covering themselves, form a "Frequent Reader Program," offer free hot-air balloon rides to long-time subscribers, and pay every reader's parking tickets throughout April.

After just three months, our operation expanded to seven days, and most of us saw overtime increase significantly, with 12- to 14-hour days the norm. We'd get up, fight traffic, get to work by 9 a.m. or so, stay until 10 p.m. or later, go home, watch a *Seinfeld* rerun, then wake up to do it all over again. It was exhausting – but exhilarating – for many of us in a real, live newspaper war. The need for editors was so great with the expansion that I soon moved up to assistant city editor and Sunday editor.

Most worked Saturdays; that Saturday of the first week, Gary and Lawrence, avid sports fans and participants themselves, allowed me to take off for an hour to play for my church hoops team in the regional championship game, which happened to be about a five-minute drive from the office. After I helped the team build a substantial lead, I requested out of the game and changed back into street clothes well before the contest ended. "I gotta get back to work," I told my surprised teammates. No time to celebrate.

Our launch made the radar of more national media outlets than the Times, including American Journalism Review and Editor & Publisher. The Times wrote that the "gambit in Arlington is one that publishers around the country are watching carefully." The article noted that papers had invaded each other's circulation areas before, but quoted an analyst who said it was unusual, even "perilous," to form a freestanding daily in a competing area. AJR called it "a different kind of fight," where "one city's newspaper moves in on a nearby city's newspaper market." [9]

By then, only one of the six Texas cities larger than Arlington featured two daily newspapers. And in El Paso, the Herald-Post was in the process of dying and would close in 1997. The Houston Post went under in 1995; San Antonio lost the Light in 1993. Austin last had two independently-owned dailies in 1924 – unless you counted the student-run Daily Texan – though the American and the Evening Statesman published separately under the same owner until 1973. The Fort Worth Press perished in 1975.

Some analysts doubted that Belo would win the Arlington battle, noting that FWST parent Disney had greater resources. But the Observer believed that the Star-Telegram was vulnerable with Disney in the process of unloading the paper and described Star-Telegram top management as "weak." The "erratic news judgment and personnel decisions" of executive editor Debbie Price, who would soon leave for the Baltimore Sun, "have driven off many talented journalists and hurt morale," the Observer charged. [10]

The Star-Telegram significantly ramped up its Arlington operation, spending about $7 million to expand staff from some 60 people to about 120, according to news reports. The paper changed its zoned Arlington edition that formed in 1992 to the Arlington Star-Telegram by July 1996. Execs gave Arlington staffers Army helmets and dog tags. Posters of the Elmore Leonard-inspired movie *Get Shorty* – a dig at the 5-foot-6 Osborne – dotted the newsroom. They slashed newsstand prices and asked advertisers to sign statements saying there was no need for another paper. Some advertisers publicly complained they raised rates if they also advertised in the AMN. Disney CEO Michael Eisner reportedly told Star-Telegram execs, "Do whatever it is you gotta do," according to a July 1996 Texas Monthly article. [11]

Many new AST staffers came from other parts of the paper, while some were recruited from outside. "This is a very serious battle," AST Editor Gary Hardee, who had been a senior editor at the Times Herald when that paper closed, told D Magazine. "When you add Arlington to northeastern Tarrant County, you come up with 54 percent of the Star-Telegram's resource base." [12]

Osborne declined to tell Texas Monthly and others – including our staff – how much Belo paid for the Arlington launch, but estimates were less than half what the Star-Telegram spent on its expansion. We didn't get dog tags but did receive some AMN shirts and mugs. Belo paid for a fancy launch party at a suite at The Ballpark in Arlington, which kept super office manager Yolanda Young, among others, busy. The budget included sending reporters to Puerto Rico for features on Rangers stars Juan González and Pudge Rodríguez and to New York to cover the team's first playoff games. For former Arlington News staffers, it was a stark contrast to when our operation was all-but forgotten in a decrepit, environmentally-questionable building that once housed a printing press in northeast Arlington's warehouse district.

By that June, the AST had about 42,500 daily subscribers, more than double our circulation. But Osborne told Texas Monthly that he was pleased: "We're much further along than our projections. It's a matter of years, more than one year but less than 50." [13]

Star-Telegram execs insisted the AMN was not its own paper but a supplement, even though we met standards such as separate registration with the Audit Bureau of Circulations. Meanwhile, they claimed the AST was more than a zoned edition. "This is not just a fight for Arlington, it's a fight for the future of the Star-Telegram, and we will never give up. Never," AST publisher Michael "Mac" Tully told the Times in 1996. But in 1999, as the battle continued amid indications showing that the AST was still comfortably ahead, he walked away to become publisher of a Florida paper. [14]

At the 1996 launch of the AST during the city's annual Fourth of July parade, Tully, dressed in a George Washington costume and sweating profusely, approached Gary and some others. He flaunted the paper's lavish float, trying to compare the AST's presence to ours, in which we just had people handing out copies of the AMN. "We choose to put the money into the editorial product," Gary told Tully, who had no comeback.

Herb's coffee passed through his nose as he stifled a laugh and noted, "Gary's response was so perfect, so utterly effortless." [15]

The last great Texas newspaper war started with a colorful upgrade in 1996. Photo by Kevin Shay

A work of art

"Why did we not have that fucking story?" Lawrence was in good form during one of several daily editors meetings. The AST had a story about the Arlington school district we didn't have. And he was livid. "How can we let the fucking Star-Telegram beat us? We're fucking better than them! We fucking own this city! We fucking own this story! We can't let this fucking happen!"

Sometimes in the midst of one of his almost daily f-bomb performances, I wanted to stand up and start a slow appreciative clap. But I never dared. I was afraid Lawrence might take it the wrong way and throw me through a wall. Some people let loose with profanity, and it seems out-of-place. Being relatively quiet and mostly business-like at work, I was among those. For others, you looked at them like there was something wrong if they didn't issue a few f-bombs every couple sentences.

When Lawrence was on a roll, some took it too personally. To me, he took venting to another level; it was a thing of beauty, a work of art. He was M.C. Hammer at Oakland Coliseum, Leonard Bernstein at Carnegie Hall, Bruno Mars at Super Bowl XLVII, Van Gogh painting Starry Night. If you looked at it objectively and weren't the direct target, you had to shake your head and marvel.

But in reality, most just tried not to make eye contact and kind of nodded along. "Yes, we will do better," we would repeat. "We will make it happen."

I met Lawrence almost a decade earlier. He was a hungry political reporter for the Morning News, having grown up in Akron, Ohio, also the hometown of John Brown and LeBron James. He became an Air Force sergeant and military policeman in California, earned a bachelor's degree in journalism from California State University, Northridge, and completed some graduate work. He worked for the Wilkes-Barre Times Leader, Arlington Citizen-Journal, and Fort Worth Star-Telegram before joining the Morning News. At the DMN, he would cover politics for four years, then become editor of the Mid-Cities bureau and rise to political editor and assistant national editor.

At the time we met, I was editor of the humble weekly Addison-North Dallas Register. We both covered the same community meeting, and I was impressed that Lawrence didn't act like I was beneath him because of where we worked. We met up more after that, including during a landmark political lawsuit trial in 1989. We both spent long hours talking Dallas politics with Roy Williams, the local dean of civil rights advocacy and one of the plaintiffs in the suit.

Lawrence was always friendly and encouraging, invoking an enthusiasm that made you know he lived and breathed the newspaper business. His passion was infectious and rekindled some of that fire I first grasped covering a speech by esteemed Pulitzer Prize-winning reporter Seymour Hersh in my 1979 college days. My then-wife, Michelle, and I sometimes dined with Lawrence and his wife, Margie. Though I attempted to stay away from political labels, believing that most people's beliefs were more complex and nebulous, Michelle and I were usually considered liberal Democrats, especially by Texas standards where even a moderate Democrat was branded a pinko-loving commie. The Young's were considered moderate Republicans but were more open than most. Margie rarely talked politics, but Lawrence – a board member of the National Association of Minority Media Executives and Newspaper Association of America diversity board, among others – was all over that subject. Sometimes, I observed diners at other tables glancing at him as his booming voice relayed a seemingly endless array of facts and opinions in an authoritative manner that likely enthralled them as much as me.

While he voiced his views passionately, he always listened thoughtfully to another side. We bonded, going to Rangers games and each other's south Arlington homes. Margie ran a travel business, and we employed her services for a cruise and other trips. I got to know and understand more about what drove Lawrence. He was as sincere and passionate about the newspaper business as anyone I've ever met. He also loved sports, especially basketball, and jazz music, so we usually found common ground.

Lori Price, who joined the AMN in 1999, sometimes called Lawrence a used-car salesman, but in a good way, writing that he had "the incredible ability of making anyone he talks to feel like they can accomplish anything." He usually had time for anyone who walked into his office, sometimes too much time. Valerie, who started as religion editor, wrote that there were many meetings with Lawrence when he said this "won't take but a minute" and ended up being an hour. He "pushed me to make just one more phone call," sometimes at midnight, "to get my stories just right," she noted. [16]

Gary had a different approach that was likely as effective. A tongue-in-cheek article written by his business staff noted that he was known as the "stealth" editor in recognition of his "uncanny ability to manage The Dallas Morning News business staff without ever visibly moving – or talking or even turning on his computer." [17]

But he moved around the AMN a lot and worked as hard, if not harder, than anyone. Gary rarely made an appearance in our editors' staff meetings, not wanting to step on Lawrence's toes. He kept busy working with Russ, Herb, and Leonidas Patterson on the editorial page, with Todd Wills, Mark Konradi, Kevin Lonnquist, and others in sports, with June in advertising, and with Osborne and downtown execs. He often left copies of our stories with encouraging notes and constructive criticism in our mailboxes, back in those pre-email days. Pennie said the notes were sparse enough to mean something when receiving them, and she had saved each one.

"It's a tough racket," was his trademark phrase that a couple sports columnists worked into their prose. "When in doubt, grin," was another Gary technique. Some called that grin a little scary and could not tell if it was really a smirk, but it was effective.

In one of my first days on the job, Gary handed me a letter from a resident complaining about columns I had written for the Arlington News and requesting that Gary not hire "an extremely negative and depressing kid." It was not just a slight against me, as I was well past the "kid" stage at 37 years old, but a campaign to derail my career. In particular, this reader attached a column on a primary election in which I made a general reference to it being "hard for me to decide whether to cast my vote with the swine that is less repugnant or sit this one out." I didn't call any particular politician swine, which would be as much an insult to pigs as pols. It was just a more colorful word that I sometimes use to avoid rewriting the same old prose.

"Here's one from someone who's not a fan," Gary deadpanned, handing me the letter. That was the only thing he said and the last I heard about it.

"Gary is the ultimate professional," Lawrence once told me. "I wouldn't have come over to Arlington without Gary here."

Michael Landauer, who joined the AMN in 1997 as a copy editor and editorial writer and continued to work with the DMN until 2016, wrote that in his first conversation with Gary, he asked about some guest columns he had submitted and whether there was anything he needed to change to get him to run them. Gary replied, "Well, who are you? Why should the readers give a shit about what you say?"

Michael wrote, "His straight talk has made me and everyone who has worked with him a better journalist." [18]

That straight talk included almost as much profanity as Lawrence issued – Wills said in his first interview with Gary he counted something like 522 f-bombs, which may have been a slight exaggeration. "He gave us story ideas and work ideas," wrote Todd. "He ripped us when we needed it. He applauded us when we needed it." [19]

Gary also visited him in the hospital when Todd broke his leg. "We went places together, like the Tarrant County judicial barbecue," he said. "We pounded down a few beers there."

Doug Pils, who not only worked in sports during his AMN stint but was business editor and night city editor for a time, recalled a closed-door meeting also involving Todd, Mark, and Cameron Maun about not meeting deadlines. Gary smiled and laughed at first, then he suddenly slammed his hand to the desk and issued "that glare," Doug wrote.

"We went back and did our best to make deadline. Of course, we busted on almost every game night, but Gary understood our plight," said Doug, who was also among those who met his future spouse, Honny, at the AMN. "He let us learn and grow in an exciting environment. He gave us the opportunity of a lifetime: To start a sports section from scratch our way." [20]

Within a few months, the AMN had not just become a real daily newspaper but moved its headquarters to a new office on Interstate 30 that was even closer to The Ballpark, Six Flags, and site of the future "Jerry World" Dallas Cowboys Stadium. It was so close you could walk to the Rangers headquarters, which I sometimes did just to take a break from the madness inside. The AMN was the largest tenant of that four-story structure, taking up most of the top floor. We put our nameplate on the outside of the building so the thousands of commuters stuck in traffic on the highway could see where to target us.

As we attempted to figure out how to best erode the Star-Telegram's Arlington foothold, top editors and reporters journeyed from Dallas to dispense advice and encouragement. Gilbert Bailon, executive editor at the DMN who broke barriers for Hispanics in the industry and later became editor of the St. Louis Post-Dispatch and WBEZ Chicago, was among the visiting regulars. So was award-winning investigative reporter Brooks Eggerton.

Awards were important to Lawrence, who earned a Lifetime Achievement Award for Education from the Dallas/Fort Worth Association of Black Communicators and three Katie Awards from the Dallas Press Club. There was always a big production about entering contests. The AMN even named a "Reporter of the Year," which created its own competition.

Lawrence Young, right, discusses politics with Dallas civil rights advocate Roy Williams and his wife, Nancy. Photo by Kevin Shay

Points of contention

The first year of any new venture was usually its most important, as about one-third of businesses go under in their first two years, according to the U.S. Small Business Administration. While some such as Tracy left before our one-year anniversary, most stayed and built chemistry.

At previous newspaper jobs, I worked such long hours I didn't want to hang out with most colleagues. But it was different at the AMN. For some reason, perhaps related to being a participant in a publicly-declared "war," many of us bonded. For a Saturday party celebrating a house in Arlington that Michelle and me purchased in late 1996, there must have been 50 attendees. Half of those were AMNers. It was awesome.

Like any "family," we had our share of disagreements, some worse than others. While the flareups could certainly hurt morale, they also got issues out in the open and even lent confidence that we would survive to fight another day.

One of the more dramatic incidents I was involved in came in early 1997. Back in those days, reporters and editors had beepers attached to their belts, rather than cell phones in their pockets. Mine went off late one Sunday night, after I had returned home to veg in front of SportsCenter.

I called the number, and Elise Anthony, a bright, young copy editor who would soon be promoted to the DMN, answered. "We're not going to run the Dalworthington Gardens story," she said.

I was taken aback. The story by Larry, who would soon join the Atlanta Journal-Constitution and remain there for 14 years, was on a third suspect named in the killing of a local couple in their 60s. Herb, who was night editor on Sundays, and I had combed through the article, made a few changes, and thought it was fine. "What? Who made that decision?"

"I called Lawrence, and he told me to take it off."

"Why wasn't I called first? I'm the Sunday editor."

"Well, I'm sorry.... I just thought it was something Lawrence should review."

I was livid. The next morning, I wrote a memo to Lawrence and Elise, whose main contention seemed to be over naming the third suspect. I pointed out that a DMN story had named him previously.

"I thought the process was that whoever edits the story on the city desk is called if there is a question on the copy desk," I wrote. "I was not called first in this case, only afterwards by Elise, who told me the decision to pull the story was already made. I do not mind so much that the story was pulled as I do that Herb and me did not have any input into making that decision."

When I came in for my night shift on Tuesday, Lawrence asked me to meet with him. "Elise was right to call me," he said. "Just because The Dallas Morning News names a suspect, we shouldn't name that suspect unless he is actually charged with a crime. We have our own standards. We're the Arlington Morning News, not The Dallas Morning News."

"That's fine," I replied. "But Herb and I are the city editors that day, and we should have been included in the process."

Lawrence shook his head. "In most cases, I agree. But not in this case. There are times when the copy desk needs to contact me directly. Elise felt the city desk wasn't going to do anything, so she called me." He was calm, not even cussing. I saw I wasn't going to win this debate and let it go.

That night was hellacious, even for our standards. City Hall reporter Kim Horner, who had started in October after Amy left and would become an assistant editor before joining the DMN directly for more than a dozen years, had her car in the shop. Somehow, I was the only person available to pick her up from a City Hall meeting so she could return to the office. Darrin, who did both business reporting and city editing, had to finish writing a story. Two other reporters were at late meetings.

About ten minutes before our 10:30 p.m. copy deadline, we still had six stories out. Two of those were being edited by Lawrence, who stormed out of his office. "How come we have six fucking stories still out?" he yelled, as the newsroom became deathly quiet. "What the fuck is going on here?" He motioned to Felicia Pinkney, a news and copy editor who would go on to work at the DMN and FWST. "Give me a printout of all stories out later than 10:30."

A few minutes later, Lawrence returned and approached me to ask what the problem was.

"We had three late meetings," I replied, not bothering to mention that two of the stories out were ones by April and Rani Monson that he was editing. "We're doing the best we can."

"It's not good enough!" Lawrence yelled. "We need to have a long fucking meeting about meeting deadlines and copy flow!"

Later after all stories were put to bed, Darrin asked if I wanted to go have a beer. "Uh, thanks, but Michelle is on me enough for coming home so late. Just wait till you get married."

Darrin, who met his future wife, Julie Miley – who became a physician – at the AMN, laughed. "That was a bullshit scene, huh?"

"Yeah, it was bullshit," I agreed.

"The last story out was April's at 10:59. That story and Rani's should have been in long before that."

"No doubt."

The next day, Martha Flores, the new deputy city editor, and Christopher told me they met with Lawrence. "We should have delayed one of the late stories until today," said Christopher, who had become a co-deputy city editor. "When we have three late meetings like that, we need to tell Lawrence beforehand."

"Did Lawrence say that two of the stories out late were ones he edited?" I asked.

"No," said Christopher, a sharp colleague who I bonded with as a fellow Lake Highlands High alum. He would leave in 1998 for a Florida paper and marry Melanie Busch, who covered transportation. He would become an editor for the St. Louis Post-Dispatch and direct media at the University of Missouri. "I know there are definitely other issues at play here. But we still need to communicate better with Lawrence about this."

At the afternoon meeting, Lawrence issued a profanity-laced spiel that was more animated than usual. "We blew our fucking deadline by 39 minutes!" he exclaimed at one point. "That was the worst fucking performance on deadline I've seen since we've been here!"

No one else said anything. So I had to say something. In most meetings, I remained fairly quiet, not wanting to add to their length. But there were times when I should have spoken up, such as when we decided to make the lead front-page story on Jack-in-the-Box releasing some "stealth fries." We justifiably got raked over in the Fort Worth Weekly over that.

"I should have pushed Cliff and the others more to get their stories in earlier," I offered. "But I also think when we have three late meetings, we need to get all non-meeting stories in well before deadline."

"We have to get all stories in early, whether they are late meetings or not," Lawrence said.

"Yes, but I think especially non-meeting stories," I responded.

Darrin then voiced a similar position. Lawrence moved on to other topics, such as a photographer who blew up at a reporter in front of people.

That evening, we pushed all stories over by 10:15 p.m. In the next day's afternoon staff meeting, Lawrence praised us for meeting deadline. But that night, we had three more late meetings. Rather than addressing Darrin, Lawrence approached Elise to ask her to message Darrin on our computer system to get in the story he was editing. Later, he returned to ask Elise if an Associated Press story on Ebonics was running. Elise said she didn't know and looked my way.

I turned. "Why don't you ask me? Yeah, it's running."

Lawrence ignored me, saying to Elise, "Can you make sure you put a reference on April's Ebonics story to the AP one?" We would soon make up. I couldn't stay angry at Lawrence for long. I knew he had a difficult job and was tasked with an almost impossible mission against an established opponent willing to spend significantly more than us in its backyard.

Off deadline, Darrin and I vented in a hallway. "If Lawrence wants to make Elise night editor, she can have it," said Darrin, who would soon leave to become the San Antonio Express-News' business editor.

"I'd like to ride it out," I said. I wanted to see how this war ended. Back in my Boy Scout days, we had toured a DMN printing press. The fast pace, noise, and smell of ink fascinated me. I had a neighborhood paper route throwing the Times Herald for a couple years in my teens. At Richland College, I caught the bug writing for the school paper. Working for the DMN/AMN wasn't my ultimate dream, but it was one goal.

In the back of my mind, I suspected it would culminate like author and former Dallas Cowboys receiver Pete Gent said, when he told a rookie during a 1960s practice to not bother reading the NFL team's playbook.

"Everybody gets killed in the end," Gent said.

Official complaints

The internal and deadline pressures were not the only forces at work. Officials not used to closer scrutiny voiced objections fairly often to upper management. Gary noted in the video that during one week in the fall of 1996, Arlington's mayor, police chief, superintendent of schools, and chamber president all called him to complain about our coverage. "That's when I knew we had arrived as a newspaper," Gary said.

Lynn Hale, superintendent of the Arlington school district from 1993 until 1998, made such complaints on a fairly regular basis. In an August 1997 letter to Martha, Hale charged that Tra, who was covering schools, deliberately "wrote negative implications about my character." Tra's "crime" was to mistakenly cite the wrong month that Hale announced she would leave the Arlington district, which Hale thought left an impression that she "was trying to benefit my future employment." [21]

Tra, who had written stories that Hale didn't like on a controversial policy that banned students caught with alcohol from sports and other extracurricular activities and on teens using liquid ecstasy, agreed to send Hale a letter apologizing for including the wrong month. But Hale wrote that she would return it "unopened" and charged that the AMN had "deliberately attempted to discredit" her. The situation would not be resolved to her satisfaction before Hale left.

In the one-year video, then Mayor Richard Greene complained about wondering at times if our role model was the National Enquirer and charged that certain reporters wrote stories on flimsy accusations that had "no basis." Arlington

Chamber of Commerce president David Sampson recalled having to field some angry calls from business execs after they read a story by Darrin and Chris about GM supplier Lear Seating Corp. seeking to build a local facility. But they also offered compliments, with Greene saying our staff overall was "very capable."

Gary noted in the video that the AMN was still "the adventure of a lifetime for me," and he liked the attitude of staffers who take an idea "and run with it." At the DMN and some other places he worked, he said he was more used to people spending "half an hour telling you why it can't be done."

He and Osborne told an Advertising Age reporter they were pleased with the paper's reception and progress a year into its birth. DeRousse also told a reporter for the Newspaper Association of America's Presstime that advertising growth exceeded expectations. [22]

By August 1997, I no longer had to concern myself with complaints and other matters as an editor since I transferred to the business department to be a reporter. I still dealt with some back-tracking officials, including one spokesperson who claimed we had never spoken about a proposed merger, when we had. The job didn't take me to Puerto Rico or New York but to Austin, where I covered some economic development commission meetings involving Sampson.

In between my AMN editing and reporting duties and writing travel articles for the DMN, I coordinated our participation in Corporate Challenge, a series of athletic competitions between area companies. Our basketball team, comprised of staffers from mostly sports such as both Mark's, Doug, Cameron, Herb, Chris Velez, Danny Woodward, and Rick Kretzschmar, placed second a couple years. We competed against mostly larger employers like Johnson & Johnson and Doskocil. Following one last-second win in which Chris tipped in the winning basket, we all returned to work as was our custom. Lawrence, of course, was there, and he razzed us mercilessly about "letting" Velez score the winning basket.

Doug was probably the best all-around athlete among us. One year, he also won medals in volleyball, golf, and cycling, and would have had a fifth in the 5K had another male participant entered. Herb also medaled in golf and bowling, while I won additional medals in volleyball and the tug-of-war. Mark Konradi, Cameron, and I also ventured to Dallas to compete in the three-on-three Hoop It Up highly competitive tournament. There were other camaraderie-building events, such as karaoke night at local bars and parties at Russ and Tra's Arlington house, which later was destroyed in a tornado, and Tamara's Deep Ellum rooftop.

While some stayed for years, the AMN did have its share of revolving doors, which is typical at most daily newspapers. City editors rarely stayed for more than a year. Numerous copy and news editors were promoted to the DMN in a relatively short time, including Marc, Elise, Felicia, Mike Luman, and Gretchen Perrenot. Others who left included photog Tony Gutierrez, who went to the AP in 1998; Chris Payne, who transferred about the same time to the Garland bureau;

Bill Swindell, who came from the Tulsa World in 1997 to cover business for about a year before leaving for publications in South Carolina, Washington, D.C., and California; and Rosa, who left in 1999 for the Cleveland Plain Dealer and later worked in California. Jason Trahan covered crime for the AMN in 1999 then soon moved over to the DMN and eventually WFAA to produce award-winning investigative pieces. Reese Dunklin interned at the AMN before joining the St. Louis Post-Dispatch, DMN, and The Associated Press. Melissa Taboada also interned with the AMN in 1997 before embarking on a long stint at the Austin American-Statesman, then becoming an editor with the Boston Globe and Austin Current.

A key loss to Lawrence was April's departure in early 1999. In a memo to the AMN staff, Lawrence wrote that "no one embraced the newspaper's values and vision more than Mrs. Washington." He praised her "tremendous work ethic, passion and commitment to excellence" and wrote that she had turned down "numerous jobs" since joining the AMN, but the Rocky Mountain News made her "an offer she couldn't refuse."

Lawrence also glowingly praised others, such as Kim, who was hired by the DMN. He mentioned how I was taking over not just April's politics beat but Melanie's transportation duties. Prior to that move, I had been doing more general assignments and plugging holes as people left, even being interim business editor for a few months. At the same time, I rewrote a book with Roy on Dallas area civil rights history that was published in 1999 by a Fort Worth company.

We quickly filled openings. Donald Lee joined as a copy editor from the Kansas City Star in late 1996 and also wrote columns. Jenni Smith transferred from the Irving News in 1998, covering tourism and transportation, among other beats. Ben Tinsley, whose father, Jack Tinsley, had been a top editor at the FWST, came aboard in early 1999 to cover police and courts. Bob Schober arrived in 1999 from the Bryan-College Station Eagle, covering city hall and courts, then business. Jennifer Arend also joined us in 1999 after completing an internship with the DMN business department.

By late 1999, I noticed signs that we were ramping down and not doing as well as hoped. Some vacated positions were combined. Hiring and travel slowed. More unpaid interns joined.

An Editor & Publisher article noted that the AST still held a significant daily circulation edge over us at some 51,000 to 27,000, though Gary said readership was about equal in certain sought-after zip codes. He was quoted in that story saying, "We've done better every year, and we're ahead of plan in many areas." Bob Mong, who would become DMN editor in 2001, was quoted saying Belo execs were still going to "be patient." Meanwhile, the Star-Telegram enticed sports columnist Randy Galloway away from the DMN and ran his column in the AST. [23]

Like me, many took on multiple duties. As a reporter, Eric covered almost every beat, from city hall to crime. When he made the move to night city editor in 1999, he still covered some court cases and wrote numerous crime-related stories. Russ transferred from editorials to business editor to city editor by 2001, and was covering Irving schools when he left the DMN in 2005. Pennie, Valerie, and Patrick Wascovich, who covered a variety of topics from sports and schools to transportation, also filled in as city editors at times.

Taking on the workload that two reporters formerly held, my expectations were high. Though I won awards for various articles and was named the AMN "Reporter of the Year" for 1999, it never seemed to be enough. I also contributed a couple articles to the DMN state desk, traveling as far as Wichita Falls, and helped with stories that made the DMN's front page, such as an Arlington police officer killed in a training exercise.

At times, my supervising editor, Judy Howard, told me I needed to do better, without giving much specifics. I liked Judy and other editors such as Robin Yearwood and Eric, and knew what kind of pressure they were under. They had been more than supportive when I proposed doing a story on stammering and other speech problems after a sports reporter had imitated a coach's halting speech to a big laugh during a staff lunch. I didn't think the joke was funny, having worked hard throughout my life to control a stutter, though many thought the joke was harmless and not directed at anyone except the coach. My response was to provide some education and awareness through a lengthy article.

I complained some when they made us do a basic reporting exercise called SPOON, which stood for "Send People Out of the Office Now." As much as once a week, editors would create movie posters like one related to *Shaft* and hang them on the wall. They would dress all in black and have us draw a theme from a bowl, then go out and pull a story from our asses, usually one that was never used.

Most of us understood what they were trying to accomplish with such an exercise in pushing us to develop better reporting skills and make sure we "hit the streets" for our stories. But most still considered SPOON more appropriate for a college course. After all, we were already overworked. We'd come up with different meanings for the acronym, such as "Shit and Piss On Other Neanderthals." Once when I was ten minutes late for a SPOON exercise, Judy lectured me on setting a better example for younger reporters. Another time when I vented too loudly to a colleague about needing to spend time working rather than doing an exercise, I had to speak to Lawrence, who agreed I shouldn't have to do SPOON as much since I had numerous complicated enterprise stories to complete.

The situation reached a point that I conducted a byline study. In a six-week period from April to mid-May 2000, I averaged five bylines a week, with my stories averaging 22 inches long and almost six sources. That ranked me fifth among 13 AMN reporters, ranging from a high of eight per week by Julie Elliott, who started interning in 1998 and joined us full-time in 1999, to a low of two a week by someone whose stories averaged 23 inches and almost five sources. I wanted some ammunition the next time I was told I needed to do better.

I figured Judy, Robin, and Eric were under increasing pressure from Lawrence, who was under increasing pressure from Gary, who was under increasing pressure from Osborne and others, as finances tightened and they didn't see the results they had once expected. I soon tired of the added workload in covering two beats and in 2000 moved back to business, which faced a significant void after Tamara and Rani left for the Delaware News Journal and Yahoo, respectively.

Then my son, Preston, was born two months prematurely. My world and priorities were in for a drastic shift. And so was the AMN.

The AMN/DMN staff picnic in 2001, shortly before the end of the newspaper war. Photo by Tom Fox, DMN

Belo buying binge, then retreat

Belo execs were not content with starting a newspaper war on their western front. About a year after launching the AMN, the company paid $1.5 billion for The Providence Journal Co., comprised of nine TV stations and Rhode Island's largest daily newspaper. It was the largest transaction in company history. Also in 1997, Belo acquired The Press-Enterprise, a daily newspaper outside Los Angeles, as well as TV stations in San Antonio and St. Louis.

When Belo's net earnings dropped by 5 percent to $83 million in 1997 and then fell another 22 percent to $65 million in 1998, shareholder pressure intensified. But when earnings rose to $178 million in 1999, Belo continued buying properties, such as the Denton Record-Chronicle and an Austin TV station.

The company also debuted the Texas Cable News channel in 1999, broadcasting to some 600,000 area households. Belo even invested in the Dallas Mavericks NBA team and a new sports arena.

In 2000, buoyed by a $151 million profit, Belo went too far with its $37 million investment in Digital Convergence Corp., which made something called a CueCat. The hand-held device was designed to allow readers to scan a bar code on a newspaper and get more information online. Perhaps Belo execs and CueCat designers failed to take into account that not many people then wanted to read a newspaper while sitting at their computers, much less scan for more details. They should have known something was funny when the CueCat's inventor, J. Jovan Philyaw, wanted to be called J. Hutton Pulitzer.

In 2001, Belo had to write off the CueCat investment, among the reasons why it showed a $2.7 million loss that year, the company's first yearly loss in more than a decade. In 2006, PC World ranked the CueCat 20th on a list of the "25 Worst Tech Products of All Time." But it wasn't deemed to be worse than some, including America Online, which topped that list. Later, some partly blamed Radio Shack's $30 million investment in the CueCat for the retailer's 2015 bankruptcy filing. [24]

Meanwhile, the AMN's circulation had not grown as much as Belo execs hoped. Almost five years after our launch, we had increased daily circulation by only about 9,000. While that was a slightly higher growth rate than the AST, the other paper still held almost a two-to-one readership edge.

In early 2001, Belo announced we would cut back to five days a week and become a DMN zoned edition starting in April. In a memo, Mong wrote that the DMN's "daily and Sunday penetration [in Arlington] are at an all-time high," but only "a couple of thousand" readers had subscribed just to the AMN while DMN subscribers automatically received the AMN. Eliminating AMN-only home delivery and single sales "will allow our circulation department to concentrate on what has been the main event all along – the combination paper," he said. Cutting back to five days "makes a lot more economic sense."

Mong praised advertising sales and editorial content. "With the advent of the AMN, Arlington went from being one of the worst covered cities of its size in America, to one of the best covered," he said. He pledged that the AMN will continue to be "just as ambitious, newsy and community-oriented" and play "an even bigger role" in the DMN's growth.

But most didn't read that as good news. Belo had included the Arlington Morning News in its annual report from 1997 to 1999, but in 2000 wrote only that "the company has other operations in Arlington" and stopped mentioning Arlington entirely beginning in 2001. And then we retreated from our highly-visible office building off a major freeway to the environmentally-challenged warehouse where the Arlington News had holed up. All that was left to do was to raise the white flag.

Publicly, Gary insisted we were not backing away from the area. "We're still going to cover the hell out of Arlington and Grand Prairie and Mansfield," he told Editor & Publisher. [25]

But the main problem we faced was that most readers in Arlington "lean west," Hardee, who had been promoted to AST associate publisher, told the Dallas Observer. "They identify with Tarrant County. Most of them in Grand Prairie, where I live, lean east. I don't know how many times Belo has come into Tarrant County, tried to convince readers to switch papers, and failed. But I do know this: We won't come into Dallas County and try to do what they've done. It doesn't work." [26]

Privately, most of us were in job-searching mode. Eric moved over to the DMN in March to be assistant Metro editor, a position he would retain more than seven years. Ben switched to covering police and courts for the Star-Telegram that same month. Others, such as Julie, joined the DMN.

By August 2001, Lawrence found a new job, returning to California as managing editor of the Press-Enterprise in Riverside. His going-away reception wasn't in a Ballpark suite like in our heyday, but at a local hotel ballroom.

Gary left that same month for an editor position back at the DMN and would retire gracefully to Austin in 2015. In early 2001, features writer Kathy Goolsby, a veteran of the Grand Prairie News who wrote for the DMN until 2009, asked him while riding to a Rotary Club meeting what he'd like to do after the AMN. He replied he'd like to start another newspaper, that he enjoyed that excitement and challenge. No AMN founding staff members she had spoken with "ever seemed anxious to return to those [early] days – no one, that is, except Gary," Kathy wrote. "But he wistfully admitted that today's economy means newspapers are cutting down rather than expanding into new endeavors, so he didn't foresee such a job opening up for him."

Great job, here's your pink slip

A month before September 11 hit, the DMN's business section decided to take over the suburban business coverage. I started reporting to the DMN assistant business editor, traveling to downtown Dallas headquarters for regular staff meetings.

The tragedy was felt in many ways, including on the bottom line at newspapers like ours. In a letter to employees ten days afterwards, Belo CEO Robert Decherd praised our coverage but noted that advertising had already slowed before Sept. 11 and was expected to really decline in the next few months.

"Just as many of Belo's customers are reducing advertising expenditures to accommodate unwelcome shifts in their businesses, we must also calibrate our expenses to reflect revenue production in today's environment," he said. "Everyone is being asked to rethink the ordinary way of doing business, and in most cases, to curb hiring, expenses and equipment purchases for the foreseeable future." [27]

On October 10, Decherd penned a more ominous letter in which he said advertising revenues had "retreated to 1999 levels." He announced eliminating 160 jobs "later this month" and a one-year wage freeze, saying that would "accelerate the crucial process of aligning Belo's expenses with expected revenue generation."

Though the company showed a relatively small loss that year, profits would return in 2002 close to the 2000 level. Decherd himself pulled in $1.6 million in total compensation in 2001, about one-third less than in 2000. But in 2002, his bonus of $1.3 million more than doubled his bonus in 2000, and total compensation ballooned past his 2000 level.

Meanwhile, Osborne left that year for an AP position, though Belo paid him almost $1 million in 2002 to be a consultant. Sadly, he would pass away in 2012 at the relatively young age of 75 following a sudden illness.

In early October, I traveled to Austin with my dad to accept an award from the American Cancer Society for some stories on new treatments at an Arlington center. Dad, who was battling prostate cancer and other ailments, also accompanied us on a long weekend trip to New Mexico in which he, mother-in-law Adele, and Preston viewed the largest hot-air balloon festival in the world for the first time. Michelle and I had gone there several times, including a 1998 trip that involved a ride in a balloon at that festival that I chronicled for the AMN.

In late October, I received an email from DMN Business Editor Ed Dufner, who wanted to meet in person. I knew that wasn't good news. I wrote an email to Kenny to alert him about the meeting, as if he didn't know, and to say, "Been nice working with you, if I do get laid off." I took my time on the drive to Dallas, not in any hurry to make this meeting. Walking through the DMN newsroom towards Dufner's office, I could feel the heat of colleagues' eyes upon me as if I was a death row inmate. From the corner of the newsroom, beneath the eerie glow of incandescent lighting, I could almost hear a guard yell, "Dead man walking!"

I don't remember much of what Dufner said, except it seemed like he was reciting a script he had memorized, which was pretty much the case. Deputy Business Editor Dennis Fulton was also there I guess in case I went ballistic, but he didn't say much. Some HR employee handed me a packet. They asked if I had any questions.

I asked if the termination had anything to do with my performance. Dufner replied that it had to do with "several factors" but declined to say much more, except to stick to the script that its main cause was a "workforce reduction." I didn't want to prolong this exchange. I just wanted out of there. I was especially mad at how Dufner made me drive the round trip between Arlington and Dallas, rather than him venture out there to break the news.

As I suspected and later confirmed, I was the only one laid off from the DMN business department that day. And, to make it worse, this guy was not only terminating me, but making me drive an extra 30 miles just to hear that news. I would have rather he had emailed the news than force me to walk back through the DMN newsroom humiliated.

In a 2004 "workforce reduction" action that affected 65 people in the DMN newsroom, people stayed glued to desks for news and cried with coworkers as they received the call, according to a story in American Journalism Review by Charles Layton. Those layoffs occurred as Belo disclosed that the DMN had overstated circulation figures and agreed to reimburse advertisers by $23 million, another report in Columbia Journalism Review by Craig Flournoy and Tracy Everbach reported. Belo also withdrew from its cable partnerships after spending $10 million annually on them. [28]

The drive back to Arlington did allow me to clear my head somewhat. Some in that bureau were in tears, but I didn't feel that type of emotion. I actually sported a weird grin to the point that Kathy, in tears herself over the layoffs though she was among survivors, asked how I could be smiling.

I didn't have a good answer. "Aw, it's not worth crying about," I finally said. I actually felt more relief than anything else on that day. In some odd way, I appreciated Uncle Belo. He did pay me more than any other paper I had worked for, some of which didn't even reimburse for mileage for driving my own car to meetings and events. Still, there was a dark side to Uncle Belo, one whose victims usually didn't identify and prepare for until it was too late.

Later in my daydreams, I stormed into the Belo board room and told off some execs. But those were mere dreams, scenes that mostly only play out in the movies. My last action before leaving the Arlington bureau was to rip down an award plaque I won for some air pollution stories that had been placed on the wall. It appropriately left a hole among the other plaques still remaining.

Bob, who survived the layoff but soon took a position with a Colorado paper, wrote an email to Belo exec James Moroney III, who had sent a message to employees saying, "While I regret the need to take this [layoff] action, I am confident this was the right decision on behalf of The Dallas Morning News." Bob replied that he had been a sales representative and business owner who had to lay off workers, before deciding to enter journalism at age 48. He wrote that it was bad judgment to eliminate strictly by positions and not by low-performing individuals.

"The company cut highly-skilled reporters, who were unfortunate enough to occupy positions that were determined to be expendable," Bob said. "That decision undoubtedly leaves other less-skilled, less-motivated and less-tenured employees in jobs. How choosing slot over competence will improve the company, morale and especially journalistic excellence escapes me." [29]

Besides such moral support, we received financial support of about $1,000 each from a fund drive headed by DMN columnist and author Steve Blow, who retired in 2015, and Pulitzer Prize-winning investigative reporter and author Howard Swindle, who tragically died of cancer in 2004 at age 58. The support was great, but the anger did not subside much as I tried to figure out what to do next. I soon learned that my position was not really being eliminated, but a younger reporter replaced me while also covering northeast Tarrant County. I couldn't just move on.

I consulted a lawyer and in January 2002 filed a complaint with the Texas Commission on Human Rights, alleging discrimination based on my age and speech problem. I charged that I was essentially fired since I had almost ten years of service with Belo and had a speaking difficulty that would not lend me as a good candidate to go on on Belo's cable station to talk about stories I wrote, though I had done that before. I attempted to come up with anything to make a case, though I knew winning this in Texas' right-to-work environment would be extremely difficult. But winning wasn't my goal. Making some managers squirm, admit more of the truth, and examine more closely what they were doing were among my goals. And finding a way to stand up for myself.

It was only by filing that complaint that I confirmed I was the only one laid off among 54 people in the DMN business department. Of the 160 terminated employees, about half came from the Morning News. Besides me, Pennie, Gene Abrahamson, who had 29 years at mostly the Belo suburban papers and once told me he felt more like an outsider at the AMN, and Shelly Moon, who had worked for the News for almost seven years, were among casualties.

Dufner and Fulton chose me to be laid off because they judged me to possess "the weakest writing skills" among suburban business reporters, according to a response to my complaint by Belo human resources manager Sandi Scott. I didn't buy that. I had won my share of awards. Kenny had written praise for my work on the response to the Sept. 11 terrorist acts and the American Cancer Society award. Kenny had only supervised me for about three months and never told me I needed to improve my writing skills or even did a formal evaluation of my work. There were less-experienced reporters who did not get laid off, including some I had supervised as an AMN assistant editor. [30]

I kept some Belo lawyers and human resources and editorial managers busy for almost two years, detailing responses to their points and objections. Besides the state office, I got the federal Equal Employment Opportunity Commission to review my case. In late 2003, the state commission and EEOC finally gave up and closed their reviews because investigators were "unable to conclude that the information obtained establishes violations of the statutes."

But the offices allowed that they could not certify that Belo was "in compliance with the statutes." I considered that a moral victory and wasn't aware of anyone else among the 2001 layoff class fighting Belo to the extent I did.

In 2006, some 18 former DMN employees who were terminated in 2004, including columnist Larry Powell, editorial cartoonist Bill DeOre, and feature writer Linda Jones, filed an age discrimination lawsuit against Belo in a federal court. Like me, they were told their positions were being eliminated, then they were replaced by younger people. They kept the case alive for five years before a judge dismissed it.

About the same time I filed the complaint, I won $500 in a national book manuscript contest for my 700-page account of a transcontinental walk for peace I joined in 1984 and 1985. I started a website called Layoff Watch in which I monitored major job layoffs nationwide and traced them to company performance to show if the business was really doing as bad as execs claimed. I wrote articles for the Fort Worth Weekly, Dallas Business Journal, Dallas Child, Dallas Examiner, and other publications. I received a contract to write *A Parent's Guide to Dallas-Fort Worth* from a Los Angeles publisher of similar books nationally, which was released in 2003. The time away from the daily grind also allowed me to bond more with Preston. I taught him how to throw a baseball, dribble a basketball, walk our dogs, mow a lawn, and steer clear of too much trouble.

The latter would prove to be the most difficult.

California tragedy

By mid-2002, Lawrence had led the Riverside paper for almost a year with the same passion, work ethic, and enthusiasm that he did the AMN. He could tell when an employee felt down and needed a pep talk, or chat. He told some that he wanted to one day own and publish his own paper.

On a sunny Saturday in late July, Lawrence drove down Central Avenue in Riverside about 6 p.m. when he could tell something was wrong. He felt chest pains, parked his Jeep, and turned on the flashers. He called his father, Charles Young, on his cell phone.

"Dad....I'm not feeling well. I need help," he said. Then the line went dead.

A motorist spied the flashers and stopped to tap on the door. When Lawrence failed to respond, the passerby called 911. Emergency workers tried to revive him and took him to a hospital. Lawrence was pronounced dead at age 47 of an apparent heart attack.

"He never let me down in 47 years," Charles told the Press-Enterprise. "I used to brag so much my friends would get mad at me." [31]

Lawrence faced other pressures besides the usual ones at work. He and Margie had divorced in May, according to his obituary. And he and April were expecting a son named after Lawrence, who would be born in August in Dallas. [32]

At his memorial, musicians played Miles Davis jazz tunes, and an actor read a 1919 speech by civil rights advocate and singer Paul Robeson. Speakers included Mong and Dallas County Commissioner John Wiley Price. Part of me wanted to attend the memorial service, and part didn't want to see anyone from Belo. The latter part won out. I wasn't in the mood for a reunion.

Some six months later in early 2003, the AMN officially died, quietly publishing its last zoned edition. By that time, my anger towards Belo had subsided enough that I accepted some assignments from the state section. My marriage unraveled, and in the split, I agreed to move close to Michelle's hometown in Pennsylvania. We put our custom house on the market, which sold in early 2004. The buyer, unbeknownst to us, was a reporter who had joined the DMN from the Star-Telegram about a year before Belo terminated me.

Return to Arlington

In 2015, I found myself back in Arlington. I had just been laid off from another journalism job with a chain of Maryland newspapers affiliated with The Washington Post, one I held for more than 11 years. It was eerily similar to the 2001 layoff, with the larger party Post deciding that the suburban operation needed to be put out of its misery.

In that layoff, I wasn't nearly as mad as I had been in 2001. Sure, Post execs lied to us – which I viewed as a normal societal practice that seemingly increased in the Internet age – telling us they could not find a buyer for The Gazette newspapers that covered Montgomery and Prince George's counties. A few hours later, a Washington Post reporter released a story quoting one potential buyer saying his offer was ignored. [33]

It had been another good run, though less intense than the AMN experience. My features on the Kennedy assassination and businesses' responses to the Great Recession were judged by the Maryland-Delaware-D.C. Press Association to be better than any the Post, Baltimore Sun, and larger operations produced. Some stories ran in the Post. But the atmosphere just wasn't quite the same. For one thing, profanity-laced tirades were discouraged. One staffer who issued one later sent out an apologetic email to the entire newsroom. Never in my wildest imagination could I see Lawrence or Gary making anyone apologize for cussing in the newsroom.

The AMN was a defined war between two large media competitors; the Gazette was also involved in a war, but a less-defined, sometimes-invisible battle to survive in a Titanic-like media environment that continued to downgrade newspapers. My colleagues were hard-working and pleasant. The job allowed me to have most nights and weekends off so I could spend time with my kids, which I appreciated. But I definitely felt the bottom-line influence as layoffs and unfilled positions increased towards the end of my stint there.

By 2015, mass layoffs at newspapers became so common that few raised their eyebrows or bowed their heads when they heard that another paper was shedding its workforce. Newsroom positions across the country declined by 51 percent between 2008 and 2019 to some 35,000 workers, according to Pew Research Center. They would continue to fall throughout the subsequent decade, including a 17 million drop between 2015 and 2022, to about 21 million. [34]

At the same time, some segments of the industry, such as cable television and digital media, added jobs. The Internet, with its social media and seemingly endless blogs, may offer a flashy, though mostly less substantive, alternative. We may have lost many good journalists, but we might know more about what goes on since it gets online so fast through direct sources. And there are platforms that publish detailed reporting.

One of many problems is figuring out what online reports are more truthful than others. People who don't like certain news automatically dismiss such reports as fake, which is usually a smokescreen. The enormous pressures on journalists – intensified during the Trump administrations with more physical assaults and death threats against media members – has at least somewhat eroded that age-old mission of the media to hold those in power accountable. On the other hand, many working journalists still labor towards that goal, though their multi-millionaire bosses often purposely rein them in, as Jeff Bezos did the Washington Post in 2024.

Part of the way I dealt with my latest layoff was to drive across the country with the kids. We played hoops on the Venice Beach outdoor courts made famous by Woody Harrelson and Wesley Snipes in the 1992 movie, *White Men Can't Jump*. We rode "Jurassic Park: The Ride" at Universal Studios, observed a live studio taping of Dan Patrick's *Sports Jeopardy*, climbed to within 40 feet of the Hollywood sign, sat on a bench used in *Forrest Gump*, explored Batman's cave, and drove down the street that Michael Scott made famous in *The Office*. We visited friends in Phoenix and refueled in the desert air.

Driving down Interstate 30 as we approached Arlington, I couldn't help but glance at the building where I had spent so many long days and nights near what later became Globe Life Field. The AMN sign was long gone. I didn't notice a replacement. A staffing firm and behavioral health agency were among the occupants. There were no signs of life there as I passed by at about 8 p.m. on this

Sunday. A prominent sign proclaiming "Available" was its most striking feature. In our day, Lawrence, me, and many others would still be there, even on a Sunday night. For all I knew, Lawrence's ghost haunted that place, barking orders laced with f-bombs to shocked janitors and security guards.

Winding down a 680-mile drive that day from Las Cruces, N.M., I had to stop to stretch and walk around somewhere. The Rangers were in Seattle, and their Ballpark appeared deathly quiet, a sleeping behemoth monster against the Texas sky. Jerry World looked equally tomb-like as twilight approached. Six Flags and some nearby restaurants and bars were the only signs of life in that area.

"I have to get a Pink Thing," I announced to Preston and McKenna. I didn't know if Six Flags still sold those cherry-flavored, ice cream concoctions the theme park first unveiled around 1965. I loved those things in my youth.

Preston didn't want to leave the car, as he was dealing with hives. McKenna laughed and followed me out the door. We showed our passes obtained at Maryland's Six Flags America that were good at any of the firm's parks, a great deal. We passed the Aquaman Splashdown, Pandemonium roller-coaster, and Runaway Mine Train. We didn't want to get wet or stand in a long line. The Gunslinger, some swings that launched riders into the air, was perfect. There was not much of a line, and we were soon perched on a swing. It didn't propel us to the lofty heights of the Texas SkyScreamer, but we flew high enough.

I asked McKenna if she wanted to ride it again, but she shook her head. "Preston is going to get mad. We better go." She was right. On the walk back to Six Flags' entrance, I looked unsuccessfully for a Pink Thing among the ice cream carts and stands. As we were about to exit, I spied one last ice cream cart. Sure enough, it sold Pink Things, and they were only $2.

McKenna devoured hers right away. I kept mine, trying to savor it, to keep it from melting for as long as possible. Reaching the car, I asked Preston if he wanted to try the Pink Thing. He did, of course. It was gone in a flash.

As we waited in a parking lot vehicle line, I glanced again at our old AMN building, which I spied in the distance. For a 1987 Texas Monthly piece, A.C. Greene wrote of his Dallas Times Herald days by starting with a question: "Why is it you never remember the good things about certain jobs, only the bad – and yet the sweetest times, the days of your life you think you'd rather live over, are those seasons when salaries were lowest, the bosses were cruelest, your fellow workers were the most problematic?" [35]

There were times I loathed working at the AMN. I certainly despised the way Belo management discarded me. But despite the layoff, the insanely long hours and pressure of a newspaper war, the screaming, the drama, I might not trade that experience for an authentic 1909 Wagner card. Well, perhaps I would if it was a highly-graded Wagner card. I'm not a complete idiot.

Salaries, at least compared with places I worked previously, were good for the most part. AMN bosses weren't really cruel, just competitive and motivating in their own ways. Certain fellow workers were dramatic and problematic. But most were smart and interesting and people who I didn't mind seeing off the clock. I had lived one dream there for a few fleeting moments. Such dreams often become nightmares, though those, too, eventually pass. Neither the finer moments nor the nightmares last. The trick is not to let your fear of the latter swallow your visions of the former whole.

Some said all we were doing was carrying the water of the Belo bigwigs in their fancy boardrooms who staked out the next acquisition territory like it was their Manifest Destiny right. Such critics had a point. When those bigwigs were done with us, they spit out pawns like me without a second thought. Gent was joking with his quip to the rookie about the Cowboys' playbook, but like most jokes, it contained some truth. Some Cowboys died earlier than they should have because they read and bought into that playbook, as observed in CTE reports. And at least portions of some were killed in the midst of the Great Arlington Newspaper War of 1996–2003.

Yet, when we were in those trenches, there were times when it felt like we were in the middle of something bigger than ourselves. We were trying to rekindle the glory days of newspapering, fighting to save that art from going the way of the dinosaurs and the Edsel. Across the country, there were other newspaper wars occurring around the same time as ours, including in California and Florida. Such wars continue to this day in a more muted tone in cities like D.C. and New York City, even smaller places such as Wilkes-Barre, Pa.

Our war came before the Internet changed media and life as we know it, before Craigslist, Twitter, Facebook, Google, Yahoo, and the Wall Street hedge fund-driven recession devalued and killed many a newspaper, reducing the number of U.S. daily papers to about 940 by 2025, from some 1,600 in 1990. Ours was in a city small enough to have community leaders and readers who still cared, with the players, territory, and stakes large enough to gain the attention of national media. With corporate media mergers escalating, it's easy to foresee a few companies owning every major newspaper in the country one day soon. Perhaps they will continue to stage newspaper wars in attempts to boost readership, but will they be real ones?

In 2008, the Morning News and Star-Telegram started throwing each other's papers in their back-yard counties. The following year, the former heated rivals began sharing some coverage and photographs. In 2014, Belo started printing the Star-Telegram at its Plano plant, a development ironically chronicled by Gary. Driven largely by the recession, bitter enemies had softened their stances, resulting in a kind of peacetime merger after a war that neither media company had really won. [36]

These days, the DMN and FWST are shells of their former selves. Belo spun off broadcasting properties in 2008, then morphed into DallasNews Corp. That entity continued to lose millions of dollars, leading to a 2025 merger with Hearst, owner of the San Francisco Chronicle and Houston Chronicle. Other former Belo-owned papers, including ones in Riverside and Providence, were sold. The DMN newsroom, which had about 400 employees in 2007, numbered less than 200 by 2020. Daily print circulation shriveled from some 520,000 in 2000 to about 45,000 in 2024. [37]

Photographer Randy Eli Grothe, who was among those caught in 2009 cuts, penned a poignant remembrance. "I was lucky enough to experience print journalism when the cotton was high and [The Dallas Morning News] was a bad-ass newspaper firing on all cylinders," he wrote. "We were all living way above the cloud line. At that time the possibilities at this outfit seemed limitless." [38]

The decline was similar at the Star-Telegram and most other large dailies. In 2024, the Fort Worth paper ceased being a daily print one, publishing only three days a week. Daily print circulation had dropped to about 13,000 in 2024, from almost 300,000 in the early 1990s. McClatchy Co. which bought Knight Ridder in 2006, held onto the Star-Telegram and 28 other shrinking papers. The company filed for bankruptcy in 2020 and was purchased by a hedge fund. [39]

In 2024, every U.S. newspaper on the Press Gazette's top 25 list lost print subscribers, led by the Los Angeles Times 25 percent decline. The only papers with more than 100,000 print subscribers were the Wall Street Journal, New York Times, New York Post, Washington Post, and USA Today. At most, digital subscriptions increased.

The print demise of the DMN and other papers can be directly attributable to newspapers being owned by publicly-traded companies, wrote Ed Bark, the News' longtime TV critic who was among those who took a buyout in 2006. He quoted Lorraine Branham, former director of The University of Texas at Austin's School of Journalism, saying that newspapers being beholden more to shareholders than readers was "the worst thing that could have ever happened to journalism." [40]

Bark also pointed out how trying unsuccessfully to focus on young readers and "soccer moms" hurt the readership base of older adults. Letting people read the paper online free was another ill-advised strategy, and it likely would have been better to devise a system where print subscribers could access the website while non-subscribers had to pay, he wrote.

In later years, DMN editors also began to worry too much about offending people, with the exception being sports under former editor Dave Smith, who retired in 2004, Bark said. For most at the paper, "raising hell wasn't an option," and it was "safer to be folksy," he wrote.

Paul Gillin, founder of the blog, Newspaper Death Watch, believed newspapers will never recover. Google was a "game-changer," he wrote on his blog in 2018. Some print media companies could survive as smaller properties with a "new model of journalism" focused on digital aggregation and reader-generated content. Ironically, his blog died in 2018. [41]

Some view that as positive, with citizens having quicker access to information and fewer trees being used in the print process. Yet, electronic devices use electricity and emit chemicals, not to mention their impact during the manufacturing process. It's like replacing paper towels in public restrooms with electronic hand dryers. You may save some trees, but you also use more electricity and materials in making the dryers. You can recycle electricity, but how many people really do that?

To me, it's a sad story. Rather than take glee in Belo's fall from power, I felt emptiness. Not so much for top execs; DallasNews Corp. CEO Grant Moise still made $1.5 million in 2023. Those left at the DMN didn't need pity, even though they were more overworked than ever and had to concern themselves with concepts such as webpage clicks and social media followers.

Most had done well, either at the DMN or elsewhere. Tom Fox and Brad Loper were part of a DMN team that won a Pulitzer for Hurricane Katrina photos in 2006. Mark Konradi rose to director of DMN newsroom operations before becoming executive editor of the Clarion-Ledger in Mississippi. Jason Trahan became investigative producer for WFAA-TV. Marina Trahan Martinez freelanced for The New York Times and ABC News, after a long stint with the DMN. Eric became assistant metro editor at the DMN, then city editor of the Temple Daily Telegram. Doug went on to be sports editor of the San Antonio Express-News and general manager of student media at Texas A&M. Darrin became the Star-Telegram's deputy sports editor, Dallas Business Journal's managing editor, a Houston Chronicle reporter, and a law firm media relations rep. Christopher was national and political editor at the St. Louis Post-Dispatch. Matt Mosley and Todd worked for ESPN. Russ was a public relations coordinator for UT-Southwestern Medical Center. Herb worked for the DMN through 2006, then moved to media relations at UTA. Pennie became editor of some community papers in Denton and Tarrant counties and an assistant professor at Tarrant County College. Shelly edited Dallas Child and other magazines. Longtime AMN advertising rep Chris Johnson returned to the DMN in 2004 but later transferred to the FWST.

I was among those who moved the farthest away from Arlington, though Steve Quinn and Bob both spent time in the more distant land of Alaska. Ben ventured west to write for the Las Vegas Business Press before returning to work in Texas. Tamara covered technology for the Orange County Register and then Denver Post. Danny was director of executive communications for Virginia Commonwealth University. April moved to Denver and then Atlanta; Kelly migrated to Virginia.

What mostly made me sad was the AMN's demise seemed to coincide with the end of the Great Newspapering Era. In the end, I just wanted to know if what we tried to do in that I-30 office building really mattered in the grand scheme of things. And as I sat there, waiting in the parking lot of Six Flags for my turn to exit some 15 years after Texas' last significant newspaper war died, I wanted to believe it did. But that notion was likely built on as much solid foundation as a Trump public statement.

Traveling towards downtown Dallas, it would have been appropriate if the Stones' "Can't Get No Satisfaction" played on the radio as I drove into the sunset. If I would have been an NBA or MLB player, that would have been my walk-up music. I turned off the radio as the kids fell asleep. I tried to think of nothing.

As we passed the Dallas skyline, I noticed Reunion Tower and other structures. I didn't look for the all-too familiar letters of The Dallas Morning News sign close to that tower. Near that sign was a saying, supposedly uttered by longtime News titan Dealey, etched in large letters in stone: "Build the news upon the rock of truth and righteousness. Conduct it always upon the lines of fairness and integrity. Acknowledge the right of the people to get from the newspaper both sides of every important question."

I didn't exit to view those words again. It wouldn't be long before the News would abandon that building with the outdated etched message for a smaller headquarters. I kept moving forward on North Central Expressway, the downtown lights growing dimmer in my rear-view mirror.

After The Dallas Morning News laid him off, Shay was mad enough to conduct a short protest outside its headquarters. He tried to look tough with the old leather jacket and sign, but not sure the backwards baseball cap helped. The News moved from this visible building, which featured an etched saying important to journalism, in 2017. Photo by Michelle Shay

Government Power:
A Strange but True Tale

First published in the Addison/North Dallas Register, July 11, 1991; and in *Death of the Rising Sun*, Random Publishers, 2017

Just because you're paranoid doesn't mean they aren't after you.
— **JOSEPH HELLER**, *Catch-22*, 1961

In the early 1990s, University of North Texas professors took a beating. Bill Cathey, an adjunct English professor with an interest in theft, con games, karate, mind control, and guns, kidnapped a young woman he found walking along a Dallas highway in the wee hours of a May 1991 morning. He hoped to break her down and rebuild her into the "perfect woman."

Cathey reportedly kept her chained in a closet, making her repeat, "I will obey," thousands of times, only letting her out to be paraded blindfolded through a store. After a shootout with police in a small Oklahoma town, Cathey was convicted of numerous charges and sentenced to life in prison. [1]

More reports surfaced about bizarre dealings by UNT profs. As a somewhat proud but distant alumnus of the Denton college, I figured that was a good time to write publicly about my strange encounter with a professor towards the end of my senior year in 1981. As a college reporter, I had broken a story in the NT Daily on how university officials covered up important details of a UNT education professor convincing students who had virtually no climbing experience to rappel down the 60-foot football stadium wall as a "confidence-building exercise." One student had died in a fall during the activity.

But that wasn't the strangest professor I had met. In 1991, I detailed the most bizarre story I knew about a UNT prof in a weekly column for the Addison/North Dallas Register.

One late spring afternoon in 1981, I was minding my business trying to write a final "Sports Jerks of the Week" column for the NT Daily when the phone buzzed. Being the only one in the office, I picked it up. A man identified himself as a representative of a Washington, D.C., public interest organization.

"Do you know a political science professor named Stephen Gorman there?" he asked.

I replied negatively. "We have information that he's doing some work for the CIA," the man continued. "We think he might be relaying information on some students or using his students' term papers as background for his reports. You haven't heard anything like this, have you?"

My heart raced as my curiosity level intensified. "Uh, no. But I'll look into it," I assured him. "Call me back next Wednesday." I should have taken down his number, but like I said, I was preoccupied with a sports column at the time.

I checked Dr. Gorman's background with university records. The California native earned a doctorate in political science from Cal-Riverside in 1977. He had been an assistant professor at Purdue University, SUNY, and Dickinson College before joining UNT in 1979. A member of the prestigious Latin American Studies Association, he had lived in Peru, Ecuador, British Honduras, and Mexico. He had published research in numerous scholarly journals and co-authored the 1981 book, *The Yom Kippur War*.

Could such research be of interest to the CIA, an organization known to influence Central and South American politics? The CIA's Dallas office declined to confirm anything.

A few days after taking the strange phone call, I confronted Gorman in his office. After I detailed the call, he laughed off being on the CIA payroll. "Nothing that any students have written would be worth relaying to the CIA, if I even worked for them," he said at one point.

Gorman's eyes gave away nary a hint of surprise or connivance. I left not fully convinced of his sincerity, but understanding the blanket denials.

Further investigation around the poli-sci department and other places revealed exactly zip. The D.C. source never called back. I dropped the matter as one of those weird, road-to-nowhere lures, thinking more about what I would do after college.

Two years later, I glanced through a Dallas newspaper as a daily custom. My eyes glued onto a short, inside-page story under the headline, "NTSU prof struck by train, killed in Denton County."

Gorman was only 32 and had traveled through dangerous territory in Central and South America. At one point, he had been held at gunpoint for 45 minutes by an army patrol in El Salvador and had narrowly escaped being blown up. Yet, he met his demise by being hit by a train early one Saturday morning in a rural part of North Texas.

Gorman's death was ruled an accident, according to an Associated Press story. He was hit by the train "while walking on a railroad track adjacent to a state highway," the story read. Among the unanswered questions that story raised was:

How many other adults in that area went for walks on the railroad track at 3 in the morning? [2]

Colleague C. Neal Tate, who became chairman of UNT's political science department in 2003, refrained from mentioning how Gorman died in an obituary. Gorman was a "skilled and popular teacher" and a "prolific writer on the politics and international relations of Western South America and on the revolutionary governments and conflict in Nicaragua and El Salvador," Tate wrote. "At his death, he was completing final revisions for a new anthology on 'Leftist Opposition in Democracies.' His expertise and frequent travel to the region made him a popular resource for local and, indeed, national media concerned with events in Central America." [3]

In early 1991, I remained concerned enough to call a professor in UNT's poli-sci department about Gorman. He mentioned then that Gorman's "weird death" eight years earlier was still a mystery, that he had no answer as to why he would be walking on train tracks in the wee morning hours. He stated that Gorman had done "consulting work for the CIA." But that was all he would say.

Dr. Gorman backs cruise missile

Q. Considering the U.S. arsenal of strategic weapons, could the United States successfully counter a Soviet thrust anywhere in the world?

A. No, we couldn't unless we're willing to go to a full-scale nuclear war. The United States has not developed a counterforce (first-strike capability). If we went to a nuclear confrontation, we would have to shoot off our missiles or lose them. The Soviet Union, with its counterforce capability, could pick off our missile silos until we were ready to say "uncle."

This type of limited confrontation has been envisioned by strategists as happening fairly soon. The Soviets have developed a counterforce capable of knocking out our land-based ICBMs, and blowing up our missile fields would not be provocative enough for us to launch a countervalue attack against Soviet cities.

Gorman

systems. To keep pace with the Soviets, any program must be ongoing.

Q. What must be done to ensure the security of the United States?

A. We must have mass production and stationing of the cruise missiles in Europe and get a fleet of Trident submarines on line. The X-1 missile system in the Western deserts is optional.

The United States should phase out its land-based ICBMs. They're obsolete and too vulnerable to Soviet counterforce attacks.

The cruise missile, because of its relatively slow speed, would not allow you to sneak a punch in, but it is cheap to build. I think you could build 20 cruise missiles for the same price they could build one anti-ballistic missile vehicle.

Because of their slow speed, from 600 mph to 700 mph, the cruise missiles are extremely accurate. You could even mount a camera on the missile's structure and fly it from the base right into the target.

The X-1 missile, scheduled to be stationed in the Western desert, would be a large ICBM with great accuracy. It would move on a 10-mile, oval, un-

military, and the United States spends only 5 percent of its GNP. But you have to remember U.S. GNP is twice as large as the Soviets'.

If the United States increased military spending to 10 percent of GNP, then we would be outspending the Soviets considerably. But to stay ahead, you must first get ahead. The Soviets know that in a democracy the people will not put the military ahead of social services, and that has paid off for them in terms of gaining superiority.

Q. With the ailing condition of the 53 remaining Titan II missiles pointed out by last week's explosion, how much longer should the United States continue to rely on the Titan system?

A. Until the Trident submarines come on line in 1985. Then the Titans should be phased out, and the manufacture of MARVs (Multiple Adjustable Re-entry Vehicles, warheads that can be guided after they separate from the missile) should be the priority.

But it remains to be seen whether Congress will appropriate the money for the development and, later, the deployment of the MARVs.

Stephen Gorman was interviewed by the North Texas Daily about U.S. strategic arms capability for this article, published in October 1980.   Photo by Kevin Shay

Close ties between CIA and academia began in 1940s

Close ties between the CIA and American colleges and universities have existed since the 1940s, according to a 1983 article in the CIA's Studies in Intelligence journal. William Donovan, President Franklin Roosevelt's coordinator of information, recruited academicians to aid him as early as 1941, the report stated. James Baxter, president of Williams College in Massachusetts, and Harvard historian William Langer were among leaders of that effort. [4]

With the CIA's formation in 1947, numerous academicians, including MIT economist Max Millikan, served as research analysts and managers. "As the agency expanded, its recruiters turned to established figures in the academic world for leads and referrals to the best among their students," according to the CIA report. The links with Ivy League universities were particularly strong.

During the 1950s, relatively few professors and students questioned the CIA-academia links. That started to change after information leaked out about the CIA's involvement in the Bay Pigs fiasco in 1961, and the opposition intensified the longer the Vietnam War continued. Groups such as Students for a Democratic Society began organized campaigns against professors aiding the CIA. Some academicians continued their intelligence work but tried harder to keep it secret.

A committee chaired by LBJ Administration official Nicholas Katzenbach recommended that the CIA end covert relationships with universities and nonprofit organizations. Student protests also targeted CIA recruiters starting in 1966, causing such efforts to go underground.

In 1976, the Church Committee, a U.S. Senate committee headed by Idaho Sen. Frank Church that examined U.S. intelligence agencies' activities, released a bombshell report that President Gerald Ford tried to withhold from the public. The report detailed the CIA's attempts to assassinate foreign leaders, spy on U.S. citizens who opposed certain government policies like the escalation of the Vietnam War, and recruit college professors, journalists, and others as part-time spies.

The action resulted in Ford issuing an executive order banning U.S. agents from engaging in political assassinations but did little to stem the academic links. The CIA's recruitment of professors and journalists might have slowed, but certainly did not stop. [5]

In 1977, journalist Carl Bernstein, fresh off Watergate fame, wrote an article in Rolling Stone that showed how the matter went far beyond the committee's findings. Just about every major media outlet, including The New York Times, The Washington Post, CBS, ABC, and The Saturday Evening Post, had reporters or executives who fed the CIA information, according to Bernstein.

"Many CIA officials regarded these helpful journalists as operatives," Bernstein wrote. "The journalists tended to see themselves as trusted friends of the agency who performed occasional favors – usually without pay – in the national interest." [6]

The Times even provided about ten CIA employees newspaper credentials in the 1950s and 1960s, he wrote. The CIA operated a formal training program for its agents in the 1950s, providing tips like how to "make noises like reporters," Bernstein said.

After the release of the Church Committee report, some academic leaders attempted to increase transparency on professors working for the CIA. Harvard President Derek Bok formed a committee to prepare guidelines on how professors should deal with the agency. A key concern was using scholars to prepare propaganda material, while the committee recommended that faculty and staff who worked for the CIA should report that to their deans.

Most universities did not emulate the Harvard guidelines. I don't think the University of North Texas – then called North Texas State University – had any such guidelines in the late 1970s and early 1980s. The Soviet Union's invasion of Afghanistan in 1979 "opened new doors to cooperation with CIA on many campuses," the CIA reported. [7]

By 1983, the agency had rebuilt "reasonably good relations with academe" and gained "much from its contacts with faculty and students." In 1982, more than two dozen professors attended a three-day CIA conference, 14 college presidents traveled to Langley for a briefing, and more than 60 agency officials spoke at colleges. CIA employees actively recruited students at some 300 universities. Middlebury College in Vermont was among the few where students protested such CIA efforts in significant numbers.

By 2000, CIA employees openly taught at universities, as more professors funneled research to the agency. While in the 1960s and 1970s the hint of a professor working for the CIA was enough to spur student demonstrations, fewer students cared about such ties in subsequent decades.

"Today's students on the whole are much more politically conservative," according to a 2000 Los Angeles Times article. And many have only become more conservative during the Trump years, as he attempts to starve the supposed "wokeness" out of colleges and remake intelligence agencies into his personal spy firms. [8]

To this day, young college professors, like Gorman in the early 1980s, remain of particular interest to CIA handlers. There appear to be few other professors thought to be working for the CIA who died mysterious deaths.

There was the case of Frank Olson, a research scientist who worked for the U.S. Army's biological warfare program in the 1940s and 1950s, a project in which numerous humans and animals became the unwitting victims of ghastly experiments. Olson died in a suspicious 1953 fall from the tenth floor of a New York hotel. In 1975, the federal government admitted that Olson had been dosed with LSD nine days before his death by a leader of the CIA's MKUltra brainwashing program since he was reportedly a security risk.

Several alleged CIA assets died mysterious deaths in the aftermath of John F. Kennedy's assassination, but none of them were academicians. Some were reporters, though not ones believed to have worked for the CIA.

I have yet to read about another CIA-connected professor who died as he supposedly walked along train tracks in the wee morning hours. I'll keep searching, though.

Getting More Personal

Healthcare and Death: The Aspirin Strain

First published in the Richland [College] Mandala, November 1978; and Medium, April 13, 2018

What is life? It departs covertly. Like a thief, Death took him.
— **JOHN GUNTHER**, *Death Be Not Proud*, 1949

When I was five in 1965, my nine-year-old sister became ill, as kids frequently do. Most get better. Sharon didn't.

I went on to spend much of the subsequent six decades wondering why. Sharon went on to an eternal resting site in Arlington National Cemetery.

For most of my life, I could only speculate on the cause of my sister's death. Dad thought it had to do with some pesticides-sprayed fruit she could have eaten. Mom collected newspaper clippings on various diseases and conditions, including Reye's syndrome, a rapidly progressive disorder that causes swelling of many organs, particularly the brain and liver.

Medical officials cited the cause of Sharon's death to be encephalopathy – a brain disease – due to "cause undetermined," according to her death certificate. The interval of the encephalopathy between onset and death was only three days.

Notes Mom took of what happened during Sharon's illness lent more clues as to what happened. On February 24, 1965, Sharon complained of a headache and had a slight temperature. Under the family doctor's recommendation, Mom gave her baby aspirin, which our physician also authorized for me and siblings Kathy and Patrick when we had fevers during those years. That was the common recommendation then, but not now. Most parents back then didn't question doing that. Why should they? The advice came from medical professionals, right?

The next day, Sharon's temperature rose to 102 degrees so Mom took her to see the physician. The Tampa, Fla., doctor told Mom to give Sharon *adult* aspirin, going beyond what most physicians recommended even back then.

The following day, Sharon's temperature regressed to 99 degrees. But another day later, it rose again to 101 before declining to 99.

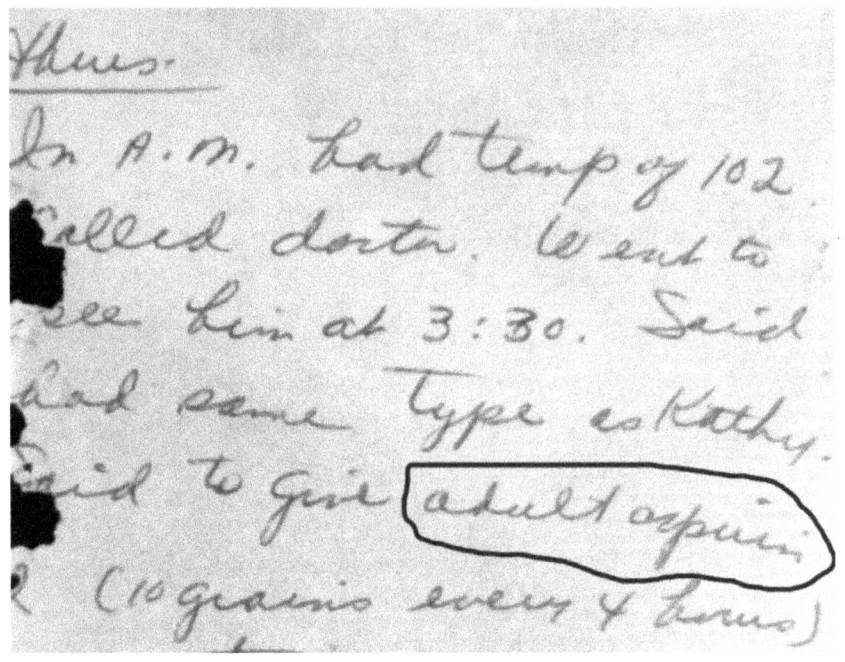

About a week before Sharon died at age nine in 1965, her doctor told Mom to give her adult aspirin, according to notes Mom took at the time.

On Sunday, February 28, Sharon's temperature remained near normal, but she complained of a stomach ache and vomited several times a few hours later. On Monday morning, she threw up twice more, so Mom took her to the doctor. He said Sharon had acidosis and was dehydrated. He suggested she take a solution of water, baking soda, sugar, and lemon every 20 minutes, as well as a suppository to control vomiting. He also advised taking milk.

In later decades, some nutritionists would recommend not combining lemon with dairy or sugar.

Between feedings, Sharon seemed drowsy. Mom called the doctor that evening, who said to let her sleep and call Tuesday morning, March 2. Around 5 a.m., Sharon awoke and started to scream like she was having a nightmare. She would not answer Mom or Dad or let anyone touch her. They called an ambulance, and Sharon screamed all the way in the ambulance and during the exam in the emergency room, according to the notes. They gave her a sedative and admitted her.

The doctors could find little wrong, even doing a spinal tap to check for a brain hemorrhage. At one point, they told my parents that it "seemed like a detective mystery" where they were "piecing all clues together."

> Awoke 5 A.M. moaning & started to scream. Would not answer or let us touch her. Called police for ambulance & called doctor. Police took pulse said - normal. Doctor said to have hospital doctor check & call him. She screamed all way in ambulance & during exam in emergency room.

They raised the possibility of toxicology, while saying there was a "slight diminution" in Sharon's liver. One thought it was an "extreme metabolic reaction."

On Wednesday, March 3, Sharon experienced trouble breathing and continued to vomit. Doctors considered doing a tracheotomy but held off. On Thursday, March 4, Sharon shook with tremors, and doctors proceeded with the tracheotomy around 1 p.m. Her breathing improved, but Mom noticed about 2 p.m. that she had a convulsion and her mouth twitched. Doctors asked Mom and Dad to leave the room.

Around 4 p.m. – eight days after she first complained of a headache and two days after being hospitalized – doctors told my parents that Sharon was gone. Like a thief, Death took her.

Years later, Mom told me that a public health study was conducted on Sharon, but she was only told the results were inconclusive. She suspected Reye's syndrome, though I could tell she didn't want to do so. The symptoms were there – vomiting, headaches, drowsiness, nightmares, screaming, sensitivity to touch, confusion to the point of not recognizing family members, the noticeable change to her liver.

But confronting the horror of giving your child something on doctor's orders, and that turning out to be what caused your kid's death, was almost too much to consider.

Yet, that was what likely occurred to not just Sharon, but to hundreds, perhaps thousands, of other kids.

Sharon poses with Kathy and Kevin in the backyard of their Florida home in 1965. This was one of the last photos taken of her.   Photo by James Shay

Colleague: Reye 'sat on this for ten years'

Drug maker Bayer began mass marketing aspirin to doctors and their patients in 1899, after being founded as a dye factory in Germany in 1863. The drug's use as a pain reliever and flu treatment quickly caught on. In a typical practice, Bayer lobbied physicians to prescribe patients aspirin to the point it obtained an exclusive patent. Other drug companies tried to hone in on the lucrative product, but Bayer's trademark allowed it to win legal claims forcing doctors to only be allowed to prescribe Bayer aspirin. By 1915, aspirin became available without a doctor's prescription, helping to make it one of the most widely used drugs in the world, according to medical researcher Jan McTavish. [1]

Amid the aspirin sales boom, medical researchers began noticing odd conditions in children who died. In 1929, **British neurologist W. Russell Brain** published a report in The Lancet medical journal, describing brain swelling and fatty liver tissue in six children who passed away after a brief illness. Brain described the condition as "acute meningo-encephalomyelitis." [2]

In 1951, Douglas Reye, the Australian pathologist credited with discovering the syndrome, started observing some puzzling cases at the Royal Alexandra Hospital for Children in suburban Sydney. In one instance, a 10-month-old boy screamed and vomited for more than a day before dying. Reye found no evidence of infection in the infant but noticed liver and brain damage. Other physicians reported children with similar brain and liver conditions in medical journals between 1954 and 1961. [3]

In 1961, Harvard neurologist Gilles Lyon headed a report in Oxford University journal Brain that called attention to infants and children who acquired fevers, experienced convulsions, and fell into comas. Some patients were retrospectively believed to have Reye's. [4]

Lyon and his team "identified Reye syndrome before [Douglas] Reye did but gave it a broader clinical description that was not retained by the neurology readers of the time," wrote Harvard neurologist Allan H. Ropper. [5]

By 1960, U.S. retail sales of aspirin climbed to $81 million, then kept rising to $107 million in 1970. That trend continued despite an increasing number of medical researchers linking aspirin to children's deaths. Edward A. Mortimer Jr., a pediatrician at Western Reserve University in Ohio, and others proposed in 1962 that salicylates like aspirin caused hypoglycemia in four infants who died after contracting chicken pox. [6]

Meanwhile, Reye himself did not publish findings in The Lancet until 1963. Colleague Jim Baral told journalist and medical doctor Lawrence Altman that he and chief resident Graeme Morgan had to push Reye to write about it.

"Dr. Reye sat on this for ten years," said Baral, who began training at the Sydney hospital in 1961. [7]

In more than half of the 21 cases reported by Reye, Baral, and Morgan in 1963, children had taken aspirin. That information was not included in the medical journal because they did not realize that link until later, Baral said. [8]

Another 1963 report led by U.S. physician George Johnson detailed a flu outbreak of 16 children in North Carolina who died after developing neurological problems similar to those described by Reye. Some gave credit to Johnson by naming the disorder Reye-Johnson syndrome, though most leave him off. [9]

In 1964 and 1965, reports in medical journals raised the possibility of a link between salicylates and Reye's. H.L. Utian and other South African doctors wrote in The Lancet about 14 cases between 1955 and 1964 of mostly infants who acquired hypoglycemia, metabolic acidosis, and an "extensive fatty change" of the liver. The illness usually began with an upper-respiratory tract infection and proceeded to convulsions, coma, and death. The doctors suggested salicylate intoxication as a possible cause. [10]

Then in 1965, as children like Sharon continued to die, H.M. Giles further explored in The Lancet the link between Reye's and salicylates, suggesting victims' enzyme system might be hypersensitive to that substance. In 1968, Canadian doctor M.G. Norman published a study of 21 cases at The Hospital for Sick Children in Toronto between 1954 and 1966. The cases were similar to the ones in other parts of the world, starting with respiratory infections and proceeding to vomiting, convulsions, and death. [11]

"These children usually were hyperventilating, suggesting salicylate intoxication and prompting an estimation of blood salicylates," Norman wrote. "As death approached, respirations became irregular and finally failed.... Nine children were delirious." [12]

Parents lobby for government warnings, then Reye's cases drop

In 1972, the mother of Mark Largent took her two-year-old son to an upstate New York hospital. He was vomiting and hallucinating, barely hanging onto life. Pediatrician Bernard Musselman told Largent's mother that her son had "a very rare condition called Reye-Johnson syndrome that no one really understood or knew how to treat." He said Largent had a "50-50" chance of surviving. [13]

Musselman knew not to do a tracheotomy or blood transfusion, or remove skull pieces, as some physicians did in attempts to treat the condition then. He opened an IV in Largent's ankle to pump fluids, glucose, potassium, and dextrose, treating the symptoms. Largent fell into a coma, then his condition stabilized the following day. He was released within a few days, fully recovered. Largent would become a professor and dean of undergraduate studies at Michigan State University.

Numerous others were not so fortunate. Soon after five-year-old Tiffini Freudenberger died of Reye's, parents John and Terri founded the Ohio-based National Reye's Syndrome Foundation in 1974. The group became a clearinghouse for devastated parents dealing with similar tragedies that established chapters across the country. Among its resources was a list of other products that can contain salicylates to avoid giving children, such as anti-nausea medications. [14]

As the number of reported Reye's cases and studies increased, parents started to pressure medical groups and government agencies to issue public warnings about giving children aspirin. In 1976, the U.S. Food and Drug Administration made a general-public "preliminary warning" not to use aspirin to treat symptoms of the syndrome. Then in 1980, the U.S. Centers for Disease Control and Prevention, which reached many more people and medical professionals than the FDA, warned parents and physicians to use caution in giving aspirin to kids. [15]

That year, the number of new Reye's cases reported nationwide by the CDC peaked at 555, though the figure was "believed to be a fraction of those that did occur," reported Altman. Many incidents went unreported or misdiagnosed, such as Sharon's. [16]

The percentage of victims dying in 1965 was believed to be around 80 percent, though that was hard to ascertain since reporting of the syndrome was so inconsistent. It didn't help that the CDC did not keep detailed records on the disorder until 1977.

In 1981, a year after the CDC issued specific warnings to not give aspirin to kids, new Reye's cases declined almost in half to below 300. While many welcomed that development, Big Pharma executives were concerned about sales of children's aspirin, which then topped $50 million annually in the U.S.

Big Pharma strikes back, eventually loses label battle

The slow nature of moving from studies to general public warnings to product warning labels was hampered by more than mere medical professional caution. Desperate to distance itself from Reye's syndrome, the aspirin lobby employed legal threats, outright payments, and misleading public campaigns to counter and hide the findings by Reye and other medical researchers.

Behind the scenes, the relationship between numerous physicians and drug companies became tighter. Many doctors accepted payments to speak at drug-makers' conferences and consulted for them on the side. The money spent on marketing drugs to doctors and the general public would balloon from $17.7 billion in 1997 to $29.9 billion in 2016, according to a report in the Journal of the American Medical Association. [17]

As in most other industries, money doesn't just talk in the medical field. It controls.

In January 1982, representatives from Schering-Plough, which made the orange-flavored St. Joseph's Aspirin for Children, threatened the executive director of the American Academy of Pediatrics with a lawsuit. The academy's crime? Publishing a small item in its newsletter about a suspected aspirin-Reye's link. [18]

M. Harry Jennison, then the academy's executive director, succumbed to pressure and pulled the item. But in the next month's newsletter, he included an academy committee's recommendation that warning labels be required on aspirin bottles.

Schering-Plough then sent out a letter to pediatricians, saying that there was "no valid scientific data" linking aspirin and Reye's. "Therefore, you should feel confident in continuing to recommend aspirin for the reduction of fever in children," they wrote. [19]

About that time, Ralph Nader's Public Citizen organization and the American Public Health Association joined parents' advocates. They sent letters to FDA officials asking for warning labels on aspirin bottles, desiring to go beyond the general public warnings by government officials. After the FDA responded that it organized a "special working group" to review the data, Public Citizen and APHA filed a lawsuit against the agency in May 1982. [20]

The following month, U.S. Health and Human Services Secretary Richard Schweiker publicly called for warnings on aspirin bottles. Then, lobbyists for the International Aspirin Foundation reportedly helped convince an official with the Reagan administration's Office of Management and Budget to torpedo the proposal. In addition, the Committee on the Care of Children, which included physicians and was mostly financed by the aspirin industry, threatened a lawsuit over the warnings.

Faced with such industry pressure, Schweiker caved, calling for additional studies in November 1982. A few months later, he resigned to become president of the American Council of Life Insurance.

Meanwhile, the pediatric academy's executive board overruled an internal committee that supported warning labels and issued a statement calling for more research. Mortimer, co-author of the 1962 ground-breaking study, resigned in protest from the AAP committee. So did committee chairman Vincent Fulginiti, head of the University of Arizona pediatrics department.

The AAP and government agencies were succumbing to aspirin industry pressure, Mortimer publicly charged. "A signal is being sent to cool it," Mortimer said. He added that there was not enough proof to say for sure that aspirin caused Reye's, but there was enough "to justify a warning. I'm 90 percent to 95 percent [certain] of this." [21]

In 1983, aspirin lobbyists successfully stopped almost 500,000 FDA pamphlets on the issue from being placed in supermarkets. A new version of the pamphlet was created, changing some answers to reflect the aspirin foundation's positions. Later that year, the Committee on the Care of Children sent a letter to broadcasters demanding equal time if stations ran the FDA's public service announcements on Reye's. The letter cited the "Fairness Doctrine of Federal Law." [22]

The committee then issued a statement: "No medication has been proven to cause Reye's." Even a federal health official denounced that campaign as misleading. [23]

Big Pharma was successful in delaying labels for a few years, but eventually, the tide turned. In early 1985, the CDC released preliminary results of a study that showed children with the flu or chicken pox were 12 to 25 times more likely to develop Reye's when given aspirin than were sick children who did not take the drug. Margaret Heckler, who took over as U.S. health secretary in 1983, then asked aspirin manufacturers to place warning labels on bottles "voluntarily."

The aspirin lobby delayed the matter for months, then released a label that merely suggested that parents consult a doctor. The FDA had little choice but to finally issue a stronger requirement in 1986.

The language on the required label was "essentially unaltered" from Schweiker's original proposal in 1982, according to a Public Citizen report. "The only major difference was that hundreds of children had died or become brain-damaged in the interim while the government and the executive board of the AAP bent over backwards for industry," charged Sidney M. Wolfe, co-founder of the Public Citizen Health Research Group, and Peter Lurie, former deputy director of the research group. [24]

By 1986, some 42 percent of the total known cases of Reye's in the U.S. had resulted in deaths, while about one-third of the others suffered serious brain damage, according to a UPI report. Only a few victims of Reyes were older than twenty. "None of these [aspirin] companies has been anything but horrendous about this," Wolfe told a reporter. [25]

By 1994, the number of new cases dwindled to almost nothing. Most of those with the disease "appeared to have taken aspirin," CDC officials stated in a media release. [26]

Repercussions and more PR campaigns

After losing the major label battle, the Committee on the Care of Children soon disbanded. Aspirin lobbyists and public relations agents pivoted to other campaigns, such as encouraging more people with heart problems to ingest the drug.

Medical researchers continued to feel the impact of the aspirin lobby. Some researchers who spoke to a UPI reporter in 1987 requested anonymity. "I'm already in enough trouble with the aspirin industry," one revealed. [27]

In subsequent studies, most researchers steered clear of placing blame, while noting that other over-the-counter medications such as acetaminophen and ibuprofen didn't seem to cause complications in Reye's victims. In 1999, CDC researchers in The New England Journal of Medicine only dryly noted that following 1980, the number of incidents "declined sharply after the association of Reye's syndrome with aspirin was reported." [28]

As of 2024, the U.S. National Institutes of Health still merely said on its website that "the cause of [Reye's syndrome] is unknown. Studies have shown a link between aspirin [salicylate] and the onset of Reye's syndrome. Because of this association, healthcare professionals do not recommend the use of aspirin for children. There is no cure for [Reye's]. Treatment focuses on preventing brain damage. Recovery is directly related to the severity of the swelling of the brain. Some individuals recover completely, while others may sustain varying degrees of brain damage." [29]

Some outright dismissed a link between aspirin and Reye's syndrome. A 2002 study in Drug Safety by doctors at a Tampa, Fla., hospital near the one where Sharon died claimed that "no proof of causation" between aspirin and Reye's was "ever established." Their report claimed that it was "clear from epidemiological data that the incidence of Reye's syndrome was decreasing well before warning labels were placed on aspirin products.... Reye's syndrome was probably either a viral mutation which spontaneously disappeared, or a conglomeration of metabolic disorders that had not been recognized or described at that time." [30]

But the statement by the Florida doctors that Reye's syndrome declined due to unexplained factors "well before" 1986 was misleading, if not wrong. The bottom line was that new cases peaked in 1980 and declined to almost nothing in about a decade after the CDC began warning the public not to give kids aspirin in 1980.

Granted, it was confusing that many children, including me and my other two siblings, were given aspirin for fevers before the government warnings, and we survived. However, most kids were not instructed to take adult aspirin when we were as young as nine, as in Sharon's case. Apparently, the reactions vary from child to child, perhaps depending on the dose, perhaps depending on the individual's characteristics and sensitivity.

While most general public websites on aspirin mentioned the link between Reye's and aspirin in 2024, a few could be found that minimize the connection.

WebMD only included a brief sentence under the precaution tab on aspirin. Gale Research's Encyclopedia updated its information on aspirin to include Reye's syndrome a month after my essay was published in Medium in 2018. Still, even the International Aspirin Foundation admitted on its website in 2024 that aspirin "should not be used in children as it can produce a rare but dangerous Reye's syndrome resulting in coma and liver damage that can prove fatal." [31]

However, the Bayer aspirin website only said in 2024 that a "possible association between Reye's syndrome and the use of salicylates has been suggested but not established. Reye's syndrome has also occurred in many patients not exposed to salicylates." It adds that the risk of acquiring Reye's "may be increased when ASA is given concomitantly; however, no causal relationship has been proven." Aspirin remained one of Germany-based Bayer AG's best-selling products with worldwide sales of $674 million in 2023, according to its annual report. In the U.S., where Bayer has a regional headquarters in St. Louis, 17.7 million aspirin prescriptions were written to patients in 2021. [32]

Some were less afraid to step on powerful toes. David Michaels, an epidemiologist and professor at George Washington University, did not mince words in his 2008 book, *Doubt is Their Product: How Industry's Assault on Science Threatens Your Health*.

The decline of Reye's syndrome cases in the 1980s after government warnings was bittersweet because of the "untold number of children" who died or became disabled while the aspirin manufacturers "delayed the FDA's regulation by arguing that the science establishing the aspirin link was incomplete, uncertain, and unclear," Michaels wrote. "The medical community knew of the danger, thanks to an alert issued by the CDC, but parents were kept in the dark." He praised Nader's group, adding that "thousands of lives have now been saved – but only after hundreds had been lost." [33]

Bill Sardi, a nutritional health advocate and author, added in a 2011 report, "It appears modern medicine was the cause and not the cure for this deadly syndrome." [34]

Families pursue lawsuits

Parents' efforts to combat Big Pharma's misleading public campaigns were buoyed by actor Dick Van Dyke, who started making public service announcements after his 13-year-old granddaughter, Jessica Van Dyke, died in 1987. She had taken aspirin while having a fever and chicken pox. "We had no conception that Reye's was a disease that could affect a 13-year-old," said Roger Heller, the stepfather of Jessica. [35]

A few lawsuits filed by parents of Reye's victims against aspirin companies and medical providers have been successful.

In what was believed to be the first successful case filed by victims, attorneys for Gary and Judith Fox of Shell Lake, Wis., reached a $2.6 million settlement with Sterling Drug, which manufactured Bayer aspirin, in 1989, ending four years of litigation. Their daughter, Jacqueline, contracted Reye's in 1981 as an infant after being given aspirin to treat the flu. She lived but suffered brain damage and other problems. [36]

Also in 1989, a California jury sided with aspirin manufacturers, awarding no damages to the family of Larry Bunch Jr. His parents, Larry and Isabelle Bunch, filed a $50 million lawsuit in 1985, saying that their son acquired Reye's when he was nine in 1983 after taking aspirin when he had chickenpox. Bunch also experienced brain damage. Doctors testifying for the companies said his condition was encephalitis or hepatitis, not Reye's. [37]

In 1992, the family of Sherry Fugler won a $7.8 million verdict against Sterling Drug, after a Louisiana appeals panel trimmed a $9.3 million award by a lower court. A doctor advised Fugler to take adult aspirin and an antibiotic for a fever in 1981 when she was five. She contracted Reye's and suffered "severe permanent brain damage resulting in moderate mental retardation," according to court documents. [38]

In 2003, Chicago attorneys for the family of a boy who suffered brain damage after acquiring Reye's in 2001 reached a $5.5 million settlement with medical providers. The boy was admitted to a hospital for a viral infection but started vomiting a few days later. He was discharged and continued to vomit at home. He was later diagnosed with Reye's, and attorneys said the delay in treatment led to brain damage. [39]

Reviving lost memories

In 2007, I took my two young kids to Van Dyck Park within a short walk of the Fairfax, Va., house where I lived for my first two-and-a-half years with Sharon and my parents. In 2003, we had moved to the Washington, D.C., area from the Dallas area.

Preston and McKenna played tag and make-believe games with other children at the Van Dyck playground, mostly in harmony. At times, Preston tried to upstage others, while McKenna followed her older brother's orders. More than four decades previously, Sharon and I likely played similar games in that very neighborhood.

From my spot under a tree, I could nearly see the house where we lived until we relocated to a Maryland suburb in late 1961. Mom and Sharon cried the day they moved from that house; it had everything they wanted, including the St. Leo the Great Catholic Church and school within walking distance. The Army Navy Country Club was just down the road. Relatives lived nearby.

But Dad wanted a shorter commute to work. So we moved 28 miles away from the western side of D.C. to the southeast burbs. The move probably saved Dad 40 minutes a day of commuting time. Then, Dad became tired of shoveling snow and sought warmer weather a few years later. He also had a rambling trait and would travel through 49 states, including as a professional truck driver after his FBI career.

So we pulled up stakes again, this time to Florida, moving 902 miles away. Mom was lukewarm about moving from Maryland to Florida, where we had far fewer relatives. Do I wonder what might have been had we remained in the D.C. area, where medical doctors might have been more versed on the latest research about aspirin? Sometimes, perhaps a little more than sometimes.

I tried to locate the District Heights, Md., house where we lived, but the street and address changed. The old home could have been demolished to become something else. The Fairfax one hadn't changed much, besides becoming worth much more, from about $20,000 when we lived there to $646,000 in 2024. The school and towering spire of St. Leo, where Sharon and me were baptized, blocked my view of our old place. I squinted harder and looked with my memory more than my eyes.

In my mind, I saw Sharon and me chasing each other in a field like this one, with Mom not far behind, trying to spot more flying birds than the other. We settled down for a picnic lunch that included cake. That was enough to quiet us, finally. Can a war or illness or cover-up or money grab be stopped, even if just temporarily, if someone is there handing out cake?

I knew that scene since Sharon memorialized it on paper in comic-strip form. The comic strip more than made me laugh; it made me wonder what the creator might have done with her life had she been given more than almost a decade on this planet.

Six months before she died, Sharon surprised Dad on his birthday by baking a cake from scratch. She must have really loved cake – she baked it from scratch and incorporated it into a comic.

Joan, a friend of Sharon's in Maryland, described in a letter to Sharon when we lived in Florida what it was like to meet the Beatles in person in a D.C.-area music store during their historic 1964 U.S. tour. "I don't know what to do without you," Joan wrote. "I got kissed on the cheek by Paul [McCartney] the Beatle and by John [Lennon] the Beatle the day I saw him at Clarks music store. Only little kids could see them. The four Beatles kissed me. I fainted when Paul kissed me, but John caught me."

Sharon also must have loved the Beatles. Like many young girls, she had cards and posters of them. She must have really been sad to miss out on a chance to meet them. Getting those letters must have helped soften the blow of the long move and having to acclimate to another new school. But she wasn't in that school long enough to really adapt.

Sharon wrote numerous lists. One of the last ones detailed contests and other activities for a girls club, such as who could draw the prettiest picture of a girl and horse, and who could name the most dog and horse breeds and types of fish. Organizing a fashion show and compiling a poem book were other activities. There was not any indication of activities completed, but I also found numerous poems and mentions of dog and horse breeds among her writings.

I only took my kids to the Fairfax park that one time. That was enough. I thought it might help me process the situation, but it really didn't. Sometimes I think about attending St. Leo's, but then, I realize that nothing will bring Sharon back, at least not anything the way it was then. As Michael Palin said in his *Full Circle* documentary series, "The trouble with traveling back later on is that you can never repeat the same experience."

It took me almost another decade before I could force myself to drive by the old Florida house, the last neighborhood where I lived with Sharon. Closure, which I doubt I'll ever get in this case, didn't drive me there. It was curiosity more than anything. After visiting cousin Barbara and her husband, Mike, I found myself in that area in 2016.

The house and yard looked smaller than I remembered. The park and church behind it seemed closer. There were no empty fields to explore, just nearby strip malls and office complexes.

I stopped in front of the old house, remembering something as I spied the carport. "I let a young neighborhood kid take Sharon's guinea pig out of its cage on that driveway under the carport," I told the kids, pointing towards the structure. "It looked sad in the cage. We thought it might like to walk outside. But a cat got it, right in front of us."

"I bet she was mad at you!" McKenna exclaimed.

"Yeah, she was. But not as much as you might expect." Sharon was a saint. I can't recall her mistreating me, only watching over me, reading to me even when I scribbled in her books, teaching me some things. In photos, she was always smiling and often had her arm draped around me. And I never really thanked her. I never got to say goodbye.

She didn't deserve to die the way she did when she was nine, delirious, with no one but doctors and nurses around her, cutting her neck, trying to save her. She deserved to live a long, happy life. Sometimes that thought makes me so mad I can't see straight.

Sharon created comic strips like this one shortly before she died.

But who do I blame? The aspirin companies? The medical profession? The cruel hand of fate? God and Sharon's guardian angels apparently being busy somewhere else at the time?

Perhaps, as John Gunther wrote, "God, standing by us in our hour of need, God in His infinite wisdom and mercy and loving kindness, God in all His omnipotence, was helpless, too."

Allowing that younger boy to let her guinea pig go was the last thing I remembered about my time with Sharon at our Florida house, before that dark day when my parents tearfully told us in the living room that she was gone. For years after my older sister died, I thought I would die by the time I turned nine. Like Sharon. Like her guinea pig.

I climbed out of the car and took some pictures. "How long are we going to be here?" Preston asked.

He was right. We'd been there long enough. We drove more than an hour to a happier place, Silver Springs State Park, and rode a glass-bottom boat, a tradition in those artesian springs since 1878. I know I did that at one point with Sharon, viewing gators, flamingos, turtles, fish, sunken boats, and more.

It was fun to do with the kids, to relive a bit of my childhood, to remember someone and something lost long ago. But I could only smile about the good times for so long, before I was left feeling hollow, once again.

Sharon's grave site at Arlington National Cemetery was a few miles from a home where we lived in Fairfax, Va.   Photo by Kevin Shay

Death and Loss: Bye, for Now

First published in The Dallas Morning News, April 24, 2008; Milford Mirror, May 1, 2008; Fairfax Connection, May 1, 2008; *It's a Mad, Mad, Mad, Mad Trip*, 2024; accepted to *A Cup of Comfort for the Grieving Heart*, 2009, but not published there

We'd only been on the road for a few hours, but it was almost dark as Dad drove the station wagon over the Texas border into Arkansas on our way to visit relatives in Pennsylvania. *Why couldn't we fly in a plane to Pennsylvania?* I thought. I could only read a map, observe the highway sights, wonder how other folks out there lived, and play the alphabet game using signs for so long.

Lying in the back of the station wagon with my younger sister, Kathy, and brother, Patrick, I did the only thing that made sense to a young boy. "In Arkansas, you have to be really careful," I solemnly told them. "There are ghosts and goblins and……..CRICKETS there." I knew how much Kathy loathed crickets.

"Daddy! Mommy! Kevin says there are crickets and ghosts in Arkansas. Is that true?" Kathy pleaded.

"Knock it off, Kevin," Dad said in a somewhat stern, somewhat amused tone. "Hey, look at those deer!" He pointed to the side of the road. I strained my eyes but didn't see anything unusual. Only pine trees. And the highway that seemed to stretch endlessly.

By the next day, we were well into Tennessee and its more mountainous views. Whenever our sibling rivalry almost boiled over, Dad stopped the station wagon at a mountainside or odd roadside attraction. We had a look and signed a temporary truce. Towards the end of the day, the station wagon sputtered, and Dad steered it off the shoulder of the highway.

"You're not out of gas?!" Mom demanded.

"I thought I could make it to the next exit," Dad said, his eyes straight ahead. Then, he turned to us, with a hint of a twinkle in his eyes as if he almost enjoyed this situation. "I'll be back soon." He climbed out of the station wagon and retrieved a metallic portable gas can from the back near our suitcases.

I watched him walk down the highway until he became a dot on the horizon. This was 1970, long before most people owned a cell phone, before even Sony

Walkmans, when people thought little of walking down a highway, leaving their family stuck in a car by the side of a road.

Eventually, someone stopped to ask if we needed help. Mom pointed in Dad's direction and thanked the driver. About an hour later, Dad returned with the full gas can. He ignored Mom's lecture about keeping the gas tank at least one-quarter full.

"Life is not always smooth sailing," he later told me. "Sometimes stuff that you don't like happens. And you have to figure out what to do."

Last visit

In April 2008, I was on a plane with my five-year-old daughter, McKenna. We moved from Texas to Maryland when McKenna was a baby and were flying to visit Dad in the hospital. "I wish Preston could be here," McKenna said, referring to her eight-year-old brother. I knew her bored look all too well.

"Preston has to go to school," I replied. Then, I told McKenna about our family road trips when I was young. She laughed at the part about us being stuck waiting by the side of the road for Dad.

Through more than four decades, I had waited by my share of roads and had yet to get everything I wanted. Still, I had two great children, a career that held my interest, and enough spare cash to take a few road trips each year.

At the hospital, Dad looked different from the previous summer when I had last seen him. He was thinner, more tired and pale, with dark circles under his eyes. At age 84, Dad had dementia and Alzheimer's. He had to be reminded who McKenna was. But he still remembered those road trips that seemed so long ago.

"Remember when you ran out of gas?" I asked, laughing.

Dad laughed. "We drove so far. I didn't like to stop if I didn't have to."

By the next day, Dad's condition improved enough to allow him to return to a nursing home. We spent the next week looking over old photographs of our road trips, gazing out the window in a second-story sunroom, and doing jigsaw puzzles. His eyes lit up when he looked at the photos, remembering a moment.

His life had been memorable. Born in Milford, Conn., before the Great Depression, he graduated from Rye High School in that New York City burb in 1942 and immediately joined the FBI as a fingerprint technician in D.C. The following year, he joined the U.S. Army Air Corps, serving in the South Pacific region during World War II until 1946. He advanced to the rank of sergeant and earned a Good Conduct Medal and other honors.

In photo at left, Dad poses in Rye, N.Y., with his brother and parents around 1930. At right, Preston and McKenna pose at a memorial in Rye that includes Dad's name. Left photo from Jim Shay collection, right by Kevin Shay

At the FBI, he became a fingerprint unit supervisor, then a research analyst, and a special agent. Along the way, he took accounting classes at Georgetown and Southeastern universities, obtaining a bachelor's degree in 1950. Working in the FBI's accounting division, he investigated violations of federal laws and handled a variety of cases. In 1965, his picture was in the Tampa Tribune newspaper while interviewing a clerk about a diamond robbery case. [1]

By 1968, he sought more control over his schedule and left the FBI to pursue stock investing, truck driving, and a vending machine business. He traveled to every state except Alaska and completed his federal retirement with the IRS. He spent much time helping with historical projects like restoring a 19th-century Galveston ship, cycling and driving around White Rock Lake, and participating in numerous activities at his local VFW post. We took a few road trips, including to New Mexico to see the world's largest hot-air balloon festival.

Soon, it was time for McKenna and me to return to Maryland. On our last day together, I wanted to do something Dad would really enjoy. He always was up for a road trip, no matter how short or long. We pushed Dad's wheelchair out the nursing home's front door into the sunshine.

Dad was like a kid in the sunshine and breeze. "Hallelujah!" Dad exclaimed in his trademark phrase in his later years.

**Dad, right, relaxes with other soldiers at a Florida training base in 1943.
Photo from Jim Shay collection**

We wheeled over to a nearby senior center. There, we watched people play pool and do jazzercise. McKenna entertained us with some impromptu piano playing. But Dad soon tired and asked to go back to his room.

We stayed with Dad as he napped, surrounded by his photos and mementos. McKenna and I tried to finish a puzzle that depicted the streets of D.C., where Dad had lived for two decades. We couldn't get it all done. After Dad woke up, we went to the dining hall. McKenna and I attempted to feed him without much luck.

Finally, we took Dad to the empty sunroom. Somehow, I knew this would be our final evening together. As tears welled up in my eyes, I shook Dad's hand and tried to come up with something that wouldn't sound too trite. I told him I loved him. I said he would be going to a better place. I thanked him for everything. He seemed to understand and said he loved me.

McKenna began to cry, as she realized, too, that this would be the last time she would see Grandpa. I tried to comfort her, telling her that things would turn out fine eventually.

"No, it won't. Grandpa will die soon, and I won't ever hear him say 'Hallelujah' to me anymore. That always made me feel happy when he said that," McKenna sobbed, sounding mature beyond her years. She knew that things wouldn't be fine right now. And she was right.

Soon, we saw that Dad had slumped over and fallen asleep in his wheelchair. I wheeled Dad back to his room and lifted him into his bed. He stayed sleeping as I grabbed his hand and said good-bye again. I let McKenna say good-bye, then hugged him again, and left.

I walked halfway down the hall, then told McKenna I had to go back. Dad was awake when I returned. "Bye for now," Dad said, as we shook hands.

I held his hand. "Bye, Dad."

"Bye for now," he repeated.

As I walked down the hall again, I felt like I was stuck by the side of another road. Only this time, as I observed Dad walk away, I knew he would not return. At least not in this life. He passed peacefully less than a week later.

Dad enjoys a Dallas outing with seven grandchildren.   Photo by Kevin Shay

Discovery in Rye

In June 2008, we buried Dad at Arlington National Cemetery. It was an impressive ceremony, with a rifle salute, bugler, and color guard. Inside the solemn, stately chapel, I gave the eulogy without choking up. Time had helped me almost digest his passing by then, as did writing his obit and researching our family background.

During the eulogy, I injected some levity by noting Dad's road games. "Dad also sometimes played a game where he'd try to see how long he could drive without having to stop to get gas," I said. "Usually, we made it to the gas stations; sometimes we didn't and had to wait by the side of the road as he walked or hitchhiked to get some gas. He called that the breaks of the game."

Laughter lightened the heavy occasion. Dad would have appreciated the moment.

In August 2008, I piled Preston and McKenna into our trusty Honda CRV that had served us well for many a road trip. Our destination this time was Rye, N.Y., the burb where Dad lived for much of his youth, and a nearby town in Connecticut, where Dad's parents were buried.

We found the cemetery and located the grave marker of Dad's father with the help of some weeding by Preston and McKenna. But we couldn't find the marker for Dad's mother, though we dug around the grass for more than an hour. Still, we were happy to unearth and improve one of his parent's markers and considered the trip a success.

Soldiers carry Dad's casket to his grave in Arlington National Cemetery in 2008. Photo by Kevin Shay

In Rye, we stopped at the town square and visited a museum that included photographs of what the town was like when Dad was young, compared with the present day. As Preston and McKenna dressed in clothes of older days, I marveled at how well-preserved many of the town's buildings were. People in Rye took good care of what they had. Things lasted. Dad had lasted for some 84 years.

We went outside and played catch in a park on the town square, a game Dad had enjoyed. Then, I spied a memorial with a water fountain, and curiosity pulled me to it. The memorial was in honor of Rye residents who had served in wars, going back to World War II. I searched the relatively long list on a plaque. Sure enough, there was Dad's name. [2]

"Grandpa!" I pointed out to my kids.

"Wow!" exclaimed Preston, as I lifted him up to view the name. "Grandpa is famous here!"

"Yeah, I never knew," I said. "He never spoke about this memorial."

We found the street where Dad lived but could not locate his old house among the well-to-do residences. We visited Playland, an amusement park formed in the 1920s that Dad frequented when young. He had taken us there several times during our road trips. I particularly liked the Dragon Coaster, which Dad also enjoyed as a boy. I let Preston and McKenna pick out one big ride in the park, and they both picked the same – the Dragon Coaster.

"That's the best roller coaster I've ever ridden!" Preston shouted, after experiencing the thrill ride.

"That's what I thought when I was your age," I smiled. "And that's what Grandpa thought when he was your age."

In my kids' faces, I saw myself 40 years ago. I saw Dad 75 years ago. That's what I had come to Dad's hometown to rediscover: the continuity of life. Perhaps a few things don't really change, at least not that much.

Driving back to Maryland, I looked in the rearview mirror at my kids sleeping. I recalled lying in Dad's station wagon myself some four decades ago, sometimes sleeping, sometimes observing the twists and turns along the highway in awe and wonder, sometimes bored. I wished I could take those moments in time – even the ones when we waited for Dad by the side of the road – and freeze them in my mind.

The vehicle's gas gauge pointed to one-quarter full, as I spied an exit sign by the highway. I toyed with the idea of driving on, trying to see how far I could make it without stopping to get gas, in honor of Dad. But I exited and filled up the tank.

My kids had many roads ahead to wait by until they got what they wanted. I didn't need to add to that total, if I could help it.

Somewhere, I think Dad understands.

Dad waves hello or good-bye at the bridge.   Photo by Kevin Shay

Death and Loss: Dancing in the Moment

First published in The Dallas Morning News, Pottsville Republican Herald, and Dallas Patch, August 20, 2021; Medium, August 21, 2021; and *It's a Mad, Mad, Mad, Mad Trip*, 2024

After migrating south from Washington, D.C., in the mid-1960s, my parents started an annual Great American Road Trip ritual. They'd pile their three kids into the station wagon and drive hundreds of miles.

They believed that these marathon trips from Dallas to Shenandoah, Pa., Boston or the Southwest not only allowed us to visit relatives much cheaper than plane tickets would before airlines were deregulated in the late 1970s, but they brought us closer together and provided a more vivid examination of our country. Among the miles of open-road boredom, sign alphabet games, and comic book readings, we'd stop at Stuckey's stores and Big Boy diners and Civil War sites and odd roadside attractions such as long-gone reptile pits.

By 1971, Dad had balked at the summer odyssey tradition. He and Mom's 24-year marriage was on the way to an amiable ending. I initially sided with Mom in their arguments and vowed to stay in Dallas after college to help out.

Mom and kids Kevin, Patrick, and Kathy stand in separate states during a 1970 road trip stop at Four Corners.   Photo by Jim Shay

But in late 1977, I wrote in a college English course assignment, "I realize that some things just do not work, and no one is really to blame. My parents tried to live together because of us, but they found out that they could not live together, and it is probably for the better that they get a divorce."

During that summer of 1971, Mom remained determined not to skip our trip ritual and discovered that Greyhound bus tickets for her and the kids – ages 12, 8, and 6 – were within budget. So we embarked on a 30-hour bus ride to Shenandoah. Then after a week or so, we retraced our path on another bus.

The bus stopped at not just big cities, but many small towns. At each stop, my siblings and I would dash from the vehicle to check the station pay phones for coins. We'd also check vending machines and even restroom stalls. Mom would run after us, yelling to get back on the bus. She usually had to return and plead with the driver to wait until we finally showed.

One time, the driver and other riders helped search for me. "We found Kevin sitting on the floor of a shop reading one of those magazines," Mom would later recall. "What was it called, Mad?"

In time, she uttered her infectious laugh as she told that story. It became something to learn from, something to entertain others and make them smile. But we would not take another trip like that, though Mom later journeyed alone or just with younger sister Kathy by bus.

Doubting the move

Mom long had misgivings about moving to Florida in 1964. She had lived in the nation's capital since during the midst of World War II, leaving the declining Pennsylvania coal-mining town that she often visited to see her mother and other relatives, working for federal government agencies such as the predecessor to the Federal Aviation Administration.

The second thoughts escalated after my older sister, Sharon, died in Tampa of likely Reye's syndrome at the age of nine. Mom had known great loss before, with her father dying in a mining accident at age 35, a mere two days after her eighth birthday. The mining company and feds denied her mother's claim for black lung benefits several times due to the death being judged to be a clot in the lungs resulting from the accident, not pneumoconiosis. But by the 1960s, five of Mom's uncles who were coal miners died of black lung. [1]

Other relatives stepped in and helped my grandmother raise Mom and her brother. That's what people did in those small towns, even during the leaner-than-lean Great Depression years.

Mom never organized a pro-union or anti-coal mining campaign, as I might have had my dad died in a similar workplace accident and his employer refused to take responsibility. It wasn't that she didn't believe in standing up for what she thought was right. It's just that she figured there wasn't much she could do about that particular situation at the time, especially when she was so young, and she had to pick her battles.

For much of her career, she had daily battles to maintain her job in the male-dominated work environment, enduring sexist comments, low pay, car troubles, and worse. She graduated a year early from J.W. Cooper High School in Shenandoah in 1942, ranking 11th in her class of 234 students. She then graduated from the nearby McCann School of Business and Technology in 1943, taking subjects such as business law, bookkeeping, and shorthand. She immediately journeyed to Washington, D.C., to help with the World War II cause, joining the U.S. Maritime Commission. She worked for the commission until 1947, eventually becoming assistant manager of the investigation and correspondence unit and receiving commendations.

But after the war, the men in charge decided she was better fit as an administrative assistant, not manager. She became a medical secretary for the U.S. Civil Aeronautics Administration, the predecessor of the Federal Aviation Administration. She continued to prove her worth through other federal government departments, receiving Special Achievement Awards and other honors.

Sharon's death affected my parents immensely. Dad, an FBI agent, requested a transfer to Dallas but soon quit his dream job to become a truck driver to attempt to better control his schedule and spend more time with family. Like many dealing with the death of a child, Dad initially distanced himself from others, though he maintained close relationships with his children and later became quite the extrovert.

Mom never stopped being an extrovert. She mourned and didn't forget what occurred. She investigated causes of her daughter's death; her notes taken during Sharon's brief illness provided key evidence of her conclusion that it was Reye's syndrome. But she also didn't let those horrendous experiences keep her from staying socially active, emotionally investing in relationships, and helping her family prosper.

One of my parent's arguments soon after Sharon died was over whether to adopt a girl of about her age. Dad lobbied for this idea more than Mom, who supported "the will of God" or whatever controlled such tragedies. Mom, as usual, prevailed.

International exposure

An avid reader herself, Mom long had exposed us to different ideas and cultures. In 1964, she and Dad took Sharon, Kathy, and me to the 1964 World's Fair in Queens, N.Y. Some 80 nations were represented during that 12-month exposition, which continued into 1965 and attracted an average of more than four million visitors each month. A 12-story stainless-steel model of the Earth called the Unisphere that celebrated the Space Age had been built. Nearby Shea Stadium fell in 2009 to make room for a new stadium, but the Unisphere remained in Flushing Meadows Corona Park as a New York landmark. [2]

Most attendees received their first introduction to computers and phone modems there, not to mention new consumer products such as an electric toothbrush. Sharon was so impressed she listed pavilions and exhibits we visited in a notebook, from GM's Futurama to France. Mom kept a pen bought for Sharon there among the school work, hairbrushes, notebooks, Beatles cards, stamps, and other possessions saved following her death. I kept a brochure from Sinclair's Dinoland and an ash tray Mom bought to use for bridge games and other entertaining.

Four years later, my parents took Kathy, younger brother Patrick, and me to the World's Fair in San Antonio. That six-month one attracted considerably fewer people, about one million per month. My favorite part was riding the monorail and going up to the observation deck of the 750-foot high Tower of the Americas, which remained the tallest observation tower in the country until 1996.

We couldn't make the international fairs in Montreal in 1967 – one of the best attended at some nine million per month – and Spokane, Wash., in 1974. But when Knoxville, Tenn., landed the 1982 World's Fair, Mom led us there as part of another long car journey to Shenandoah. Attracting about two million people a month, the fair featured the 266-foot high Sunsphere topped by a five-story golden globe that remained to this day. The Peruvian mummy and ancient artifacts of Eqypt were particularly memorable. Hungary introduced the world's largest Rubik's Cube that transferred to a hotel lobby after the event. We viewed innovations like touch display screens and pay-at-the-pump gas outlets.

I had saved ten bucks – $34 in 2025 dollars – by using my freelance media pass to enter. Divorced since 1977, Mom had welcomed me back into her home after I graduated from the University of North Texas, with Kathy gone to Texas A&M. I paid some rent and even introduced them to a psychic friend. Mom was particularly interested in that field, having had unexplained otherworldly experiences.

The Sunsphere still stands in downtown Knoxville as a remnant from the 1982 World's Fair. Photo by Kevin Shay

At the fair, I put aside the paranormal to ask people about the event's energy efficiency theme. Windmills, waterwheels, hot floor heating systems, and energy efficient appliances were showcased with the latest designs and ideas. Energy saving tips were at each counter. Processes like fluidized bed combustion, geothermic power, fossil fuel recovery, undersea engineering, and synthetic fuel production were explained. Nuclear, solar and wind energy were discussed.

There was creative energy in the form of magicians, mimes, jugglers, and puppets. There was spiritual energy generated at the pop and religious concerts. There were music and dance festivals, parades, films and other outlets. There were people exchanging views with people from different backgrounds, united in a purpose larger than themselves. As barriers were torn down, people saw not color, not nationality, but people.

At one point, we stood around a Caribbean island pavilion near the Sunsphere, listening to musicians play steel-pan drums and maracas. In a spontaneous move, Mom started dancing to the beat, as we tried our best to ignore her. But in between my embarrassment, I noticed the look on her face, which revealed joy, something I hadn't noticed there in a while. She tried to get her kids to dance as well, and we largely resisted. But Mom didn't care about public perceptions at that moment. For those moments, she was free of her cares, her burdens, and was glad to be there, in the middle of this sea of diversity in this Deep South city with her grown-up kids who were still willing to embark on the traditional long summer road trip with her.

New Orleans would host a World's Fair in 1984, Vancouver in 1986. That would be the last one sanctioned by the Bureau International des Expositions held in North America. There was always Disney's more crowded and commercialized Epcot, but there was something special about these World Fairs.

Moving down the road

I married Michelle in 1995, and we had two kids, Preston and McKenna, within seven years. But then, the wheels came off. I lost my dream job with The Dallas Morning News shortly after the 2001 terrorist attacks and held things together by freelancing for multiple newspapers. But our marriage crumbled, and I agreed to move, as she wanted to be closer to family in Allentown, Pa. I was willing to move as far Northeast as D.C. Something about living in the area where I had resided with my family as a toddler appealed to me.

Mom and Dad had met in D.C., when they both worked in federal government positions and attended swing dances at Glen Echo Amusement Park's Spanish Ballroom, which they could access by trolley. They had bonded with others in the war cause, working for something larger than themselves. The energy, diversity, patriotic landmarks, and optimism of the post-war times in the nation's capital made them stay for several decades. In 1954, they married at St. Thomas Apostle Catholic Church near the National Zoo, the neighborhood where Mom lived and not far from where Dad resided in Dupont Circle. I wanted to get to know that area better. And I wished I could recreate some of that commitment to a cause.

So in 2003, I navigated a 28-foot van from Dallas to D.C., then flew back to Dallas with Preston to drive our second vehicle back. Mom wanted to accompany us on another cross-country road trip. What could I say but yes?

On the road trips of my youth, Mom always brought a huge cooler full of food. Most of our breakfasts and lunches were along various rest stops between the Northeast and Texas. This trip provided the same. We stopped at a rest area in Arkansas for lunch and ate turkey sandwiches and fruit. Preston was young enough to appreciate it. Soon, he and McKenna would have none of that tradition, believing those rest stops were only good for snacks, usually the ones they could purchase in machines.

Jackson, Tenn., became the first day's resting site, as usual, since the motels were reasonably priced – that is, before the 2020 pandemic sent prices soaring. Mom drove the Honda CR-V occasionally to give me a break and remembered incidents that occurred on previous trips. In Knoxville, we stopped at the Sunsphere, and Preston had a fun time gazing off the observation deck. I reminded

Mom of her dancing moment here, and she laughed. "The music was good. You have to kick up your heels sometimes."

We didn't stop much after that until we pulled up to the two-bedroom apartment in D.C. burb Gaithersburg. It was a little crowded, but we made it work. As Mom helped unpack boxes and clean, I worked a contract job but took off one day to drive her back to her old neighborhood near the National Zoo. We found the church where she married, as well as one of the boarding houses where she resided. We took Preston to see the pandas at the zoo, one of the oldest in the country, dating to 1889.

Then we drove to the National Mall and took in a few buildings where she once worked. We visited Sharon's grave at Arlington National Cemetery, which also included the burial sites of the Kennedys and William Howard Taft. Then came a drive to Fairfax, Va., to try to find the home where we lived when I was born.

We drove around the area for awhile, but my phone battery died and we couldn't recognize landmarks to lead us to the right neighborhood. "It's around a golf course [Army Navy Country Club] and St. Leo's Catholic Church," Mom remembered. "That was where you were baptized. We loved that neighborhood." Dad had wanted a shorter commute to D.C. so he found a house in District Heights near where his mom lived. We stayed there for about two years until the move to Florida.

Despite our efforts, we couldn't figure out the proper route to St. Leo's. We were tired and didn't stop to ask someone where the church might be. Of course, a few weeks after Mom returned to Dallas, I found the neighborhood easily enough, taking Preston and McKenna to play in Van Dyck Park, as Sharon and I had done more than four decades previously. Mom would have enjoyed that day.

Continuing the long road trip tradition

By 2010, I was officially divorced for four years and implemented an annual long road trip ritual of my own with the kids. We flew a couple times, but then the driving bug hit me. Dad died in 2008 at age 84, succumbing to natural causes that included dementia. As his condition gradually worsened, I visited him in a Dallas area nursing home a week before he passed and said my thank yous and good-byes. Despite the dementia, he seemed to understand.

Kevin, Sharon, Kathy, and Mom visit a Florida park.   Photo by Jim Shay

During the almost 4,000-mile 2010 trip, we tried to track down celebrities, including Miley Cyrus, then McKenna's favorite singer. We rode wild rides, such as a 1,800-foot-long mountain slide that simulated a bobsled ride in Gatlinburg. We hiked in the Great Smoky Mountains to a waterfall and observed a bear in the wild. We searched for buried treasure in the form of huge quartz crystals in Arkansas and rode up and down dirt mountain back roads.

We sneaked into a fancy hotel to swim at Hot Springs' best mountainside resort pool and hot tub, the same hotel where former President Clinton had his proms. Preston, then 10 years old, drove Uncle Patrick's motorboat on a Texas lake, pulling McKenna and cousins on a killer whale-shaped raft.

We made some of the usual tourist stops, including at Graceland during an Elvis impersonator convention and at the Ripley's Believe it or Not museum, aquarium, and haunted house in Gatlinburg. We made some unusual stops, such as at Stonehenge recreation Foamhenge and the Haunted Monster Museum in Virginia. We also had time to take Mom on a road trip to Patrick's lake house some 200 miles from Dallas.

On the drive, Mom made Preston and McKenna laugh with tales from the bus trip and other adventures. While Preston was enthralled with driving the boat, McKenna enjoyed the raft ride, even after cousin Julia yelled, "You have to really hang on, McKenna! There are sharks and crocodiles in this water. You don't want to fall off."

"No, she's just kidding," cousin Krystal said.

"No, for real," Julia said.

Lake Livingston had been featured on the popular Animal Planet television show, *River Monsters*, in which the hosts searched for alligator gar, a freshwater fish that can grow to more than 9 feet long and over 350 pounds. Alligator gar had been suspected in attacks on humans, though none were confirmed. The lake was one of the largest and deepest in Texas, with a surface area of 83,000 acres and a depth of 90 feet. In 2025, one angler would catch a 153-pound gar in this lake. The gars didn't stop cousins Morgan and Austin from gliding on a single ski. [3]

Back at the house, Morgan showed off his potato cannon, which sounded a little like fireworks going off. Some fell into the lake after flying high.

Dinner's barbecued chicken, hamburgers, and hot dogs tasted better than any I had in a long time. We had our own Norman Rockwell moment, sitting there eating, laughing about past incidents, watching the kids play with the potato gun, as the sun went down over the lake. I couldn't remember the last time Mom and all seven of her grandchildren had been with her together.

Preston and McKenna slept for most of the ride back to Dallas, after we stopped at Arby's in Huntsville for roast beef sandwiches and shakes. Mom was quiet for the first few miles. Then she asked if I ever planned to move back to Texas.

"I never say never," I replied. "But the kids have their friends. They don't want to move." I didn't really want to move. The thought of packing everything into a huge van and driving it back over those Tennessee mountains didn't thrill me. I had a decent job with The Washington Post Co.'s Gazette and had gotten used to being close enough to visit New York City, beaches, and mountain towns on day trips.

"Well, you could stay at the house. Preston and McKenna could go to the same schools you did."

"I don't know. I like it in Maryland."

"It is nice when you see the leaves change. That's one thing I miss," Mom said. "But I don't miss shoveling snow."

"That's not so bad. I like having four seasons." I hadn't had to mow a lawn since 2003 so shoveling snow around the CR-V wasn't much of a burden.

Mom quickly changed subjects. "I still don't know what to do about a burial plot."

"Burial plot?"

"Yes, it's something you have to think about." She looked out the window. "I'm not getting any younger."

"You have a long way to go before that."

"I'm 84. Most days, I feel good. But there are some days I'm not sure I will make it."

I laughed. "Well, I'm 51. I have those days sometimes."

"No, but really, have you thought about where you want to be buried?"

"Have I thought about *what*?"

"Where would you like to be buried? Are you planning a plot in Texas or Maryland?"

"I don't... I really haven't thought a lot about it," I half-lied. I had thought some about it. At times, I thought I wanted to find some land, maybe out in western Maryland, Virginia, or West Virginia. I could build a little house on it, live there like the Walton's, and have a burial ground. The place might give the kids some roots, if they wanted that. But at other times, such a place seemed like so many other hollow, pipe dreams. I wasn't sure I was the type who embraced putting down roots.

Dad had wanted that, too. He talked about getting a farm with chickens and other animals, a place where we all could stay. He bought some land in East Texas by a lake, but it remained empty. We had our own lives, and he didn't want to live way out there alone. So the lot remained vacant. I went out there once with him to mow it, and we couldn't even do that because it was so hot and all we had was a weed whacker and a tiny mower. He finally accepted an offer from someone with a tractor to mow it. Though perhaps Dad's dream materialized in another way; the house he bought with Mom became our roots, our shared homestead.

"I might look into Restland," Mom continued. "Everything is pretty expensive."

"Dad was lucky to get into Arlington Cemetery." If it wasn't for Sharon being buried there, he might not have been able to have his ceremony there, since plots filled up quickly by the 21st century at the country's largest national cemetery near D.C. They put his casket right above Sharon's, which was dug deep enough for three caskets to be on top of hers.

"Yeah, your father was lucky," Mom said. "It's too bad I can't be buried there because we got divorced."

"You'd think that 20-something years of marriage would mean something. I mean, they should allow you to be buried there if you lasted at least 20 years." After all, seven years of marriage is the average. Twenty years is a lifetime.

"Well, they don't. It's not a service thing.... There's nothing I can do about that."

"That's not fair."

At Dad's grave site, Mom had almost passed out, but not just from the heat. She had been to numerous funerals, but this one was different. Though they had been divorced for 30 years, Dad was the man in whom she had invested a significant part of her life. The reality of life's final moments on this planet cut too close.

Back in Dallas, I settled into the old room, which was once so familiar and now seemed more like a regular guest room. Mom maintained it nicely with new storm windows, carpet, bedding, and framed pictures of Santa Fe, rather than Farrah Fawcett and Mad posters. I could no longer sneak out the side window to leave at night, or enter when I returned from school as a kid. Still, it had some touches that reminded me of the way it was – the old chin up bar between the doorway, the special marks on the wall that wouldn't come out. Kathy's old room even had the hole in the door that Patrick had made with a broom handle after we locked the door for a more private discussion.

Other rooms in that house had undergone similar upgrades. The living room with the yellow, sunken couch that Dad often slept on had been converted to a formal area with crystal knick-knacks and picture frames, fluffy couches, and an elegant dining table. The den that I converted to my own room as a teenager featured new carpet and furniture, including a flat-screen television. But there were some hints of the past on the built-in shelves, the framed pictures of us in our youth, the glass elephant that I cherished as a kid, the old books.

Walking through the rooms, I wanted a place like this for my kids' lives but wasn't sure I would be able to give them that. Their rock would have to be me personally. Or perhaps the CR-V, which would be an appropriate symbol for their nomadic upbringing.

I tried to play multiple roles in my kids' lives. I helped coach their sports teams and was involved in their Scout dens and school activities, as Mom had been. She held positions in my Scout troop and other groups, somehow finding time as she pursued a career and performed menial household chores. Doing that in my own life lent me a greater appreciation of what she had done.

I remember Mom working a variety of odd jobs to support us, from the cafeteria at Wallace Elementary to doing Census Bureau surveys and delivering phone books. She returned to the federal government in 1973, namely Health, Education, and Welfare, and Immigration and Naturalization Services, and retired in 1990 with a decent pension. She continued to volunteer with the PTA, St. Patrick's Catholic Church, Newcomers Club, library, and more. She remained active in bridge groups and often took scenic trips with friends to Europe, Canada, and other places, visiting at least 17 other nations. Dad attended our activities but was more the outing organizer, taking us to many college and pro sports events, festivals, and parks.

On our last day in Dallas that trip, McKenna and I cut bushes and weeds and cleaned out the garage, taking a big load of unwanted books to Half Price Books' main store, one of the largest in the country. We went out to eat at Tony's, an Italian place that was a big local high school supporter.

We took a photo of the kids with their cousins by the huge fruitless mulberry tree, the traditional spot for photos of people about to depart that house. It was the only tree left standing in that place as the others' roots became too entangled with utility lines and had to be cut down. I had grown up with that tree; my roots were there as much as the tree's.

Marathon road trip

In 2013, I decided to go beyond the trips of the past. The kids were getting old fast, and I wanted to provide them a more memorable journey. Almost 7,000 miles in 17 days, with stops at Mount Rushmore, Yellowstone, Grand Canyon, Vegas, Hollywood, Football Hall of Fame, and more did the trick.

Of course, we paused at Mom's familiar house for our lone restful day. After I drove all night from the Grand Canyon, she was waiting for us with salmon steaks, rolls, salad, and corn on the table, showing her continued cooking prowess at age 87. "Well, there are the world travelers! How was your trip?"

"Long," Preston and McKenna said simultaneously.

Over dinner, we talked about the trip. "We never went all the way across the country and back in about two weeks, right?" I asked.

"No, the farthest we went is Connecticut. Or maybe Boston one summer." She turned to McKenna. "So where was your favorite place to stay on your trip?"

McKenna thought hard. "Hollywood."

"She liked seeing the stars' homes and footprints," I added.

"How about you, Preston?"

"Uh, it was all good. Las Vegas was cool. Those hotels were neat."

"He didn't do too well in blackjack, though. How much did you lose?"

"What? Be quiet, Daddy."

As they relayed more details, I was lost in recalling the summer road trips of my youth. Some nights, we would sleep in the back of the wagon as my parents drove most of the night. Some days, we would stop at a motel with an outdoor pool. I was bored for much of those trips; no iPods, portable DVD players, or even Walkmans. I read *Archie* comic books, travel guides, and sports and *Encyclopedia Brown* novels. I studied maps, teased Kathy and Patrick, and played more than my share of the alphabet sign game.

But as I thought back to my childhood, I recalled those trips more than anything. I wish I had appreciated them more when I was in their midst.

After viewing too many pictures, McKenna and Preston said good night. Mom soon turned in, as well. I should have been able to sleep, but I couldn't. I was wired, like after a big basketball game in high school and college. I ventured into the garage and surveyed the boxes and file cabinets that contained old books, trophies, school papers, and artwork. The garage was the place in this house that most resisted change. There were still many relics from our childhood, though the old catfish head I kept in a jar full of formaldehyde after catching it in White Rock Lake in ninth grade was gone.

I opened a file cabinet drawer, and one folder stood out, as if it called my name. "Sharon," it read. I suddenly remembered for the first time that day that it was my older sister's birthday. I browsed through folders, letters, photos, books, and more memories, until I ended up asleep on a chair in the den. I woke up suddenly and turned off the lights, retreating to my old childhood room-turned-guest room, where I slept better than I had in a long time.

We spent the afternoon swimming in Kathy and Barton's pool and catching up. Cousin Erika worked at a local accounting firm while attending college part-time and sporting a new Nissan Rogue. Julia was almost finished with high school. Kathy was enjoying the summer break as a teacher, while Barton was busy with his tech job, Taekwondo, and completing Kathy's house projects.

We topped off the day by playing the dominoes game, Mexican Train, which Mom – the real card shark in the family – won. A goodbye scene ensured the following day, complete with the traditional pictures in front of the big tree.

'Trying to make the most of life'

By 2017, Mom had to check into a nursing home. She had used a walker for her balance for some time before a major fall caused head damage that required surgery. She pulled through the surgery but had a long period of rehab and needed more care.

I had journeyed to Dallas alone the year before to attend Mom's 90th birthday party. She was in great spirits, quite alert, though she battled Type-2 diabetes, high blood pressure, a thyroid issue, and arthritis, among other medical conditions. I made her a birthday video that included a substantial interview, asking her queries such as the secret of reaching 90 and what advice she would give to younger people.

"I wish I knew what the secret was," she stated. "I was just trying to make the most of life. I like going places. I did a lot of different trips."

Advice included, "Enjoy yourself along the way. Develop some hobbies. Go out and socialize, especially after retirement. You have to live life in moderation. I mean, you have to be sensible about things, about what you can do and what you can't do, and what you can afford and what you can't afford. You kind of have to plan things. Still, there are a lot of things you can do."

Mom ended up in Twin Rivers assisted living community in Richardson, a place she liked. She had friends, regular family visits, activities such as bingo and card games. I visited when I could, but getting the kids there between their school and jobs became tougher. Our annual road trip became more irregular.

I wanted to block off enough time to interview Mom on video about her life, growing up in the Great Depression, picking huckleberries on the hill above Shenandoah, World War II, and changes she had seen. Somehow, that never materialized. I don't know why. I should have made it happen. When I visited, there was always something else going on, or she seemed tired so I didn't push a video interview.

After Christmas 2019, Preston, McKenna, and me found some time to make the drive, taking a longer route through Atlanta to avoid bad weather in the Tennessee mountains. We arrived about a week before her mid-January birthday in 2020. I had requested that Kathy not tell her of our visit to surprise her.

She was sitting at a lunch table in Twin Rivers conversing with some friends. I casually sat down beside her. "Hi, Mom," I said.

She looked like she saw a ghost. "Kevin! Is that really you?"

"Yep. How is the food here? Not as good as what you made at home, I'm sure."

"It's not bad. There are some good cooks here." After retreating to her room, handing out some presents like an abstract painting of D.C., and catching up, we took her outside on a walk around the campus. The sun shined, making the day seem more like a crisp autumn one than the dead of winter. We maneuvered to a basketball goal at the edge of a parking lot, where Preston showed Grandma how he could dunk.

Mom, my longtime protector, nurse, mentor, teacher, tour guide, and more, was the kid now, talking excitedly about past trips and experiences. Our Ford Fiesta was too small to put her in comfortably, but we later placed her in Kathy's minivan and went out to eat to celebrate her birthday at a local restaurant. I bought a cake and had "Happy 94th Birthday Grandma" written on it. We sang "Happy birthday" again. She beamed. She still loved a holiday, a celebration, a birthday. I thought she would have many more.

COVID-19 soon hit, and plane rides and hotel stays became risky. For her 95th birthday, Kathy, Erika, Julia, and her two young daughters had to keep a distance from Mom and wear masks.

At age 90, Mom has a birthday party at a Dallas-area restaurant.   Photo by restaurant waitress

In midsummer, Mom had some more setbacks, requiring rehab and a move to a nursing home that could provide more extensive care. I was working on a house I bought and planned to visit after getting Preston and McKenna off to college in August. I talked to Mom in late July, and she seemed in good spirits. The conversation was light, staying away from any heart-felt good-byes. Perhaps that was how we both wanted it.

About a week later on August 8, I tried to call and couldn't get through. She was having problems answering her phone. The next morning, she fell as workers tried to put her into a wheelchair. Things went downhill fast. She stayed in bed most of the day and didn't feel like talking much.

Then on the morning of the 10th, Kathy called, tearfully informing me that Mom had passed away in her sleep. The next few days were a blur of making funeral plans, writing an obituary, ironing out travel details.

At the funeral service at Restland, I tried to keep remarks light, retelling the long bus ride we took when I was 12. I spoke about resisting a college friend's requests to write in more depth about his men-are-better-than-women theory because even as a 19-year-old, I knew it wasn't true since Mom set the best example for me, showing she was as good as anyone with grace, style, and a smile. Others made better points and remembrances. We put items in her casket – photos, a rosary, cards, including a Mother's Day one from years ago in which I wrote, "Thanks for everything in life. Love, Kevin."

"At least I thanked her once," I noted.

She looked so peaceful in her casket, like she was taking a nap. As I held her hand and said good-bye, I expected her to wake up. But Mom just laid there, her normally warm hand strangely cold.

At the grave site, Preston relayed a heart-felt prayer. We laid flowers on her casket, then watched it drop into the Earth. We dispersed and attended lunch at Mom's old house that Erika and husband Sam purchased, keeping it in the family. Soon, it was just immediate family members. We took another photo at the tree in front of Mom's old house. We searched through a few boxes of Mom's belongings. I found some items of interest, including her mink hand warmers and wedding cake ornament. But my mind and heart were miles away.

We left the following day, thanking Kathy for all she did for Mom, taking over her finances and maneuvering through the nursing home process, among others. "I know she appreciated what you did," I said.

There was not much else to say. I bought some flowers and returned to Mom's grave. The canopy was still up, and the dirt around the grave was fresh. We had a little lunch picnic in her honor. Restland was our first rest area stop on our summer road trip home.

Mom's grandchildren carry her casket to the grave site at Restland in Dallas on August 14, 2021. Photo by Kevin Shay

"You'll always be with us, Mom," I said. "Come with us on another long road trip." I would soon lay some flowers from her grave onto the graves of her mother and brother in Pennsylvania.

On the journey back to Maryland, we sneaked into the Hot Springs hotel pool again, the first time we had done that in nine years, just to see if some things remained the same. We ate stew and chili in Memphis and barbecue in Nashville. We slept in an overpriced Jackson motel. We refueled at the Parthenon replica near Vanderbilt University.

Driving through downtown Knoxville, I considered stopping at the Sunsphere to try to rekindle the dancing memory. But it was getting late, and we had more than 450 miles left to drive.

In the corner of my eye, I spotted the Sunsphere among the city's less innovative structures, reflecting the setting sun. In my mind's eyes, I saw Mom suspended above it, dancing in the moment, smiling upon us, happy to see her kids and grandchildren living decent lives.

Mom and Dad wave goodbye in front of their car after their 1954 wedding in D.C.. Photo from Jim Shay collection

Epilogue: Still Searching for Utopia

After I passed my 66th birthday, I continued to display signs such as one reading, "Stop the Department of Greedy Egomaniacs," at various protests in the Washington, D.C., area. It seems I have spent my life protesting against one ill or another, pointing out life's absurdities with attempted stinging wit, standing up for injustice, for our constitutional rights to force those in power to address the grievances that plague our society.

I have done this in various forms, through writing letters, social media posts, columns, essays, articles, and books, walking, talking, questioning, arguing, standing on a street corner or in front of a government building with a sign, placing handbills in public places, distributing publications, throwing buttons over walls, smuggling books and coffees into foreign places, sheltering the needy from the rain. I have gone beyond protests and complaints to work for solutions, such as helping to start retreats and businesses and mentoring young people as a volunteer for the Boy Scouts, Girl Scouts, and youth sports. Then there were stints with the Sierra Club, ACLU, and other worthy groups.

The late James Peck, a more committed social justice advocate than me, once said, "It is my philosophy that the struggle has to be a non-ending one, because I am not one of those idealists who envision a utopia." Between the 1930s and 1980s, Peck was arrested more than 60 times for labor, social, civil rights, and environmental causes. He was beaten mercilessly more times than most. Perhaps he knew more about the pitfalls of standing up for your ideals than me. But I'm still one of those idealists who cling to a vision of a utopia.

Perhaps it is not of this world. Perhaps it still can be. There are moments when I have glimpsed that vision walking along a dusty road singing songs of uplift, driving along a lonely, twisted road overlooking a majestic scene, listening to the laughter of my kids and their friends running around a playground, getting caught up in the music, mayhem, and collective energy of a large crowd that seems to agree on a singular cause. It's here if we seek it. The question is for how long. Are they mere moments that vanish as quickly as they arise? Or can we make them remain longer than a fleeting flash in time?

I don't have the answer to that. There are always more questions than answers. I only know that the only way to make a vision a reality is to persevere during the most severe tests, to hold fast to the vision no matter what occurs. This life appears on some levels to be one long examination of will. At some point, we get tired of that and rest. At some point, we rest longer than others.

The above anti-DOGE sign appeared at protests throughout the D.C. area in 2025, including at the White House, Washington Monument, Lincoln Memorial, Heritage Foundation headquarters, Frederick City Hall, and U.S. Treasury Department headquarters. Below, Shay displays a different sign at the Capitol during the We Are America March, which he joined for six days. Above photo by Shay, below by Duane

In rereading and rewriting some of these articles, columns, and essays I have written, I renew my sense of purpose. I commit stronger to pursue a vision of utopia. I see that it doesn't have to be a grand dream-come-true with mansions and ponies for all. It can be a simple one where people are free to pursue the creative sparks within them. Yet, even that seemingly simple vision is damn hard to obtain in this life.

So it goes.

I wasn't always a liberal type in this life, but I have always been one to question the status quo, especially when that status quo goes against the concept of liberty and justice for all. In the end, I believe that standing up for that concept is the primary action that matters in this life. Don't let the bigots tell you that staying woke to authoritarianism and injustice is negative. May we all stay woke and keep striving to be up to the test.

Appendix

Acknowledgments

Putting together a memoir-like collection of essays can be a daunting task. Remembering everyone who helped get you to where you are can be even more daunting.

My parents, Dorothy and Jim Shay, taught me early in life that standing up for what you believe is important. My siblings, Sharon, Kathy, and Patrick, provided crucial support. Early childhood friends remained true, including Steve, Ken, David, and Bob.

Relatives, including cousins Mike, Barbara, and Tim, stood up for causes in the 1970s before me. Journalism professors, including Delores Griffin at Richland College in Dallas and Richard Wells at the University of North Texas in Denton, helped broaden my horizons beyond sports. Journalists such as Jim Erwin, Lawrence Young, and Jim Marrs taught me to knock on any door without fear. People who I met along the way, including Pulitzer Prize-winning journalist Seymour Hersh and JFK killing witness Bill Newman, provided more inspiration.

Dallas civil rights advocate Roy Williams became a great friend and mentor, as he tackled seemingly lost causes in the far-right corners of Texas with perseverance and grace. Fellow justice advocates Dale, Andy, Pamela, Mary, Solange, Prem, and more walked with me along a difficult road.

My kids, Preston and McKenna, their mom, Michelle, and partner Christy provided a wealth of inspiration and support. Sorry I left out many. This could go on a long time, but it's time to head on down the road.

Notes

As with other heavily-researched books I've written, I include footnotes here to detail specific sources. That's something many books get away from, but I think it's important to know the source of information.

Introduction
[1] Douglas Birch, "The U.S.S.R. and U.S. Came Closer to Nuclear War Than We Thought." The Atlantic, May 28, 2013.//
[2] John Mecklin, "Closer than ever: It is now 89 seconds to midnight." 2025 Doomsday Clock statement, Bulletin of the Atomic Scientists, January 28, 2025.//
[3] Yana Gorokhovskaia and Cathryn Grothe, "Freedom in the World 2025: The Uphill Battle to Safeguard Rights." Freedom House, 2025.//
[4] Raymond D. Gastil, "Freedom in the World, 1985-1986." Freedom House, Greenwood Press, 1986.

The Big Issues

Taking on the Big Issues
[1] Terry Gross, "Get on the Bus: The Freedom Riders of 1961." NPR, January 12, 2006; Amanda Onion, "Freedom Riders." Historydotcom, January 20, 2022.//
[2] Jeff Smith, "Grand Rapids Freedom Rider Walter Bergman." Grand Rapids People's History Project, February 22, 2016.//
[3] James Peck, Freedom Ride. Simon & Schuster, 1962; Eric Pace, "James Peck, 78, Union Organizer Who Promoted Civil Rights Causes." The New York Times, July 13, 1993.//
[4] David Halberstam, *The Children*. Random House, 1998.//
[5] "Interview with Jim Zwerg, Civil Rights Activist, United States." Peoples Century, WGBH/ PBS, May 2011.//
[6] Henry Hampton and Steve Fayer, *Voices of Freedom*. Bantam Books, 1991, pp. 87-88.//
[7] Hampton and Fayer, op. cit., pp. 136-37.//
[8] News release, "Youth and the 2024 Election: Likely to Vote and Ready to Drive Action on Key Political Issues." Center for Information and Research on Civic Learning and Engagement, Tufts University, November 29, 2023.

Housing and Society: Searching for Utopia
[1] Ben Huttash, "Denton's underground houses at Whitehawk Valley." Preserve Denton, April 2, 2014.//
[2] Herk Sampson, "Underground Homes - Wave of the Future." Eternal Flame, Dallas, February 1982.

[3] Bruce E. Johansen, Forgotten Founders: How the American Indian Helped Shape Democracy. The Harvard Common Press, 1982.

[4] Margaret Atwood, "Best Utopia: God is in the Details." The New York Times Magazine, April 18, 1999; "Experiments with Utopia." Independence Hall Association, Philadelphia, Pa., 2014.

[5] Aaron McEmrys, "Brook Farm." Dictionary of Unitarian and Universalist Biography, project of the Unitarian Universalist Studies Network, April 4, 2006.

[6] Gayla Brooks, "Oak Cliff history: How the La Reunion colony influenced the culture of our neighborhood." Oak Cliff Advocate, March 31, 2014.

[7] Tony Paterson, "In Germany's Twelve Tribes sect, cameras catch 'cold and systematic' child-beating." The Independent, Sept. 10, 2013.

[8] Foundation for Intentional Community directory; Anna Spinner, "Peace, Love, and Social Security: Baby Boomers Retire to the Commune." The Atlantic, Nov. 21, 2011.

[9] Raj Ghoshal, "Twin Oaks Community: History of a Successful Commune." Culture Change, Sustainable Energy Institute, Santa Cruz, Calif., 2002.

[10] Jonathan Costen, "Off the grid: Striving for a Utopia." WRIC ABC News, Nov. 4, 2015.

[11] Katie Gilbert, "Communes still thrive decades after the '60s, but economy is a bummer, man." Al Jazeera America, Dec. 7, 2014.

[12] Jill Ettinger, "It Took 50 Years, But The Farm's '70s Hippie Ideals Are Finally Mainstream." Ethos, July 21, 2023.

[13] Shay, Walking through the Wall. Lulu Press, 2012, p. 257.

[14] Jeanne Segal, Jeanne, Lawrence Robinson, Melinda Smith, "Conflict Resolution Skills: Building the Skills that Can Turn Conflicts into Opportunities." HelpGuide.org, December 2023.

[15] Lucy Sargisson, "Strange Places: Estrangement, Utopianism and Intentional Communities." Utopian Studies, Vol. 18, No. 3, Summer 2007, pp. 393+. From Gale Literature Resource Center.

[16] Gryffin Cook, Noah Ferguson-Dudding, Louis Macalister, "New Zealand's Last Hippie Commune." The Department of Information, YouTube, September 28, 2022.

[17] McEmrys, op. cit.

[18] Ibid.

[19] Cohousing Association of the United States directory.

[20] Karen Gimnig, "Why I'm Leaving Cohousing ... Again." Cohousing Blog, April 11, 2023.

[21] Sargisson, "Second-wave Cohousing: A Modern Utopia?" Utopian Studies, Vol. 23, No. 1, pp. 28-56. From Gale Literature Resource Center.

[22] "Why tiny houses?" Tiny Home Industry Association, 2024.

[23] Loren C. Impson, "Ferrocement Earth Sheltered Housing Projects." The Potential of Earth-Sheltered and Underground Space: Today's Resource for Tomorrow's Space and Energy Viability, edited by T. Lance Holthusen. Pergamon Press, 1981.

Public vs. Private Land: Who Owns America?

[1] Eric Kasum, "Columbus Day? True Legacy: Cruelty and Slavery." HuffPost, October 10, 2016.

[2] Vincent Schilling, "Eight Myths and Atrocities about Christopher Columbus and Columbus Day." Indian Country Today, October 15, 2020.

[3] Howard Zinn, *A People's History of the United States*. Harper & Row, 1980.

[4] Carol Vincent, "Federal Land Ownership." Congressional Research Service, 2020.

[5] Matthew Yglesias, "Nine charts that explain the history of global wealth." Vox, December 16, 2014.

[6] "Land Report 100." The Land Report, 2025.

[7] Rob LaFranco, "World's Billionaire List." Forbes, 2024.

[8] Anthony Shorrocks, "Global Wealth Report 2023." Credit Suisse Research Institute, 2023.

[9] G. William Domhoff, "Wealth, Income, and Power." Who Rules America? 2017

[10] Ralph Nader, "Who Really Owns America?" The American Conservative, May 21, 2014.

Climate Change: Where is the Will for Real Action?

[1] "The Ice Hunter." Rolling Stone, November 3, 2005.

[2] Shay, "As Earth Day approaches, where is the political will to do more about climate change?" Democracy Guardian, April 19, 2024; Shay, "Climate scientist: Change will have to be led from 'bottom up'." NewsBreak, April 20, 2024.

[3] "Global Climate Highlights 2024." Copernicus Climate Change Service, European Union Earth Observation Programme, January 10, 2025.

[4] Press release, "WMO confirms 2024 as warmest year on record at about 1.55°C above pre-industrial level." United Nations United Meteorological Organization, January 10, 2025.

[5] "Assessing the Global Climate in 2024." National Centers for Environmental Information/NOAA, January 10, 2025; "Global Sea Ice, January 1979-2025." National Snow and Ice Data Center, University of Colorado Boulder.

[6] "February made me shiver [but not the Arctic]." NSIDC, March 4, 2025.

[7] "Atmospheric CO2 Growth Rates." CO2.earth, March 5, 2025; CO2 data readings at Mauna Loa Observatory, U.S. National Oceanic and Atmospheric Administration, March 1958-February 2025.

[8] News releases, "Trump Administration Opens the Entire Coastal Plain of the Arctic National Wildlife Refuge to Oil and Gas Leasing." Earthjustice, October 23, 2025; "Latest Documents Uncovered by Sierra Club Reveal Americans Oppose Efforts to Whitewash History on Public Lands." Sierra Club, December 11, 2025.

[9] Brian Kennedy, Alec Tyson, "How Americans View Climate Change and Policies to Address the Issue." Pew Research Center, December 9, 2024.

[10] David Remnick, "Ozone Man." The New Yorker, April 16, 2006.

[11] Shay, "Plans offered to curb pollution." The Dallas Morning News, May 23, 2000.

[12] Shay, "Warming to the challenges." Maryland Gazette of Politics and Business, Post-Newsweek Media Inc., October 26, 2007.

[13] J., Ettinger Fine, et. al, "Climate Change in the American Mind: Public Perceptions of the Health Harms of Global Warming." Yale Program on Climate Change Communication, George Mason University Center for Climate Change Communication., February 28, 2025.

[14] "World's most polluted countries & regions." IQAir, 2023.

[15] Jumaina Siddiqui; Zaara Wakeel, "India, Pakistan choke on their smog. Can they clear the air?" U.S. Institute of Peace, March 29, 2021.

Natural Disasters: A Growing Threat

[1] Jeff Renner, "Inside the Red Zone: Remembering the Eruption of Mount St. Helens." Columbia: The Magazine of Northwest History, Spring 2020.

[2] Don Swanson, "A geologist remembers the Mount St. Helens eruption 37 years ago." Volcano Watch, Hawaiian Volcano Observatory, USGS, May 11, 2017.

[3] "Mud, ash inundate old Truman's lodge." UPI, May 21, 1980.

[4] Maggie Jackson Dean, comment on "As a Mexico volcano erupts, some remember the Mount St. Helens disaster." NewsBreak, May 26, 2023.

[5] Peter W. Lipman, Donal Ray Mullineaux, The 1980 eruptions of Mount St. Helens, Washington. USGS Professional Page #1250, 1981.

The summit of St. Helens was shrouded in clouds during a 2022 visit. Parts of the surrounding area were still bare, while much land supported new life.
Photo by Kevin Shay

⁶ Melanie Holmes, *A Hero on Mount St. Helens: The Life and Legacy of David A. Johnston.* University of Illinois Press, 2019.

⁷ Heidi Koehler and Steven Sobieszczyk, "New USGS map shows where damaging earthquakes are most likely to occur in U.S." USGS news release, January 16, 2024; Shay, "New federal earthquake map highlights more areas of significant activity than Alaska, West Coast." NewsBreak, March 20, 2024.

⁸ Holmes, op. cit.

Civil Rights and the Danger of Standing Up: The 1960s Assassination Conspiracies

¹ Mark Feldstein, "The Nixon White House plotted to assassinate a journalist 50 years ago." The Washington Post, March 25, 2022.

² Rick Bowers, Spies of Mississippi. National Geographic, 2019, pp. 30-32; Earnest McBride, "Honors for Clyde Kennard came after death, author says." Jackson Advocate, May 8, 2023.

³ Jeffrey H. Caufield, *General Walker and the Murder of President Kennedy: The Extensive New Evidence of a Radical-Right Conspiracy.* Moreland Press, 2015, pp. 141, 174, 197-98; FBI file, "Mary McPhilomy Davison, aka Mrs. Clyde Davison." U.S. Army Intelligence report, November 25, 2018.

⁴ "Lynching, Whites & Negroes, 1882-1968." Tuskegee University report, 2010; "History of Lynching in America." NAACP, 2025.

⁵ Jennifer Taylor, Andrew Childers, et al., "Lynching in America: Confronting the Legacy of Racial Terror," Third edition. Equal Justice Initiative, 2017.

⁶ Hampton and Fayer, op. cit., pp. 151-52.

⁷ Bernard LaFayette Jr., *In Peace and Freedom: My Journey in Selma.* University of Kentucky Press, 2015.

⁸ "Trials: Hung Jury." Time, February 14, 1964; FBI teletype, "Morning session Beckwith trial." January 31, 1964, February 4, 1964.

⁹ Reed Massengill, *Portrait of a Racist.* St. Martin's Press, 1994, p. 197.

¹⁰ Massengill, op. cit., p. 201.

¹¹ Adam Nossiter, *Of Long Memory.* Hachette Books, 1994.

¹² Jerry Mitchell, *Race Against Time.* Simon & Schuster, 2020, p. 18; Mitchell, "The case of the supposedly sealed files – and what they revealed." Nieman Reports, September 9, 2011.

¹³ Mitchell, op. cit., pp. 68-69, 80-84, 90-92, 96-97, 124.

¹⁴ David Talbot, *Brothers: The Hidden History of the Kennedy Years.* Free Press, 2007, pp. 5-7.

¹⁵ Glenn C. Altschuler, "The Devil's Chessboard, by David Talbot." San Francisco Gate, October 16, 2015; Talbot, *The Devil's Chessboard: Allen Dulles, the CIA, and the Rise of America's Secret Government.* HarperCollins Publishers, 2015; Oliver Stone, The Joe Rogan Experience. Spotify podcast, no. 1759, January 5, 2022.

¹⁶ Edwin Black, "The plot to kill JFK in Chicago." Chicago Independent, November 1975.

[17] Abraham Bolden, *The Echo from Dealey Plaza*. Crown, 2008.

[18] "Transcript of Milteer-Somersett Tape," Mary Ferrell Foundation website.

[19] Don Adams, *From an Office Building with a High-Powered Rifle*. Trine Day, 2012.

[20] Hampton and Fayer, op. cit.

[21] Mitchell, op. cit., pp. 333-34, 338.

[22] Amy Goodman, "Spies of Mississippi." Democracy Now! February 25, 2014; Rick Bowers, "Spies of Mississippi." National Geographic, 2010, pp. 16-17.

[23] Ralph D. Fertig, *A Passion for Justice*. Dorrance Publishing Co., 2018, p. 208.

[24] "Hope for three wanes as Dulles opens Mississippi talks." The New York Times, June 25, 1964.

[25] A.L. Hopkins, "Investigation of integration and further investigation into the disappearance of three civil rights workers." Mississippi State Sovereignty Commission, July 3, 1964, Massengill, op. cit., p. 206.

[26] Jerry Mitchell, "Mr. X, 'Unsung Hero' in Slaying of Three Men." Clarion-Ledger, June 12, 2005.

[27] Josiah Bates, "The enduring mystery of Malcolm X's assassination." Time, February 20, 2020; Hampton and Fayer, op. cit., p. 261.

[28] News release, "Assassination Conspiracy Trial." The Martin Luther King, Jr. Center for Nonviolent Social Change, 1999.

[29] Dan Christensen, "King Assassination: FBI ignored its Miami informer." Miami Magazine, October 1976; Becky Little, "While King's family believes Ray was not his killer." History, April 4, 2018.

[30] Tom Jackman, "Who killed Bobby Kennedy? His son RFK Jr. doesn't believe it was Sirhan Sirhan." The Washington Post, June 5, 2018; The Truth and Reconciliation Committee, "The Investigation." Justice for RFK.

[31] Edward J. Curtin Jr., "The Blatant Conspiracy behind Senator Robert F. Kennedy's Assassination." Behind the Curtain, May 27, 2018.

[32] Dave Roos, "The 1969 raid that killed Black Panther leader Fred Hampton." Historydotcom, August 11, 2023.

[33] Drew Taylor, "Was an FBI informant involved in the 16th Street Baptist Church bombing?" CBS News 42, September 15, 2023; Michael T. Kaufman, "Rowe, who informed on klan in civil rights killing, is dead." The New York Times, October 4, 1998.

[34] Jerry Mitchell, "KKK killed Ben Chester White, hoping to lure and kill MLK." Clarion-Ledger, June 10, 2014.

Social Justice: Dream Deferred

[1] Bill Minutaglio and Steven L. Davis, "The Night Martin Luther King Jr. Came to Dallas." Texas Observer, October 28, 2013.

[2] Martin Luther King Jr., "Letter from Birmingham Jail." Bill of Rights Institute, April 16, 1963.

[3] Josh Bivens and Jori Kandra, "CEO pay slightly declined in 2022." Economic Policy Institute, September 21, 2023.

[4] Tim Naftali, "Ronald Reagan's Long Hidden Racist Conversation with Richard Nixon." The Atlantic, July 30, 2019.

[5] Alice Bonner, "The 20th Anniversary March on Washington." The Washington Post, August 28, 1983.

[6] Lena Hodge, "Speaking for themselves." Hard Times News, September 1983.

[7] Clarice Bates, "Speaking for themselves." Hard Times News, September 1983.

[8] Andrea Cervantes, "Speaking for themselves." Hard Times News, September 1983.

Authoritarianism: Putin and the Rise of Dictators

[1] Shay, "Russia held 1991 coup plotters accountable. Why can't the U.S.?" Democracy Guardian, February 19, 2021.

[2] Ron Synovitz, "What Happened to the August 1991 Soviet Coup Plotters?" Radio Free Europe, August 19, 2016.

[3] Catherine Belton, "Did Vladimir Putin Support Anti-Western Terrorists as a Young KGB Officer?" Politico, June 20, 2020; Nick Walsh, "KGB 'kept in power by Putin." The Guardian, February 28, 2004.

[4] Masha Gessen, *The Man Without a Face: The Unlikely Rise of Vladimir Putin*. Penguin Group, 2012, pp. 118-23.

[5] Adrian Karatnycky, General Editor, "Freedom in the World, 1999-2000." Freedom House, February 2000.

[6] Andrei Soshinikov and Carl Shreck, "The Brutal Killing of a Reporter who Probed Putin's Past." Radio Free Europe, June 22, 2022.

[7] Gessen, op. cit., pp. 12-16, 254.

[8] Ibid., pp. 20-21, 132-34.

[9] Ibid., pp. 26-27, 38-41.

[10] Ibid., pp. 173-74.

[11] Anna Politkovskaya, "Her Own Death, Foretold." The Washington Post, October 15, 2006.

[12] Linda Qiu, "Does Vladimir Putin kill journalists?" PolitiFact, January 4, 2016; Gessen, op. cit., p. 226.

[13] Jonathan Chait, "Will Trump be meeting with his counterpart or his handler?" New York Magazine, July 9, 2018; Malcolm Nance, *The Plot to Destroy Democracy: How Putin and His Spies Are Undermining America and Dismantling the West*. Hachette Books, 2018, p. 1.

[14] Anita Kumar, "Buyers tied to Russia." McClatchy DC, June 19, 2018; Bill Littlefield, "A Day with President Trump." WBUR, May 11, 2017; Jeff Nesbit, "Donald Trump's Many, Many, Many, Many Ties to Russia." Time, Aug. 2, 2016.

[15] Paul Krugman, "Useful Idiots Galore." The New York Times, Dec. 16, 2016; Jason Hiner, "Mueller Report update." CNET, May 30, 2019; John Kruzel, "The Russia investigation and Donald Trump: a timeline from on-the-record sources." Politico, July 24, 2019.

[16] Michael Isikoff and David Corn, *Russian Roulette: The Inside Story of Putin's War on America and the Election of Donald Trump.* Twelve, 2018.

[17] *United States of America v. Viktor Borisovich Netyksho et al.* U.S. District Court for D.C., July 13, 2018.

[18] Stephanie Grisham, *I'll Take Your Questions Now: What I saw at the Trump White House.* HarperCollins, 2021, pp. 211-13.

[19] "Freedom in the World: Hungary." Freedom House, 2025.

[20] Sergei Kuznetsov, "Belarusian opposition leader on trial as Lukashenko continues his crackdown." Politico, February 17, 2021.

[21] Grisham, op. cit., pp. 210-11.

[22] "Freedom in the World." Freedom House, 2020.

[23] Heather Cox Richardson, *Letters from an American.* Substack, January 28, 2025; Thom Hartmann, "Trump's Hostile Takeover of America: The Corporate Raider's Final Heist." The Hartmann Report, January 29, 2025.

[24] David Klepper and Lisa Mascaro, "Here's a look at Musk's contact with Putin and why it matters."The Associated Press, October 25, 2024; "Conspiracy theory spreading on social media about Starlink interfering with election results." Center for an Informed Public, University of Washington, November 18, 2024.

[25] Timothy Snyder, "Why Greenland?" Thinking about… January 15, 2025.

[26] Yana Gorokhovskaia and Cathryn Grothe, "Freedom in the World 2025: The Uphill Battle to Safeguard Rights." Freedom House, February 26, 2025.

Democracy: The Valor of Vigils and Marches

[1] Nur Ibrahim, "Fact Check What Charlie Kirk actually said about Biden getting 'the death penalty'." Snopes, September 17, 2025

[2] The Atypical Witch, Threads, September 14, 2025; Art Jipson and Paul J. Becker, "Analysis: What data shows about political extremist violence." PBS News, September 22, 2025.

[3] Kathleen E. Carey, "Haverton woman co-organizing march to Washington." Delaware County Daily Times, August 30, 2025.

[4] Lillian Glaros, "Demonstrators march to show support for American democracy." Capital News Service, September 15, 2025.

[5] Yuri Perelman and Sophia Cooper, "We Are America March welcomed in Washington DC by large crowd on National Mall." American University Eagle, September 29, 2025.

[6] Kevin Shay, *Death of the Rising Sun.* Random Publishers, 2017.

[7] Andy Zipser, "The Valor of Vigils." Phoenix New Times, April 1984.

The Afterlife: Exploring What Happens After Death

[1] Lauren Canaday, "The strange and beautiful aftermath of sharing my 'death' story on the interwebs." Cognitively Intact, Substack, January 5, 2024; Alice Gibbs, "Woman Clinically Dead for 24 Minutes Shares Astonishing Experience." Newsweek, December 24, 2023.

² Canaday, "If you can't say something nice…" Cognitively Intact, Substack, October 15, 2025.

³ Aristos Georgiou, "Near-Death Experiences Can 'Totally Transform' a Person in Seconds, Says Scientist." Newsweek, March 8, 2021; Shay, "Life after death meets science." NewsBreak, January 16, 2024.

⁴ News release, "Lucid Dying: Patients Recall Death Experiences During CPR." NYU Grossman School of Medicine and NYU Langone Health, November 6, 2022.

⁵ Georgiou, op. cit.

⁶ Rick Komotar, "Dr. Bruce Greyson – Near-Death Experiences: The Science Behind the Phenomena." *The Brain Surgeon's Take*, October 18, 2023.

⁷ Robert G. Mays and Suzanne B. Mays, "Investigation of George Ritchie's NDE OBE." Self Conscious Mind, February 18, 2010.

⁸ Herk Sampson, "New Age Dawns, Psychics Go Public." Eternal Flame, January 1982.

⁹ Taylor Orth, "Two-thirds of Americans say they've had a paranormal encounter." YouGov, October 20, 2022.

¹⁰ R.D. Whitaker, *Ghosts of Dealey Plaza*. Amazon, 2015.

¹¹ Nibor Noals, "We saw John F. Kennedy in early 1990s." About, April 11, 2016.

¹² Megan Peterson, "The Ghosts of Gettysburg." *Mysterious Journeys*, Travel Channel, October 5, 2007.

¹³ Laine Crosby, "A Beautiful Mistake." *Cognitive Dissonance*, October 7, 2008.; *Investigative Medium – The Awakening*. The Redd Group, December 31, 2013; Shay, "Taking Paranormal Mainstream." The Maryland Gazette of Politics and Business, Post-Newsweek Media Inc., October 27, 2006.

¹⁴ Steve DiSchiavi and Amy Allan, "Invaded." *The Dead Files*, Travel Channel, December 27, 2013; Shay, "Spooky Texas restaurant up for sale. Medium, October 6, 2022.

¹⁵ Ann Harden, "Traveling Texas: Catfish Plantation restaurant serves 'souls and spirits'." KXXV-TV, October 26, 2022.

¹⁶ "Welcome to Texas: Catfish Plantation." CBS 11 News, February 25, 2016.

More Societal Ills

Race and Class: Why was Ruben Triplett Murdered?

¹ "Married Couples by Race," Table 60, U.S. Census Bureau, Statistical Abstract of the United States: 2011; Yanyi K. Djamba and Sitawa R. Kimuna, "Are Americans Really in Favor of Interracial Marriage? A Closer Look at When They Are Asked About Black-White Marriage for Their Relatives." Journal of Black Studies, July 10, 2014; Gretchen Livingston and Anna Brown, "Intermarriage in the U.S. 50 Years After *Loving v. Virginia*." Pew Research Center, May 2017.

² Allen Pusey, "Triplett on phone when shot." Dallas Times Herald, July 28, 1980.

³ Travis Brown, "Banker kills spouse, ex-SMU star, himself." Dallas Times Herald, July 28, 1980.

[4] Mary Barrineau, "Patrick moody, quiet, shocked neighbors say." Dallas Times Herald, July 28, 1980.

[5] Pusey, op. cit.

[6] Ibid.

[7] Brad Bailey, "Triple killing triggers more questions than answers." The Dallas Morning News, July 29, 1980.

[8] Brown, op. cit.

[9] Ibid.

[10] Ibid.

[11] "While Prewitt returns to Mustang drawing board." UPI, March 5, 1973.

[12] "10 Year Review," Gun Violence Archive, 2025; "Homicide Rate from Firearms, 2021," United Nations Office on Drugs and Crime, 2023.

[13] Tuskegee University report, op. cit.

[14] Taylor, Childers, op. cit.

[15] Roy H. Williams and Shay, *And Justice For All: The Untold History of Dallas*. CGS Communications, 1999.

Education: The Religious Right's Long Campaign to Destroy Public Education

[1] Media Matters staff, "Moms for Liberty co-founder calls for 'conservative search firms' to find 'new educational leaders' because current educators will all be fired." Media Matters for America, March 31, 2022.

[2] George N. Green, *The Establishment in Texas Politics*. Greenwood, 1979.

[3] Jennifer Jenkins, "I'm a Florida school board member. This is how protesters come after me." The Washington Post, October 20, 2021.

[4] Ray McNulty, "The stories we could tell about this mom." Vero News, July 27, 2023.

[5] Maurice T. Cunningham, *Merchants of Deception: Parent Props and Their Funders*.Network for Public Education, February 2023.

[6] Patrick Phillips, Nick Reagan, "Charleston Co. school board member issues statement amid calls to resign." WCSC 5News, April 3, 2023.

[7] Debra Hale-Shelton, "Moms for Liberty member avoids criminal charges over comment about gunning down a school librarian." Arkansas Times, June 22, 2022.

[8] News release, "Second Annual Hide the Pride Launches June 1." CatholicVote, May 30, 2023.

[9] Katherine Fung, "Republican's Wife Replaces Library Books With Bibles." Newsweek, August 8, 2023.

[10] Rachel Barber, "Moms for Liberty co-founder tells American parents they have something in common with Trump." USA Today, April 14, 2024.

[11] Nate Monroe, "In Jacksonville, one of Florida's largest school districts is crumbling." Florida Times-Union, May 1, 2024.

[12] Kirsten Slungaard Mumma, "The Effect of Charter School Openings on Traditional Public Schools in Massachusetts and North Carolina." American Economic Journal, Vol. 14, No. 2, May 2022.

[13] Jamie Klinenberg, Jon Valant, Nicolas Zerbino, "Arizona's 'universal' education savings account program has become a handout to the wealthy." Brookings Institution, May 7, 2024.

[14] Jeremy Schwartz, "Former Far-Right Hard-Liner Says Billionaires Are Using School Board Races to Sow Distrust in Public Education." ProPublica, May 15, 2024.

[15] Libby Stanford, Mark Lieberman, Victoria Ifatusin, "Which states have Private School Choice?" Education Week, February 28, 2025.

[16] Dilice Robertson, "Don't fail our children by abolishing the Department of Education." The Fulcrum, November 8, 2024.

[17] Henry A. Giroux, "The Nazification of American Education." CounterPunch, July 22, 2022.

Press Freedom: The Last Great Texas Newspaper War

[1] Judith M. Garrett and Michael V. Hazel, "Dallas Morning News." The Handbook of Texas Online, Texas State Historical Association, June 2010.

[2] Steve Kaskovich, "Star-Telegram presses roll one last time." Fort Worth Star-Telegram, March 15, 2014.

[3] Iver Peterson, "A Newspaper War, Texas Style, Grips a Suburb." The New York Times, April 22, 1996.

[4] Matt Wallace and Keith Hale, video editors; AMN photography staff. "Arlington Morning News – 1996-97 Year in Review." Video, 1997.

[5] BeloWatch, "News plans new Arlington daily; suburban newspaper war looms." Dallas Observer, March 7, 1996.

[6] Burl Osborne, A.H. Belo Corp. letter to colleagues. April 10, 1996.

[7] Ralph Langer, The Dallas Morning News office memo, to Arlington Morning News staff. April 4, 1996.

[8] Iver Peterson, "A Newspaper War, Texas Style, Grips a Suburb." The New York Times, April 22, 1996; David Pasztor, "A.H. Belo here to rescue Arlington [parody]." Dallas Observer, April 25, 1996.

[9] John Morton, "Invading Another Paper's Turf." American Journalism Review, June 1996; Dorothy Giobbe, "Lone Star Launch." Editor & Publisher, March 23, 1996; Peterson, op. cit.

[10] BeloWatch, "News plans new Arlington daily; suburban newspaper war looms." Dallas Observer, March 7, 1996.

[11] Joe Holley, "Belo the Belt: The Arlington Newspaper War Gets Personal." Texas Monthly, July 1996.

[12] Robert Deitz, "Newspaper War: Dealeys vs. Basses?" D Magazine, Oct. 1996.

[13] Holley, op. cit.

[14] Peterson, op. cit.

[15] Herb Booth, "Perfect response." Gary Jacobson, Arlington's Own Publisher. Arlington Morning News report to staff. Aug. 2001.

[16] Lori Price and Valerie Fields, "Lawrence stories." Arlington Morning News report to staff. Aug. 2001.

[17] Joe Simnacher and Michael Weiss, "Jacobson to lead the Arlington Stormin' News." The Dallas Morning News [parody], 1996.

[18] Michael Landauer, "A good question." Gary Jacobson, Arlington's Own Publisher. Arlington Morning News report. Aug. 2001.

[19] Todd Wills, "He believed in us." Gary Jacobson, Arlington's Own Publisher. Arlington Morning News report. Aug. 2001.

[20] Douglas Pils, "The Gary glare." Gary Jacobson, Arlington's Own Publisher. Arlington Morning News report. Aug. 2001.

[21] Lynn Hale, "Letter to Martha Flores." Arlington Morning News. Aug. 18, 1997.

[22] Laurie Freeman, "Ad Age Special Report: Newspapers." Advertising Age, April 28, 1997; Gyles, Barbara Z. "Arlington's wild ride." Newspaper Association of America's Presstime, Jan. 1997.

[23] Roy Hamric, "Suburban Warfare." Editor & Publisher, June 26, 1999.

[24] Dan Tynan, "The 25 Worst Tech Products of All Time." PCWorld, May 26, 2006.

[25] Lucia Moses, "Casualty of war in Texas turf battle?" Editor & Publisher, Feb. 23, 2001.

[26] Eric Celeste, "Retreat: The Morning News ends its battle in Arlington with a whimper." Dallas Observer, March 8, 2001.

[27] Robert Decherd, "Moving forward" letter. Making News @ Belo. Sept. 21, 2001.

[28] Charles Layton, "The Dallas Mourning News." American Journalism Review, April/May 2005; Craig Flournoy and Tracy Everbach, "Damage Report: Most of the two hundred journalists who left The Dallas Morning News landed on their feet. Those who stayed are not so sure." Columbia Journalism Review, July/August 2007.

[29] Bob Schober, "Email to James Moroney III." The Dallas Morning News, Oct. 26, 2001.

[30] Sandi Scott, Letter to Adrian L. Stockton, investigator, Texas Commission on Human Rights. The Dallas Morning News. Oct. 28, 2002; Steve Kenny, "The Dallas Morning News memo, 'Thank you'." Sept. 14, 2001.

[31] George Watson, "Lawrence Young, P-E editor, dies." The Press-Enterprise, July 22, 2002; Joe Simnacher, "Ex-News editor was mentor to young, inspiration to many." The Dallas Morning News, July 22, 2002.

[32] Richard Prince, "Lawrence Young Leaves Male Heir." "Richard Prince's Journal-isms," Robert C. Maynard Institute for Journalism Education, Aug. 25, 2002.

[33] Erik Wemple, "Current Newspapers made offer for The Gazette." The Washington Post, June 12, 2015.

[34] Elizabeth Grieco, "U.S. newspapers have shed half of their newsroom employees since 2008." Pew Research Center, April 20, 2020; Sarah Naseer and Christopher St. Aubin, "Newspapers Fact Sheet." Pew Research Center, November 10, 2023; Press Gazette, March 6, 2025.

[35] A.C. Greene, "Old times." Texas Monthly, Nov. 1987.

[36] WFAA staff. "Dallas Morning News, Fort Worth Star-Telegram to share sports coverage." WFAA, Oct. 16, 2009; Gary Jacobson, "Dallas Morning News to print Star-Telegram." The Dallas Morning News, Nov. 6, 2013.

[37] Kristen Hare, "In a shift away from print, The Dallas Morning News is laying off 25 and outsourcing its newspaper design." Poynter, January 27, 2017; Craig Flournoy and Tracy Everbach, "Damage Report." Columbia Journalism Review, July 2007; Bron Maher, "U.S. newspaper circulations 2024: LA Times loses quarter of print circulation in a year." Press Gazette, March 6, 2025; Belo annual report, 2000; DallasNews Corp. annual report, 2023.

[38] Randy Eli Grothe, "When a Monkey Screams, Think of Me." DMNcuts, April 19, 2009.

[39] Eric Garcia, "Star-Telegram reduces print editions to focus on digital offerings. What comes next?" Fort Worth Report, October 15, 2024.

[40] Ed Bark, "What Happened to the Dallas Morning News?" D Magazine, July 2009.

[41] Paul Gillin, Newspaper Death Watch, 2018.

Government Power: A Strange but True Tale

[1] Glenna Whitley, "The Professor and the Love Slave." D Magazine, February 1, 1993; Evan Moore, "Prison Time Denouement for Ex-English Professor." The Oklahoman, September 20, 1993.

[2] "NTSU prof struck by train, killed in Denton County." The Dallas Morning News, July 3, 1983; "Texas road accidents kill at least 18." The Associated Press, July 3, 1983.

[3] C. Neal Tate, "Stephen M. Gorman." Political Science and Politics, The American Political Science Association, Vol. 16, Issue 4, Fall 1983, p. 767.

[4] "The CIA and Academe." CIA Studies in Intelligence, Winter 1983.

[5] Church Committee, "Final Report of the Select Committee to Study Governmental Operations with Respect to Intelligence Activities." U.S. Senate, April 26, 1976.

[6] Carl Bernstein, "The CIA and the Media: How America's Most Powerful News Media Worked Hand in Glove with the Central Intelligence Agency and Why the Church Committee Covered It Up." Rolling Stone, October 20, 1977.

[7] CIA Studies, op. cit.

[8] Valerie Strauss and Vernon Loeb, "Top-Secret Teachers? CIA Agents in Demand on College Campuses." Los Angeles Times, May 8, 2000.

Getting More Personal

Healthcare and Legal Drugs: The Aspirin Strain

[1] Sally Squires, "Aspirin: The World's Most Popular Pill Turns 100." The Washington Post, August 5, 1997.

[2] W. Russell Brain and Donald Hunter, "Acute Meningo-Encephalomyelitis of Childhood: Report of Six Cases." The Lancet, February 2, 1929.

[3] Lawrence K. Altman, "The Doctor's World: Tale of Triumph on Every Aspirin Bottle." The New York Times, May 11, 1999; Ivana Dvorackova, *Aflatoxins and Human Health*. CRC Press, 1990.

[4] Gilles Lyon, Philip R. Dodge, and R.D. Adams, "The Acute Encephalopathies of Obscure Origin in Infants and Children." Brain, December 1, 1961.

[5] Martin A. Samuels and Allan H. Ropper, Samuels and Ropper's Neurological CPCs from the New England Journal of Medicine. Oxford University Press, 2012.

[6] Edward A. Mortimer Jr. and Martha Lipson Lepow, "Varicella with Hypoglycemia Possibly Due to Salicylates." American Journal of Diseases in Children, 1962; Statistical Abstract of the United States. U.S. Department of Commerce, 1976.

[7] Altman, op. cit.

[8] Ibid.

[9] G.M. Johnson, T.D. Scurletis, and N.B. Carroll, "A Study of Sixteen Fatal Cases of Encephalitis-like Disease in North Carolina Children." North Carolina Medical Journal, October 1963.

[10] H.L. Utian, J.M. Wagner, and M.B. W'srand, "White Liver Disease." The Lancet, November 14, 1964; "Labeling for Salicylate-Containing Drug Products." Federal Register, December 28, 1982.

[11] H.M. Giles, "Encephalopathy and Fatty Degeneration of the Viscera." The Lancet, May 15, 1965; Lisa A. Degnan, "Reye's Syndrome: A Rare But Serious Pediatric Condition." U.S. Pharmacist, March 20, 2012.

[12] M.G. Norman, "Encephalopathy and Fatty Degeneration of the Viscera in Childhood: Review of Cases at The Hospital for Sick Children, Toronto [1954–1966]." Canadian Medical Association Journal, September 21, 1968.

[13] Mark A. Largent, Keep Out of Reach of Children: Reye's Syndrome, Aspirin, and the Politics of Public Health. Bellevue Literary Press, 2015.

[14] National Reyes Syndrome Foundation, Bryan, Ohio. reyes-syndrome.org

[15] Michael Hinds, "Warning issued on giving aspirin to children." The New York Times, June 5, 1982; U.S. Centers for Disease Control and Prevention press release, "CDC study shows sharp decline in Reye's Syndrome among U.S. children." May 6, 1999.

[16] Altman, op. cit.; "Reye's Syndrome: A Medical Mystery." Science, March 28, 1980.

[17] Abbey Meller and Hauwa Ahmed, "How Big Pharma Reaps Profits While Hurting Everyday Americans." Center for American Progress, August 30, 2019.

[18] Larry Doyle, "Aspirin and Deadly Reye's Syndrome: Warnings Can Be Missed." United Press International, May 31, 1987; Hinds, op. cit.

[19] Doyle, "Aspirin-Reye's Chronology: Threat of Suits Delayed Warning Process." UPI, May 31, 1987.

[20] Public Citizen Health Research Group, et al., v. Commissioner, FDA, and Aspirin Foundation of America, U.S. Court of Appeals for D.C., July 27, 1984.

[21] "Administration says pressure was not responsible for aspirin warning delay." The Associated Press, November 19, 1982.

[22] Ibid.

[23] Marlene Cimons, "New Study Strongly Links Aspirin, Reye's Syndrome." Los Angeles Times, January 9, 1985.

[24] Peter Lurie and Sidney M. Wolfe, "Aspirin and Reye Syndrome." Paradigms for Change: A Public Health Textbook for Medical, Dental, Pharmacy, and Nursing Students, Public Citizen Health Research Group, unpublished.

[25] Doyle, op. cit.

[26] CDC press release, "CDC study shows sharp decline in Reye's Syndrome among U.S. children." May 6, 1999.

[27] Doyle, op. cit.

[28] Ermias D. Belay, Joseph S. Bresee, Robert C. Holman, Ali S. Khan, Abtin Shahriari, and Lawrence B. Schonberger. "Reye's Syndrome in the United States from 1981 through 1997." The New England Journal of Medicine, May 6, 1999.

[29] "Reye's Syndrome." U.S. National Institutes of Health, November 28, 2023.

[30] James Orlowski, Usama Hanhan, Mariano Fiallos, "Is aspirin a cause of Reye's syndrome? A case against." Drug Safety, 2002.

[31] "The Chemistry of Aspirin." International Aspirin Foundation, 2020.

[32] "Aspirin Product Monograph." Bayer Inc. March 2022; "Annual Report 2023," Bayer AG, Leverkusen, Germany.

[33] David Michaels, Doubt is Their Product: How Industry's Assault on Science Threatens Your Health. Oxford University Press, 2008.

[34] Bill Sardi, "Why Reye's syndrome prevailed from 1950-1980 and then suddenly disappeared." Knowledge of Health, September 18, 2011.

[35] "Aspirin Labels to Warn About Reye Syndrome." The Associated Press, March 8, 1986; Doyle, op. cit.

[36] Patrick Jasperse, "Bayer agrees to pay $2.6 million in Reye's case." The Milwaukee Journal, August 12, 1989.

[37] "Jury scuttles $50 million aspirin suit." United Press International, August 4, 1989.

[38] *Sharkey v. Sterling Drug*, Court of Appeal of Louisiana, First Circuit. Leagle, April 23, 1992. ; "Girl Stricken with Reye's gets $7.8 million award." Orlando Sentinel, April 27, 1992.

[39] "$5.5 Million Settlement for Child who Suffered Brain Damage as a Result of Medical Negligence." Rapoport Law Offices news release, October 13, 2003.

Death and Loss: Bye, for Now

[1] "James Joseph Shay Jr." Milford Mirror, May 1, 2008; "$100,000 Gem Robbery Probed." Tampa Tribune, February 12, 1965.

[2] "Shay, James J." Rye, N.Y., Veterans Project, 2025.

Death and Loss: Dancing in the Moment

[1] "Longtime Dallas government worker, community advocate passes away." Dallas Patch, October 4, 2021.

[2] Jasmine Garsd, et. al, "The park. Sunday. Queens, New York." NPR, September 11, 2024.

[3] Matt Williams, "Lake Livingston angler catches potential world-record alligator gar." Beaumont Enterprise, April 21, 2025.

About the Author

Kevin James Shay, 66, was born in Washington, D.C., and grew up in Dallas. He played basketball for the Lake Highlands High Wildcats and Richland College Lakers. After blowing out a knee in college, he figured he better learn something and obtained a journalism degree.

More than 40 years later, he is still trying to learn something.

He has worked for, or contributed to, The Dallas Morning News, The Washington Post Co.'s Gazette, Minority Business News USA, U.S. News and World Report, Online Journal, Texas Catholic, the late Dallas Times Herald, and numerous other newspapers, magazines, and Internet sites. He has been covered or mentioned by The Associated Press, BBC, CBS Morning News, NPR, The Irish Times, Le Havre Libre, Good Morning Texas, The Dallas Morning News, The Atlanta Journal and Constitution, Austin American Statesman, D Magazine, Dallas Observer, Lake Highlands Today, and more. He has written books on politics, history, travel, and more, including one released by a national publishing company and another by a regional one.

He won two "Best of Show" awards from the Maryland-Delaware-D.C. Press Association, with his stories judged to be better than even The Washington Post and Baltimore Sun. Others that have recognized his work include Lincoln University's Unity Awards in Media, Dallas Press Club, Texas Press Association, American Cancer Society, Suburban Newspapers of America, Bethesda Literary Festival, and Mental Health Association in Texas.

An Eagle Scout, he has been involved in community service, including as a Cub Scout den leader, Girl Scout volunteer, and a coach of his son and daughter's basketball and baseball teams. He has served on the board of organizations such as Rainbow Bridge, a youth advocacy group in Dallas, and the Dallas chapter of the ACLU, and been a longtime member of organizations such as the Sierra Club. He was among those chosen to hold a rope for the 60-foot Eagle Scout balloon that paraded down Constitution Avenue in Washington, D.C., during the 100th anniversary celebration of the Boy Scouts in 2010.

Shay has met the likes of Barack Obama, George W. Bush, Robert Blake, Jesse Jackson, Amelia Boynton Robinson, and Granny D. He has exposed political and business corruption, systemic racism, government waste, psychiatric facility abuse, contracting inequities, and other societal ills. He was kicked out of the former East Germany several times, detained by authorities in the former Yugoslavia, and strip searched by guards at Los Angeles International Airport. A 2013 road trip, where he drove his two kids 6,950 miles across the country and back in 17 days, was believed to be the most miles driven by one adult with at least two kids in that time period.

Shay has participated in marches and demonstrations to raise awareness for peace, environmental, and social justice issues since 1981. Those include walking more than 5,000 miles with "A Walk of the People - A Pilgrimage for Life," a project endorsed by numerous peace organizations that attempted to bridge East-West gaps by walking from California to Moscow in 1984-85. He also walked about 600 miles on an international march in 1987-88 in India, as well as some 70 miles with the We Are America March at the age of 66 in 2025.

In 1979, as a 20-year-old college journalist, Shay was fearless, ready to tackle anything and everything, with the hair and attitude. Photo by Jim Shay

www.ingramcontent.com/pod-product-compliance
Lightning Source LLC
LaVergne TN
LVHW011415080426
835512LV00005B/67